I0820118

Endorsements for *Son of the Congo*

"Tracing A.T.'s gripping story from poverty to global leadership and from political persecution to Kingdom impact, *Son of the Congo* is a tour de force testament to God's unstoppable grace. If you're struggling with trusting God, read this book and believe."

—**KEVIN SORBO,** director and actor

"In *Son of the Congo,* Kadita Tshibaka finds God's grace in a journey through a hard and inspiring life. He traveled from Congolese tribal warfare to immigration to America, to an Ivy League education and a career in finance. Then he turned his energies to giving opportunities to the poor in Africa. In his life, love and faithfulness produce resilience and redemption. This inspiring story will make you more resilient too."

—**DR. LARRY ARNN,** president of Hillsdale College

"*Son of the Congo* is an inspiring account of faith, resilience, and leadership. Kadita Tshibaka—whom we fondly call A.T.—takes us on a remarkable journey from his childhood in Congo, marked by loss, hardship, and political turmoil, to positions of global influence in Citigroup, Lloyds TSB, and international development.

"As one of the first generation of African leaders to attain senior executive roles in global banking, A.T. not only carried Africa's hopes into the boardroom but also demonstrated that integrity and perseverance can overcome the most daunting obstacles. For me personally, A.T. was a mentor and trailblazer at Citigroup whose example helped open doors for the generations that followed. This memoir is more than a personal story; it is a testament to the power of faith and purpose to transform lives and shape legacies of service."

—**ADE AYEYEMI,** former group CEO of Ecobank Transnational Incorporated

"The book you are about to read is fascinating. It unveils a truly exceptional life story, painting a vivid picture of resilience and steadfast integrity. Rising from humble beginnings in the Congo, A.T. from his very early years navigated a path through profound personal challenges, worked hard on his education, and ultimately managed to achieve a very distinguished career in international banking. His narrative is a powerful testament to principled leadership, showcasing an unwavering commitment to ethical conduct even when confronted with political turmoil, military coups, and immense corporate pressures. A.T.'s uniquely strong moral compass and devotion to God have guided him in his every decision.

"*Son of the Congo* is a story that commands deep respect and provides a timeless example of true leadership. I hope you will find it as inspirational as I did."

—**MR. ZDENEK TUREK,** chief risk officer of Citigroup

"*Son of the Congo* belongs on the desk of every corporate executive who wonders whether integrity, humility, and purpose can still thrive in today's competitive—and often cutthroat—corporate culture. A.T.'s life offers a compelling blueprint for how leaders can steward their platforms with character and conviction. His journey is a powerful reminder that true leadership is forged not only in boardrooms, but in the crucible of adversity. This book is a masterclass in leading with purpose and will inspire executives seeking to balance profit with principle."

—**DIPAK RASTOGI,** former group executive of Citigroup and CEO of Citi Venture Capital International at Citibank N.A.

"*Son of the Congo* is more than a memoir. It is a testament to God's grace, to the resilience of the human spirit, and to a man whose life has been lived with purpose. I respected A.T. deeply when I first met him. After reading this book, I respect him even more. A remarkable story of perseverance, history, finance, and faith."

—**BRENT MEKOSH,** CEP and CFP of Mekosh Financial Services

"*Son of the Congo: A Journey of Tragedy, Triumph, and Transformation*, is one of the most inspiring works I've come across in years.

"Born into poverty, displaced by conflict, and raised in scarcity, A.T. could have become a footnote in history. Instead, his life became a testimony to faith, resilience, and unshakable passion.

"What stands out to me is this: Passion is the common thread. It's what carried A.T. from hardship to hope. It's what fueled his decades-long career in finance and his service to others through microfinance. And it's what continues to drive him today as a mentor, leader, and author. Reading A.T.'s story reminded me again that passion is contagious. It inspires, it lifts, and it endures."

—**KAREN ROBINSON COPE,** managing director, Mara6, and former board member of Opportunity International

"A.T. Tshibaka has lived a life that makes dramatic fiction seem boring by comparison. From the mighty rivers and forests of the Congo, through the sedate halls of Ivy League American institutions, to the high streets and gilded boardrooms of high finance, with detours to the seamy dungeons of volatile state actors, Tshibaka has delivered an autobiography of extraordinary authenticity, range and depth, woven together by family, love, belief, and the unmistakable guiding hand of the Divine. In parts, *Son of Congo* presents a lived perspective far richer, and nuanced than the journalistic reporting that has defined most narratives from that magnificent and storied country."

—**CHINEDU IKWUDINMA,** chief risk officer of Ecobank Transnational Inc., Lome, Togo

"*Son of the Congo* is a narrative of breathtaking scope. It is the story of a fatherless boy who, through a mother's fierce love and unimaginable sacrifice, escapes a destiny of poverty and obscurity. A.T.'s professional life reads like a thrilling saga set against the backdrop of a volatile Africa and a changing global banking landscape.

"The most powerful thread woven through this entire tapestry is that of faith. This is not merely a story of a man who achieved worldly success; it is a narrative of a man relentlessly pursued by God."

—**CAMILLE NTOTO,** visionary and co-founder of Africa New Day/Un Jour Nouveau

"A.T.'s story is truly inspirational, one that proves the verse Philippians 4:13, 'I can do all things through Christ who strengthens me.' His devotion to his family, his Savior, and serving his community prove that when you put the needs of others ahead of yourself, anything is possible. A.T.'s humility comes across strong in his memoir, because the true number of people who have had their life transformed through A.T.'s story can't be expressed in words."

—**SCOTT GOEDEN,** managing partner, reference point, and board member of Africa New Day

"Thank you, A.T., for sharing your remarkable journey. For many of us that served with you and experienced your leadership at Citi, and as one of those that had the privilege of being directly mentored by you, I know how impactful your memoir will be. To paraphrase a statement A.T. once shared with me, 'it's not about where the journey begins, it's about how we travel despite the odds.'"

—**ÉRIC ITAMBO,** president at CoBank

"A.T. Tshibaka's proven intelligence could not have been all that was required to navigate this journey. Minus a divine force propelling him, he would have remained forever the smartest fellow in the village, maybe the province. The consistent fundamental in this entire miraculous journey has been A.T.'s Christianity, commencing with the divine inspiration of a mother's unselfish love and family sacrifices, which were so generously given at critical events leading out of the village.

"This is a unique story which will inspire the non-believers to question their skepticism and will reinforce the believers' faith that there really are angels on earth doing the Lord's work in the belief, not just hope, that their efforts will make many more stories like this become possible."

—**JAMES ("JIM") HAWES.** Jim is a former Navy Seal, author of the book *Cold War Navy SEAL: My Story of Che Guevara, War in the Congo, and the Communist Threat in Africa.*

"I enjoyed every minute reading about this remarkable man whose faith and family supported him through the challenges and celebrations of a truly global life."

—**MARK T. ROBINSON,** CEO of BSP Financial Group Limited, Papua New Guinea

"*Son of the Congo* goes far beyond an autobiography: it's a meditation on life, faith, resilience, and a sense of duty. You demonstrate that a personal journey, when guided by conviction and grace, can become a source of collective inspiration. It is both a testimony and a journey."

—**MICHEL LOSEMBE,** founder and managing director of Tshinu Consulting in Kinshasa, DRC and former CEO of Citibank (Congo)

"Nowadays who's got time for God if you care deeply about your career and your family? But why not? What if we make Him room in our lives? This very personal book, through a collection of life stories, is an invitation from a successful banking professional to change our way of seeing the reality and to work through reaching our goals in life while following superior principles, investing in our communities, and really making a difference while not losing passion for life."

—**MAR TURRADO,** founder and managing director of Findango, Spain

"A rich story in which many anecdotes are similar to the trajectory of my own life and past."

—**WILLY MULAMBA,** managing director of Equity Banque Commerciale du Congo

"What a beautiful, amazing account of the Lord's sovereign, remarkable unfolding of his gracious, powerful design for your life."

—**STAN AND MOLLY DOLAND,** former pastors at Centro Cristiano in Vida Nueva, Spain

"There is an elderly man in Virginia who understands the essence of America. His name is Athanase Tshibaka. He has written an extraordinary book called *Son of the Congo*.

"Mr. Tshibaka's words are directed to the doubters; of God, of Country, of themselves. His rise from incredible poverty and deprivation in Africa, to Dartmouth, and on to powerful corporate jobs, is so stunning it's hard to describe.

"If you read *Son of the Congo*, it will enhance your life."

—**BILL O'REILLY,** journalist and historian

SON OF THE CONGO

SON OF THE CONGO

A Journey of Tragedy, Triumph, and Transformation

KADITA TSHIBAKA

Son of the Congo: A Journey of Tragedy, Triumph, and Transformation

Collaboratively written with D. R. Jacobsen (www.jacobsenwriting.com)

Some names and identifying details have been changed to protect the privacy of individuals.

Published by Resolve Editions, an imprint of Forefront Books, Nashville, Tennessee.
Distributed by Simon & Schuster.

Library of Congress Control Number: 2025921400

Print ISBN: 978-1-63763-479-0
E-book ISBN: 978-1-63763-480-6

Cover Design by Bruce Gore, Gore Studio, Inc.
Interior Design by Bill Kersey, KerseyGraphics

Printed in the United States of America
26 27 28 29 30 31 RR4 10 9 8 7 6 5 4 3 2 1

To my wife, my love, my partner, my confidante, and cheerleader who has faithfully supported me for more than fifty years of an incredible adventure together, Priscilla Madlyn Tshibaka.

Contents

Part Three:
The Indomitable Banker:
Persevering Through Political Imprisonment, Professional Betrayals, and Coups D'état, 1972–2007

Author's Note

I WRITE THIS FROM MY HOME IN SPOTSYLVANIA, VIRGINIA, AN UNLIKELY spot considering I grew up across the Atlantic Ocean, in a tiny village in the Democratic Republic of the Congo (Congo).

There are difficulties in telling such a wide and wandering story as mine, a story that spans more than seven decades. As with any memoir, these recollections are mine alone and imperfect. I have no doubt that others perceived events differently, but I will leave it to them to write their own versions of the story. And as with any memoir, conversations, interactions, and events have been recalled to the best of my ability. That is all I can offer.

I have made two stylistic choices that I believe will assist the reader. First, the names of several characters in this story are quite long. My own full name, for example, is Athanase Tshibaka Lumbala Kadita Baya Bakaji Wa Ngandu. Even my shorter name has proved difficult for some, leading to my nicknames "Atha" and "A. T." Therefore, after my youth, I've referred to myself often as "A. T.," even when I was called another name.

Second, I have simplified the name of the country of my birth. Throughout its history, Congo has been known by various names: the Congo Free State, the Belgian Congo, the Republic of the Congo, the Democratic Republic of the Congo, Zaire, and once again the Democratic Republic of the Congo. Similarly to the way I am streamlining my own name, I will interchangeably refer to my native country as "the Congo" or "Congo." However, during the period of time it was known as Zaire, that is how I will refer to it.

I recently returned to the Congo for a board meeting at Equity Banque Commericale du Congo accompanied by my grandson, Athanase (also known as Josiah). While he connected with his Congolese roots, Athanase was struck by the resilience of the Congolese people and the difficult living conditions they experience every day. As his eyes were opened to the overwhelming needs of the family, he was also moved with compassion and a desire to help. My heart is full, knowing that yet another generation of my descendants will not forget our family or our people.

But let us get to the story! It is not giving away anything to say this is a tale of God's grace, although to discover exactly how that grace unfolded, you will have to keep reading.

Athanase Kadita Tshibaka
Spotsylvania, Virginia
June 25, 2025

Introduction

I knew you before I formed you in your mother's womb.
Before you were born, I set you apart and appointed you
as my prophet to the nations.
JEREMIAH 1:5 NLT

YOU HOLD THE STORY OF MY LIFE.

It is a tale that spans six continents and nearly eighty years. It will travel between health and sickness, birth and death, peace and war, freedom and prison, and nearly every element of the human condition. There are mundane moments just as surely as there are unexpected and life-changing surprises.

Yet by itself, such a story would be relatively unimportant. What has happened to me has no more intrinsic value than what has happened to any other individual. Nearly eight billion of us inhabit this planet. My life is not the most noteworthy or the most deserving of attention.

Nevertheless, I am convinced that my story must be told.

Why?

Because the story of my life is the story of God's grace, operating not only on a single life but on countless lives.

I look back with gratitude on those who were placed along my path, by the grace of God, for the glory of God, just as I am humbly grateful for the opportunities I have been given to share that grace with others.

If that sounds grandiose, I ask for your forgiveness. I confess that the greatness of the story I have been granted is not of my own making or doing. Rather, it is a testament to God's goodness and love, operating in and through the lives of His children, changing and transforming everything, charting and shaping destinies.

God's goodness and love *do* change everything.

But all this is counting the chicks before the chicken has even laid any eggs! Before one can reach a destination, one must begin the journey. And my beginnings, like the countless streams and rivers that are the lifeblood of Congo, were subject to the whims of larger forces, often beyond my control.

Indeed, if my life bears similarity to a river, its course was forever altered while I was a small boy. I had been flowing in a particular direction when, suddenly, I was shifted irrevocably into a new course. What changed my life so early on were the twin facts of the untimely death of my father and the words he spoke to my mother before he breathed his last.

The year was circa 1949. He lay in hospital in Tshikapa, the diamond mining town thirty kilometers northwest from our village of Mai Munene.

"I do not want you to marry any of my brothers, Ngalula Kayibabu Wa Kanda," he said to my mother. She was commonly known as Julienne Bilonda after marrying my father, but because she came after three boys, she earned the birth title of *Ngalula*. In our tribal practice, the name Ngalula would also be given to a boy born immediately following three girls. To that was added *Kayibabu* (abandoned, away from one's own siblings), and *Wa Kanda* simply meant daughter of Kanda.

"You must not," my father insisted, "no matter how they pressure you! We have five children. Spend your attention on them, and not on a new husband. My brothers have their own wives and children. You and our children will be neglected, or worse."

His unexpected words shocked her into silence.

Mother understood, and she wholeheartedly agreed. She knew her in-laws quite well. But my father's proposal was taboo. It went against countless generations of tribal custom. By tradition my mother should marry my father's younger brother, Matthieu Nkongolo. If he did not wish to take her as his second or third wife, she would marry the next in line, my father's next youngest brother, Sebastien Muzemba. This would continue, all the way down the line of his brothers and cousins, second cousins, and other extended relations. A husband would be found eventually on *some* branch of my father's family tree. Remaining unmarried after his death would be unthinkable.

Yet that is exactly what my father instructed my mother to do.

And despite the strangeness of my father's words, my mother honored them. When he died in hospital, my mother returned to Mai Munene alone and remained alone. We knew what had happened, the five of us siblings, with my older siblings even more cognizant of the situation than I. Even being the youngest, I understood that life could not remain the same.

It was not long until the uncles arrived at our two huts to speak with my mother.

When they understood what she intended, their speech became threat. They could not tolerate such flouting of tribal tradition. Things were done a certain way, and things were not done any other way. Their egos were enormously bruised. They felt that lessons needed to be taught and learned.

What did I do while my uncles slapped my mother with open palms? Did I speak when they hit her with closed fists, or intervene when they upended her three-legged iron stove and scattered a pot of food across the dirt?

I could not. I was too small, incapable of defending my beloved mother.

My sister and three brothers were teenagers but were even more terrified than I was. They stood frozen in fear and silent horror, helpless to intercede on my mother's behalf as well. How could they? Their intervention would have constituted a severe *tshibindi* (taboo), and if any of my uncles cursed them, who would then come to their rescue? Fearing the curse and potential for severe beating themselves, they too watched the spectacle of our mother being abused by family, the very people who were candidates to take care of her…and us.

Meanwhile, my mother clung to one of the posts of her hut as my uncles repeatedly struck her. One tried to pull her away, then two, and still she clung to the wooden post. Guttural sounds of pain and hopelessness cascaded from her, conveying her defenseless agony.

When my uncles left at last, they carried with them our goats, our pigs, and our chickens, whatever little we had. We had been reasonably well-off by the standards of our village. Now we were doubly poor. Our resources were depleted, and my father would never return.

I expressed nothing beyond my wordless tears.

Beating my mother and taking away our few possessions did not prove cruel enough for my uncles. Later, they forced me, along with my brothers Antoine Tshiyombo Muka and Honore Ngandu Kashala, to abandon her and move in with Uncle Sebastien Muzemba, the uncle who lived closest to us. This was a traumatic experience for me as a seven-year-old boy. It left an indelible mark on my heart. Even though I have forgiven, I have never been able to forget.

Papa Sebastien Muzemba, my father's next youngest brother after Matthieu Nkongolo, lived not far from his mother's hut. He was a subsistence farmer and constantly struggled to produce enough to feed his own large family. He did own several pigs, and when one was slaughtered, many in the village expected a piece of meat. Because of the challenges raising his family in Mai Munene, he moved to Kananga in the 1950s, where he had secured a job with the main Belgian slaughterhouse. During that period, I was privileged to eat a Belgian sausage for the first time. Papa Sebastien had brought some goodies from the butchery, and all of us feasted!

That is my only memory of a good meal during the time we stayed with Papa Sebastien. We had not only been forced by our paternal uncles to stay with Papa Sebastien but had also been forbidden to visit our mother. Yet even if Papa Sebastien had been willing to take care of his own family *and* the three of us school-going boys, he was simply not able to do so with his very meager means. We were lucky when we could have a single meal each day, usually in the evenings. And the smaller you were, as I was, the less you were likely to eat, given that we shared from the same pot. Eventually this arrangement became unsustainable, and so we were at last sent back to our mother!

So it was that the course of my life was forever altered.

Of necessity, I would leave Mai Munene, flowing to places I did not know existed. Places elsewhere in Congo, yes, but also places like Spotsylvania, Virginia, where I now sit on my screened porch, listening to the whine of mosquitoes and the whir of cicadas. Even now I can taste the *saka saka* (cassava leaves) cooked by the hands of my mother, eaten with *bidia* (a dough-like paste made of manioc flour and corn flour). I can feel the grit of red-brown soil beneath my bare feet in Mai Munene and smell the scent of the large grapefruit tree that blossomed in front of our two huts. I still picture our few goats and chickens, rushing to and fro across the dirt or into the bushes by the huts.

Life, just as love, is a many-splendored thing.

Yet before I learned that truth, I remained a small boy, growing up in Mai Munene without a father.

PART ONE

SON OF THE CONGO

A STORY OF TRAGEDY AND TRIUMPH 1947–1966

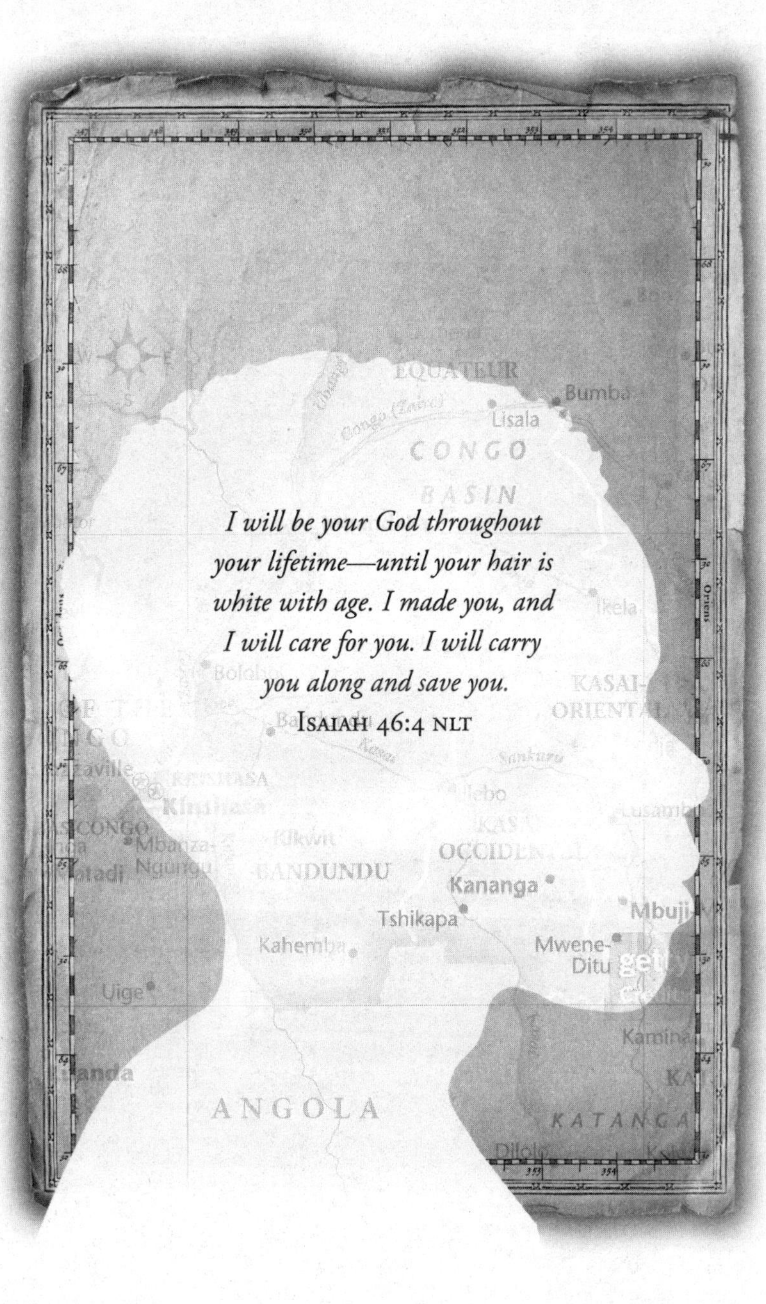

I will be your God throughout your lifetime—until your hair is white with age. I made you, and I will care for you. I will carry you along and save you.

Isaiah 46:4 NLT

CHAPTER 1

A Mother's Love Always Finds a Way

Southern Congo

EACH BREATH I TOOK SYNCED WITH THE RHYTHM OF MY MOTHER'S footfalls. I was being carried into the bush, on her back, away from our village. Each step my mother took lifted my scrawny frame, then dropped it, bouncing my cheek against the back of her shoulder. A pagne or wrap (*dipupila*) bound me to her back, and on her head she carried empty bottles in a basket (*tshisaka*). A dented kerosene lamp swung from her right hand.

On she walked. Ten minutes. Thirty minutes. Long enough to reach a hidden clearing amid the thick tropical trees. The space was removed from the routes of farmers and hunters, and sheltered by vegetation on three sides, creating a pocket of deep darkness in which my mother could do the work that helped to keep us alive.

We had left our village when the last glow of light faded from the sky. Once in the quiet dark of the clearing, her practiced hands undid the knot of the pagne. I slid down my mother's back and dropped to a crouch. Cool dirt pressed between my toes. A nearby brook whispered from somewhere in the darkness. I could see nothing beyond the circle of yellow light cast by the kerosene lamp. The surrounding trees were so black as to be an absence rather than a presence, sensed only by the irregular shapes their upper branches cut into the million-starred sky.

I watched as my mother conjured a fire and extinguished the flame in the lamp. Shadows began to dance as she set to work.

From a hidden spot in the trees my mother removed a large barrel. She dragged it across the dirt toward the fire. Several weeks earlier, on a night nearly twin to this one, I had seen her fill the barrel with manioc peelings (*bikuluidi*), which she had boiled. Then she had added dried corn sprouts (*misela*). Now she was ready to transform the contents of the large barrel into the fiery alcohol *kabumwe* that certain men of my village loved to drink. This *maluvu a kapia*, this drink of fire, was the secret to our survival.

It was a process that seemed like magic.

She stoked the fire; attached various tubes between a barrel, smaller calabash gourds, and the empty bottles; and seemingly endless bottles would fill with *cinq cent.*

I watched until my eyes began to close. Soon all that remained was the orange of the fire, the bustling and blurred silhouette of my mother as she passed between the fire and me.

I woke to the hiss of the fire being extinguished. My mother had relit the kerosene lamp, and by its glow she dragged the large barrel back to its place of concealment and carefully bundled together the now-full calabash gourds. She crouched and I climbed on her back. The pagne was retied. She stood, lifting the gourds and the lamp, and we set off toward our village.

In the darkness I allowed the rhythm of my mother's steps to once again close my eyes, fearing to see the bright eyes of foraging bonobos, or any other wild animals, outside the lantern's ring of light. As we approached the village, I heard the welcoming *kokoriko* of the roosters. I knew I was now safe from wild animals and mamba snakes, just as my mother knew her illicit alcohol would soon be safe inside our hut, hidden from the authorities.

I woke outside our huts just as dawn crept into our village. My mother, free of my burden, moved quickly to hide the calabash gourds inside her hut. Most in our village would not be interested in reporting an indigenous brewer to the Belgians, whoever they were, but some might, and any disruption in our *kabumwe* production would mean less food for us, or none.

At sunset I watched two, three, four men walk in from the fields, passing their own huts and families and arriving at ours. Each carried the farming tools required by the season. "Ah, the *bidia* [manioc and corn paste] smells so good!" one said, reaching hopeful fingers toward the burbling pot, only to be met with a verbal slap on the wrist from mother.

"Not yet, not yet, the stew is still cooking!" my mother admonished.

A perfect pause, a friendly look exchanged, and then my mother would extend an olive branch. "But I think I have something to quench your thirst while you wait. Although...perhaps I should give the first sip to another who is waiting more patiently? Perhaps he harvested more in the fields today for my family. Does he deserve an extra portion of chicken and *maluvu a kapia*? As Scripture says, 'The worker deserves his wages,'" Mom said.

And so would pass the next quarter hour. My mother encouraged gentle competition among the men, plying them with meat and with alcohol, both of which they would not otherwise enjoy. The men, having spent a tithe of their day working the fields for my mother, left sustenance on the floor of her hut: peanuts, manioc, beans, *saka saka* leaves.

I watched from the children's hut. It did not take long for the men to stand, rub their bellies in gratitude, and walk toward their own huts. One thoroughly satisfied with the meal would proclaim, *"Ngadi ngukutu, tualaku muela untapa!"* ("I have eaten and am satisfied, bring the machete, and cut off my head!") This was meant as the ultimate compliment for a great meal, as if to say, "What other reason do I have to live? You could chop off my head now and I will go contented."

The routine was always the same. Soon our huts were ours again, we children free to examine the pot for leftover bits. Mother, meanwhile, would sort and store the harvest the men had brought, always careful to ensure there were enough bottles of alcohol.

If mother had lived on the pagan side of our village, she perhaps could have been more open about her brewing. But then, if mother had lived on the pagan side of the village, it would have meant remarriage—to one of father's brothers—since on the pagan side were my paternal grandmother and my paternal uncles, along with their immediate and extended families.

Mai Munene, after all, was a village divided.

On one side, the south, closer to the Mai Munene River, lived the pagans. This word, often used by the priests on our side of the village, seemed to mean people who had not yet joined the Catholic faith and who did not go to church.

On the other, the north, on the higher ground away from the riverbank, lived the Catholics. Born on the Catholic side, I was christened Athanase Tshibaka Lumbala Kadita Baya Bakaji Wa Ngandu.

My name began with *Athanase*, named for a second cousin to my father. He and his wife did not have a child, and so my father decided to help his cousin's name live on. (His wife, Wa Mukeba, was a fine woman who spoiled me at every occasion.) *Athanase* was also Saint Athanasius, Archbishop of Alexandria and one of the early defenders of the Christian faith. *Tshibaka* meant "man of many wives" or "one who marries many," a description that applied to my uncles and was meant to apply to me when I grew older.

Lumbala was after my uncle Lumbala, the wild one in our family. He was reputed to be one of the fastest runners in Mai Munene, and legend had it that he could chase a *nkuadi* (guinea fowl) so long the *nkuadi* would tire, allowing Uncle Lumbala to snatch it up. He died years later while mining diamonds illegally, though whether he was murdered by other artisanal miners or bitten in two by the local hippopotami we never learned.

The second half of my name began with *Kadita*, my mother's preferred term when I was naughty, such as when I would snatch a tiny piece of goat meat from her hand while her attention was elsewhere. *Baya Bakaji* followed, redundantly meaning "one with many wives." Next came *Wa Ngandu*, meaning son of Ngandu, and (with the same spelling but a different intonation) meaning crocodile.

Thus, I was a small boy with a prodigious name, the quasi-literal translation of which was close to Bishop Lover of Many, Chaser of Guinea Fowls, Mischievous Man of Many Wives, Son of a Crocodile.

My mother gave birth to me in the main hospital in Tshikapa, some thirty kilometers away, before returning immediately to Mai Munene, her newest son strapped tightly to her body with her brightly colored pagne. Our village of Mai Munene, meaning "great waters," was less expansive than my name. The village itself was not worthy of note, apart from it being my home for the early years of my life.

When my mother returned to Mai Munene from the hospital, she observed a village much like any other in that region of south-central Congo, or indeed like countless other villages in our country. Families lived in one or more huts, each surrounded by a variety of accoutrements such as fruit trees, farming tools, goat pens, and chicken runs. Our family possessed two huts. In one we children slept, finding room around the edges of the kitchen, and in the other slept my parents.

The dirt was red, the surrounding jungle was green, and the Mai Munene River that flowed past was a roiling, muddy brown. The Mai Munene River ran into the Kasai, Congo's second-largest river, which in turn proceeded nearly one thousand kilometers north before spilling into the great Congo River, one of the world's major waterways.

However, unlike other villages nearby, ours was home to a Catholic mission church. Easily the largest structure for many miles, the church was constructed of red bricks in a traditional Belgian design, including a steeple that rose several stories above the surrounding huts. Its cross was the highest point in our village, and walking the path up toward the front door caused one's neck, almost inadvertently, to tilt backward and one's eyes to look up to the heavens.

The presence of the mission church had resulted in a fractured village, and in some ways it may have been the cause of my fractured family.

My father, while alive, served in church on the Catholic station. We attended Mass each week, dressed by my mother in my literal Sunday best. For me that meant thirdhand slacks, brown, ironed with a sharp crease down the front of each leg, and a yellow collared shirt with pearl buttons up the front. Inside the building it was always dark. As my eyes adjusted to the gloom, familiar details would emerge: dim stained glass, dark wooden pews, and weighty expectations of holy behavior.

Around one hundred of us attended from the village each week. The priest led Latin chants, the organ led Latin hymns, and my mother ensured we sat as still as statues. The only movement I allowed myself was to run the edge of my thumb along the crease in my slacks, back and forth like a sewing machine.

It was this same church where I was circumcised, and along with the official Catholic doctrine there was a bit of local lore that had evolved. Each year the older boys impressed on the younger boys that they ought *never* to scream for their mothers when the painful moment came, but rather to shout, *"Tatu wanyi, tatu wanyi!"* (My daddy, my daddy!)

Legend held that any boy who mistakenly cried for the wrong parent would suffer the lifetime shame of a crooked manhood.

When my time arrived, I forgot to heed my elders' advice. Blessedly, however, I did not yell, *"Mamu wanyi, mamu wanyi!"* (My mama, my mama!) Rather, I cried out, "My God, my God, my God!" *(Nzambi wanyi, Nzambi wanyi, Nzambi wanyi!)*, which was perhaps the most appropriate reaction on that painful occasion given the downside risks had I uttered the wrong cry!

I say this not entirely in jest. The fear of God was driven deep inside me from my earliest days. Years later, as I looked back at my faith journey, I would conclude that the Catholic Church taught me the fear of God and the Presbyterian church taught me the Word of God when I was finally able to read the Bible for myself. The ultimate realization of eternal consequence occurred after I accepted Christ Jesus as my personal Lord and Savior, an occurrence I will discuss later in this tale.

Once in Mai Munene, after we had just finished a meal of *saka saka* with a small amount of goat meat, I observed my mother place the few pieces of leftover meat inside a container in the hut. Soon thereafter a visitor stopped by, and naturally my mother offered her a helping of bidia (also known as *fufu*) and *saka saka.* My eyes narrowed: She had neglected to bring out the goat! I stepped closer to her and, hands folded behind my back, inquired why she had not brought out the meat to our visitor as she ought to have done. Her anger warring with her embarrassment, my mother complied. For my part I was able to escape the predicted punishment because I had acted with integrity, just as my mother required of me.

This honesty would have been lost on one of our frequent visitors, a Congolese *Frère* (friar), always dressed in his ankle-length cassock that was tied with a piece of rope. The stains on his clothing were one indication of his limited mental capability, as were his constant repetitions of certain prayers.

Dieu te bénisse…

Le règne…

La puissance et la gloire, aux siècles des siècles…

"God bless you…

The kingdom…

The power and the glory, forever and ever…"

To this one might respond, "Good day, *Frère*, and how are you?"

To which he would certainly answer:

Dieu te bénisse…

Le règne…

La puissance et la gloire, aux siècles des siècles…

We were instructed to be kind to him, and we generally honored that request. He was gentle and harmless. The priest we loved, though, was *Père* Denis. I recall him leaning through the doorway of our hut and offering greetings as he arrived, week in and week out, to sit with my father. At the time I failed to understand why he did not visit our neighbors with the same frequency, just as I could not understand the extent of my father's illness and suffering.

For my father was slowly dying of untreatable back cancer, and I was too young to appreciate what his absence would mean for the remainder of my life.

As I reflect on my upbringing, it is clear how fortunate I was to avoid being raised by any of my father's brothers during my formative years. They had shown the true colors of their characters when they viciously attacked my mother upon the occasion of my father's death. Certainly, to have a father would have been better still! Yet being cared for by my mother, sister, and brothers aligned the trajectory of my life with love and grace, even in the midst of hardship. I was fatherless, yes, but left in the care of an incredibly resourceful family who made untold sacrifices for me.

And perhaps I should say *especially* in hardship, for from the time of my birth I was tutored by tears and trials.

Recall my mother's *tshisaka*, used for transporting bottles of alcohol to and from her hidden brewing location. This basket, when turned upside down and topped with a plank, became a makeshift café table outside our huts.

I can see my father sitting across from me at that table. Whenever we could afford it, my mother would cook for him the best goat stew in the whole of Mai Munene. As *Tshibaka Mukala* (the baby of the family), I had the privilege of being the sole invitee at the *tshisaka* table with my father. Even when the meal was not goat stew, Mother always made sure my father had the best there was to eat on any given day, whether *nzolu ne tshiluabenyi* (chicken cooked with *tshiluabenyi*, a plant whose leaves smell like a mixture of rosemary and thyme), *kaleji* (manioc leaves, also known as *matamba* and *saka saka* depending on where you were from in the Congo), *bitekuteku* (spinach), *nkunda* (beans), *tshilunga* (leaves of sweet potatoes), and other local veggies. I remember this period of my life as one when I ate relatively well—or at least better than my siblings!

In those days, my father, still in his mid-forties, was for the most part bedridden. The wound in the lower part of his back was incurable. The suspicion was that the abscess represented a cancer that had reached an advanced stage. The doctors at the hospital in Tshikapa had tried what they could to save him. In the end, they were forced to give up and send my father home to die in his village. He suffered from 1946 until November 1949, when he passed away.

By way of background, Ngandu Alphonse, my late father, was born circa 1904, of Kanyiki Mpwanya and Ntumba Wa Katshinga. Kanyiki Mpwanya, my grandfather, had four wives, including Ntumba Wa

Katshinga, the wife with whom he had six children. Ngandu Alphonse was the eldest out of Ntumba Wa Katshinga's line. As such, he was the next in line for the chieftainship of Bena Kadiamba, my clan, but he could not reign as chief because of his sickness. Nor before his sickness, because of his work responsibilities at Forminiere.

Ngandu Alphonse was the head of a forestry and mining camp of Forminiere, a Belgian diamond exploitation company, at Basanga, not far from Mai Munene. This was a paying job and quite prestigious to boot! As chief of Bena Kadiamba, he would have been expected to attend to the myriad needs and demands of his subjects, using whatever little we had to survive, and, as would become a regular fallback for a chief, he would have had to cajole, seeking the support of some of the council members and elders of the clan who had means.

He made the right decision by opting to work for Forminiere.

As was the tribal custom, Grandmother Ntumba Wa Katshinga found a wife for him, Bilonda Ngalula Kayibabu Wa Kanda Julienne, otherwise known as Bilonda Julienne. She was from the sub-clan of Bakwa Bilonda, clan of Bena Mpuka. Her last name was to be later changed to Ngalula Julienne in her official documents. (Recall that Ngalula is the name given to a girl who comes after three boys or a boy who is born after three consecutive girls.)

Father being sick meant the next in the succession line, his younger brother, Matthieu Nkongolo Mumpela, could choose to step in, which he earnestly did. And at Nkongolo Mumpela's passing, the chieftainship passed to my older brother, Antoine Tshiyombo Muka, in 2003. He was chief of Bena Kadiamba into his eighties. My brother passed away in October 2024, following years of struggles with illnesses. One of his sons, Jean Muimbi Tshiyombo, has succeeded him. His honorific title is Mulonda Mbuji VI.

Jean Muimbi is the fourth of twenty-one children born to my brother Antoine. He shattered his leg in 2021 and needed multiple operations before he was able to walk again three years later. His surgeons had told him that his leg would have to be amputated. As has been the case when catastrophic situations occur in the family, a call came in for me to intervene. My wife, Priscilla, and I took care of his medical and hospital bills during the three-year period of uncertainty for him. The men's Christian fellowship and couples' Bible study in our community prayed consistently in our weekly meetings that the doctors would find alternative solutions to amputating his leg.

By May 2024, he could walk with a cane, and by July 2024, he did not need one!

He still walks with a limp today, but praise God, he walks!

Yes, the men in my family were many, and they all influenced me in their own ways. Yet none was more influential than my father, although our time together was cut short.

As I recall that supper, sitting across the basket table from my father, it strikes me as a last supper of sorts. Even after all of these years, the memory of that meal and others like it remains vivid in my mind.

Father was to die with Mother by his side.

My mother never remarried.

My life was never the same.

I could tell you a hundred other stories about my years in Mai Munene, but I wish to end this part of my account with an image: Woven through everything I did, everything I thought, was the dark thread of my father's absence.

CHAPTER 2

My Wayward Years

Southern Congo

MY MOTHER, EVER LOVING AND FIERCELY PROTECTIVE, CARRIED the heavy burden of raising me after we lost my father when I was just three years old. Determined to give me some sense of stability, she sent me to live alternately with my eldest sister, Godelieve Kayowa, in Tshikapa; my older brother, Robert Vianney Kanyiki, in Kananga; and one of my maternal uncles in a nearby village. During these years, I drifted between these homes—living a kind of nomadic childhood.

Perhaps this lack of stability was unsurprising, given the twin realities of my father's untimely death and his unlikely instructions to my mother regarding remarrying.

In addition to my father's death, which was tragic enough, my family endured other dramatic incidents. My sister Ngalula, born three years before me, was gored to death by a male goat. This would not be the only family incident during my formative years. Godelieve Kayowa, the eldest sibling, was by now married to a man named Kamanga Pius, who had a clerical position with Forminiere in Tshikapa. One day, Pius came back from work and, for reasons that my little mind could not grasp, violently beat my sister. Once again, I found myself incapable of defending her. All I could do was to hide and cry, wondering who would come to our rescue.

Many years later, Mother shared with me that whenever my sister would run from her home back to Mai Munene, Mother would ask whether she was coming for a normal visit or if she was trying to escape her husband. If the reason given was the latter, my sister would be fed and given water to drink, but she was not allowed to stay. She'd be sent back to her husband, if not the same day, then at the latest the next day. Mother desired to see my sister work out her issues with her husband.

My heart aches as I think about the sufferings my sister endured. I loved her beyond words. She was a second mother to me. When I had a cold and suffered from a stuffy nose, often she would suck out the snot from my nostrils with her mouth!

Writing from the perspective of an aging man, I cannot help but feel the weight of *all* my years, tempting though it is to dwell in childhood memories. The only other detail I will recount from these nomadic years centers on sugar—yes, sugar!—and the trajectory of my education, especially in regard to my motivation.

When I lived with Godelieve in Tshikapa, I took a strong liking to school…or at least to Wednesdays! This was owing to the habit of our teachers providing us with milk and cookies on Wednesdays, a powerful incentive for me to be present. Suffice to say I never missed that treat, but the other four and a half days of education were very much optional in my young mind.

One such Wednesday, on my way back home, I walked too close to an electricity tower whose massive poles and wires were not properly grounded. The pull and shock I experienced have remained engraved in my mind. It was the scariest moment for me at that time.

Thank You, Lord Jesus, for sparing my life. You had Your plans for it and did not desire that it be snuffed out so early!

My education proper began in the unlikeliest of ways.

My brother Robert was the station chief of a public transport company. And here I will briefly recall why Robert was working there: He had been kicked out of the seminary! A priest had caught Robert admiring himself in a mirror, dressed in his ironed seminary uniform. Unfortunately for him, pride was a no-no in that rule-bound institution. Now, I will admit to not knowing if that was the only reason my brother was kicked out of the seminary, but for the family and me, that departure proved a blessing in disguise. Robert was forced to apply for work and start contributing to my upbringing, proving once again the saying "In all things God works for the good of those who love him" (from Romans 8:28).

Robert's position as station chief was considered reputable and influential, allowing him and his wife to maintain a fine hut and send me to a local Catholic school. While most of my first-grade peers were learning to read and do sums, I had been busy doing something very different and decidedly nonacademic. I had what some would have called an *adventurous* spirit. Each morning, when I left Robert's hut, I carried my folder under my arm, inside of which was my school notebook and my best pencil. I must have resembled every other schoolboy headed toward our Catholic school. Unlike most other schoolboys, I met three of my friends at our secret place near a small brook. Once hidden from the road, we would carefully remove our school clothes, folding them and placing them in neat piles atop dry, clean rocks. Our folders were similarly cared for, leaving no evidence of where we had taken them.

What followed were delightful hours of play, sliding on pineapple leaves down a mud-slicked hillside and splashing into the creek. When the slanting sun informed us the afternoon was waning, we would begin our farewell procedures. Each of us would wash in the brook before clambering up the bank, careful not to muddy ourselves. Then we would don our school clothes, collect our notebooks, and return via secret paths to the main road. There, like a brook flowing into a stream, we would rejoin the other children returning from a day at school.

On school days this occurred more often than not.

What had *not* occurred to my young mind was the idea of a reckoning. Each day presented itself as brand-new, a playground for my fancies. If most of my peers were content to be cooped up in a classroom, that was their business!

As that academic year neared its close, however, a startling realization came to me: Proclamation proceedings were coming.

Tradition dictated that each school in Kananga assemble its students in the local soccer stadium, where each class would be called to a stage at the center of the stadium. The top three in each class would be presented with coveted prizes, such as a small toy car or a ball. Of more concern to me, however, was what happened further down the list of students. Even with my limited engagement in the educational system, I knew the worst-performing student in each class received a notorious distinction: *tshiamsho*.

While the origins of this expression had been lost in the murky past, its meaning was clear. If I were to be *tshiamsho*, I could count on my classmates following me home from the assembly, chanting at me all the way. The shame would be unbearable. Some tormentors would go even further, I knew, throwing dust or pebbles at the unlucky student.

It was far too late in the year to change my standing. All I could do was pray in earnest that I would avoid notoriety.

I woke up on the dreaded day and immediately wished I had not. Heightening my misery was the arrival of my mother. She had come to see me, of course, but even more to cheer on my two older brothers, Antoine Tshiyombo Muka and Honoré Ngandu Kashala, both of whom were excellent students. As the four of us walked to the stadium, I was one person inside and another person outside. When we reached the gates, I said goodbye and good luck to my brothers, hugged my mother, greeted my classmates, and took my place on the pitch near my instructor. All this time my insides were working to tie themselves into knots.

The event proceeded as if in a fog. I paid little attention to who in each class was top and who was *tshiamsho*, other than to note my two brothers had both achieved top-three status and been awarded prizes. At last, it was time for my class. The director announced names from first to last. There were fifty-four children in my class, including me, and with every name called my heart accelerated.

"Number thirty…"

Of course, I would not be near the top… but I simply could not bear to be at the bottom!

"Number forty…"

I calculated that I did not have many more chances to avoid humiliation. When the director reached number forty-five, a drop of moisture stung my left eye. I touched my forehead and found it covered in sweat. I glanced to my left and then to my right. Could I make a break for freedom? Probably. But what then? Even if I managed to make it home without being tormented by my classmates, an even greater shame would await me. How would I explain to my brother Robert that I was *tshiamsho*? He and his wife, Jeanne Mulanga, had taken me into their home. He was as close to a father as I had.

Still worse, what would my mother say?

Help me, God, I prayed, *I* cannot *be last*. This, by the way, is one of the earliest prayers I can remember, and it remains one of my most passionate, despite everything that has occurred in the intervening seventy-plus years. (The only other cry to God carrying the same fervor and passion was at the time of my circumcision. I was a few years old already and was given nothing to eliminate or numb the pain!)

Forty-six, forty-seven, forty-eight.

Help me, God.

Forty-nine.

Please, God, please!

"Fifty, Athanase Tshibaka."

I was fiftieth! What joy and relief! Never in my young life had I felt such elation. A grin split my face and I felt as if my feet were lifting off the dirt pitch. The rest of the ceremony flew by in what seemed an instant, and soon I found myself reunited with my mother and my brothers, clapping their backs in congratulations and examining the prizes they had been given. I glimpsed several *tshiamshos* shuffle off in shame, already enduring jeers, but I could not bring myself to participate so soon after my own escape.

When I returned home, however, my joy was broken like a dry twig being snapped in two. Robert was there, but he appeared to be a different brother. He rarely disciplined me, choosing more often the brotherly carrot than the fatherly stick. In this case, however, I had crossed a line. No doubt he had been informed of my narrow escape from *tshiamsho,* and unlike me did not consider fifth-from-last something to celebrate.

"You cannot continue on this road, Athanase. You *cannot!*" Robert glared at me, his hands resting on his hips. "From now on you will study. And I will know if you do not!"

That evening, I prayed again. My words were not born out of fear like my earlier prayer, yet they carried the same conviction. I knelt on my mat, clenched my hands tightly, and vowed before God to apply myself to my schoolwork. I prayed that God would give me strength and thanked Him for the chance to do better. When I said "amen" and opened my eyes, I sensed that my plea had been heard and that it would be answered.

As I fell asleep, I considered my day. It had ended well after beginning with such terror, and I had certainly deserved a tongue-lashing from Robert. My brother was right: It was time to put childish ways behind me. There would be no more playing hooky at the creek for *this* student.

And then a wonderful thought occurred. My vow would have to wait because school was out of session for the summer.

Tutu Robert was friends with Mr. Albert Kasanda, a first-grade teacher at the newly founded *École Officielle de Luluabourg* (Public School of Luluabourg). Luluabourg is today known as Kananga, a town about two hundred kilometers from Mbuji-Mayi. My brother's connection with Mr. Kasanda helped to secure a place for me in first grade at that public school.

My prayer, and my brother's scolding, had worked. Having escaped the ignominy of *tshiamsho,* I attacked my studies with gusto. The Belgians had introduced a nationwide system of public schooling, *École Officielle,* and Robert had moved me from the Catholic school to the local government school. It was a fresh start for me in two senses: new instructors *and* the brand-new language of French. I had heard French being spoken by the *Pères* in Mai Munene, but now I was old enough to learn it.

At the end of that year, after first grade (repeated!), I stood facing a mango tree with squared shoulders. After clearing my throat, I began to speak to the tree.

"Bonjour Monsieur le manguier!" ("Good day, Mr. Mango tree!")

There was no reply forthcoming from the mango tree, so I continued my end of the conversation.

"Comment allez-vous? Je m'appelle Athanase. Et vous?" ("How are you? My name is Athanase. What's your name?")

The mango tree did not provide me with its formal name, nor a description of how it was doing. Undeterred, I continued practicing every bit of French I knew...and even some I made up on the spot!

So passionate was I about this new language that I seized any opportunity to practice, even if my conversation partner happened to be a mango tree. Unbeknownst to me at that moment, my brother Robert was observing me from a nearby window. His intrusion in my language practice caused me to stop, somewhat embarrassed that I had been caught talking to a tree.

Robert was so proud of my burgeoning language skills that he began taking me on trips to visit his friends. I recall being asked to converse in French, much to the delight of the gathered adults. No doubt Robert relished the opportunity to showcase his little brother. In a way he was responsible for setting me on the path to academic achievement and excellence, and I never looked back. From that year onward, I always finished in the top two in my class, often capturing the top spot.

But lest you imagine me as fully reformed, I must report that I was very much a work in progress.

I remember once fighting with a girl, Veronique Tshibola, whose parents lived two houses across the street from us. I do not recall what had provoked the altercation, but I remember her parents' reaction.

"Athanase, why would you beat up your future wife?" her dad asked.

We had been neighbors since my mother moved us to Tshimbi, just on the outskirts of Kananga. They were from the Bena Lulua tribe. I was a Muluba (from the Baluba tribe). Veronique Tshibola was one year older than me, and I was one year older than her younger brother. The three of us were friends. We used to gather with other kids from our neighborhood at night under the bright shining moon, singing and dancing to traditional songs. We would hold hands and one of us would be in the middle, blindfolded. We would sing and move up and down, circling around the lion, the child in the middle. The song was known as *"Ntambwa Kuata Weba"* ("Lion, catch your prey!"). The person in the center would be positioned in a crouch, jumping up and down as a lion, trying to catch one of the people in the circle. The one touched would replace him in the center. Sometimes we would divide into teams of two and play hide-and-seek.

Veronique had both her parents, while I had lost my father when I was still very little. Looking back, I simply thank God that her father did not teach me a lesson of a lifetime. Instead, he was fatherly and forgiving.

Yet it seems that I did not learn from the fight with Veronique. That same year, when I was still in sixth grade at a public elementary school in Tshimbi (*École Officielle de Tshimbi*), I got into another fight, this time with a boy who was bigger than me. We were in the last period of our class that day. He folded his hands as if forming binoculars around his eyes and stared straight at me. I knew exactly what he was calling me. He was calling me a crocodile because I had eyes that appeared too large for the size of my head.

Now that was an insult I could not ignore without responding!

I took my hand and placed it below my lip, signaling that my classmate had larger-than-normal lips. By this point in the pantomimed war of insults, other classmates began to observe and laugh. My interlocutor did not find the situation funny, and his next signal was a clenched fist that he gently placed against his cheek. That meant I was in trouble. I had just provoked a fight I could not possibly win.

At the end of class, we were all to line up and march to where the teacher would dismiss us to go home. As one of the younger and shorter members of my class, I was always number two from the front of the line, while the danger lurked somewhere back in the line. I thought I would be able to escape and avoid confrontation with him, until he caught up with me some fifty meters from the school.

"Oh, help me, Lord!" I prayed.

"What did you do in class?" he demanded.

I was so frightened that I could not speak.

The next thing I felt was a punch, very hard and at the exact place on my cheek where my adversary had pointed during class. I suddenly found myself on the ground, with him on top of me. Before he could inflict more damage, an older boy from my neighborhood separated us and held my aggressor tight, signaling to me to punch him back. Yet how could I? That would simply have meant more beating for me the next day. I went home with a red eye and a few markings on my face, which I could not hide from Mother. She grilled me, then scolded me and told me she never wanted to hear that I had engaged in a fight with anyone ever again.

And, happily, that was the last time that I ever fought with anyone.

Three elementary schools operated within an hour's walk of my home in Tshibombo: a public school (*École Officielle*), a Presbyterian school, and the Catholic school I was attending. As Catholics, my family put me in the Catholic School of Tshibombo when we first moved as refugees to that village near Mbuji-Mayi, a move I will discuss in greater detail later. The year was 1960, and the transition was jarring. The Catholic school was more than a kilometer down the road toward Mbuji-Mayi. The Presbyterian and public schools were a shorter distance in the opposite direction, on either side of the road that joins Mbuji-Mayi and Kananga, passing through Tshibombo.

I was still keen to improve my academic performance, but our instructors believed in preparing us for life after graduation, which in their minds meant farming and animal husbandry. We were moved from classroom to field and back again, and this became a routine of my school experience, day after day.

One afternoon, our teacher's announcement that we would be moving to the fields was met with groans. Outside, it was nearly forty degrees Celsius, over a hundred Fahrenheit. Inside, it was not any cooler, but going into the fields would mean hours of sun blazing down on us, not to mention the tiring manual labor. We had been working in a particular field for the last several weeks to prepare it for spring planting. That meant hoeing, and a great deal of it.

Despite the grumbling, in which I was a vocal participant, we soon found ourselves outside. After less than one hour of labor, I suddenly stopped. Straightening and leaning on the hoe, I surveyed the field. A great deal of work remained, and it felt even hotter than when I had begun. When I had vowed before God to buckle down and commit myself to school, this was certainly not what I pictured.

"I cannot keep this up," I said to myself. "Forget it!"

That sounded right. I was not nervous. So without further deliberation I stopped working and turned to face my teacher.

"I am done hoeing," I announced.

"What are you doing, Athanase? Keep hoeing!"

"No, I will not."

"What do you mean you will not? You will!"

"I will not. It is hot and I am tired."

My teacher took two steps toward me. All the other students had taken advantage of our dispute and were leaning on the handles of their hoes. My stubbornness was buying them a moment of rest and providing them with entertainment.

"Listen to me, Athanase. You will keep working. Do you know why? Because if you refuse to work you will be expelled from school. Is that what you want?"

I glared at him.

He pressed his point. "If you are kicked out of school, then where will you go? You will be a failure. And you will have to work in the field anyway! So you may as well hoe now."

I was far past the point of thinking clearly. He was attempting to put the fear of God into me with threats of expulsion, but I was so tired and overheated that expulsion sounded almost pleasant in comparison! I did not want to spend one moment more in that field.

I flung down my hoe. "I quit!"

There were a few gasps from my classmates. "What did you say?" demanded my teacher.

But I was already walking away from him, and I did not stop until I reached home.

My oldest brother, Robert, was visiting at that time. As soon as I saw him, I began to complain. "Robert, do you know what just happened to me? My teacher is impossible!"

He grinned at me. "Okay, okay, little brother, tell me this big thing that happened to you."

I launched into my tale of woe, ending with the worst part of the whole event. "And then he kicked me out! And I quit!"

Robert did not react the way I had supposed he would. At the wise old age of thirteen, I believed I had been wronged by my teacher. My brother ought to take my side. Instead, he frowned at me and seemed to be deep in thought. Would this be a repetition of six years earlier, when he had scolded me so severely about nearly becoming *tshiamsho?* I waited nervously.

I knew he had reached a decision when I observed his face relax. Yet instead of speaking kind words to me, he took my arm and pulled me from my hut. We walked onto the road, turned left, and began marching… yet stopped almost immediately. I stared questioningly at Robert.

He said, "Mbiya Jacques's parents live in this hut. Jacques is the principal of the Presbyterian Elementary School of Tshibombo. And *that* school is where you are going to be attending, little brother, beginning tomorrow morning. Now wait here."

Robert entered the hut, and that same afternoon I was officially enrolled at the Presbyterian school.

Our God operates in mysterious ways. At that time, I could not have known the significance of changing schools. Yet in the course of the following six years, it would become apparent to me that God's hand had been touching me in the parish field that roasting afternoon. Or perhaps touching my hoe to help me cast it down! In Genesis 50:20, Joseph speaks to his brothers for the first time in decades—the same brothers who, out of jealousy and fear, sold him into slavery when he was only a youth. "You intended to harm me," he tells them, "but God intended it all for good."

Some six years earlier, in Kananga, Robert had been instrumental in moving me from a Catholic school to the *École Officielle de Luluabourg*. Now, he had just maneuvered me from the Catholic School of Tshibombo to the Presbyterian Elementary School of Tshibombo. Through it all, God was good. He had plans for me, and His plans were good.

In fact, I was soon to learn that God may transform *anything* into good, including the impetuous decision of a boy to quit working in a hot field.

CHAPTER 3

Refugee in My Own Country

Southern Congo

LEARNING SUCH A LESSON, THAT GOD MAY TRANSFORM *anything* into good, was neither immediate nor painless.

Before my circumstances were transformed into good, my family and I endured a decidedly terrifying season. In 1959, even as I completed elementary school and prepared for my secondary schooling, I underwent a far more traumatic transition. At the close of that decade, I became a refugee, and that status would in many ways define my life throughout the years that followed.

While a part of me wishes to skip over my time as a refugee, both because of its evil and because I do not wish to be pitied by my readers, another larger part of me understands it is crucial to discuss. Sometimes it is the darkness that enables us to see the light more clearly.

To understand how I became a refugee in my own country, a small amount of background information is in order. This is not a textbook of history, and in any case, others tell the story of that time with more detail and perspicuity. Nevertheless, here is a broad sketch of the key events.

The modern history of my country began in 1885 when, at a conference in Berlin, King Leopold of Belgium was personally awarded the "rights" to the Congo. Through the lens of history, such a development is as unsurprising as it is barbaric. Nevertheless, King Leopold seized his new power with both hands and directed it toward a single goal: wealth. With only a few hundred Europeans and a few thousand collaborating Congolese, organized into what was called the *Force Publique,* Leopold forced the locals into economic and working conditions that amounted to torture and slavery, all in the name of providing *him* with valuable ivory, rubber, and eventually Congo's rich minerals. Millions died in the following decades, even as Leopold became one of the wealthiest individuals in Europe.

In 1908, under pressure from many countries to end his exploitative stranglehold on my country, King Leopold formally transferred control to the Belgian government. The transition to being owned by a small country more than six thousand kilometers to the north was, shockingly, an improvement on the previous twenty-three years of economic exploitation that had been literally murderous.

The Belgians, though, were clever when it came to maintaining their hold on power. Devilishly clever.

Congo was a vast, sprawling nation, roughly seventy-five times the size of Belgium. And then there were the people. Us! For every Belgian there were ten times as many Congolese, living mostly in the same tribal lands for hundreds of years. So perhaps it was unavoidable that the Belgians turned to nefarious means to consolidate their power and to cling to it when the edifice of their power began to crack.

By the late 1950s there was a spirit of change in the air of Africa. Nations were throwing off their colonial shackles and walking toward independence. Our foreign occupiers chose to foment discord and hatred between tribes, reasoning that a divided populace would be unable to unite against a common enemy.

In many cases, to our shame, this strategy proved all too easy. Tribes were tragically willing to be exploited if it meant an opportunity to expand or consolidate power, or even to settle a long-standing grudge or feud.

My Baluba tribe was on the receiving end of this new power dynamic, and the Bena Lulua on the giving end. Instigated by the Belgians to "divide and conquer," ambitious, power-hungry politicians became colonial mouthpieces with rhetoric that further inflamed already brewing tribal tensions. "The Baluba must return to their land of origin!" intoned our Lulua brothers and sisters.

To enforce that message, attacks were launched against the Baluba in and around Luluabourg (today's Kananga). The Baluba responded in kind. The ensuing fights and skirmishes were waged with machetes, rocks, and hand-to-hand combat. My brothers Antoine and Honoré joined the other men and youth in the fights that erupted throughout Tshimbi. My sister Godelieve, who was visiting from Tshikapa, ran after them, screaming and begging them to return and hide at home with the rest of us. Antoine was to return that evening, bleeding from the head after being hit with a rock.

How could we continue to live in Tshimbi? Given the instability and perils surrounding our situation, my mother decided to send us kids with the last batch of refugee trucks leaving Luluabourg to Mbuji-Mayi, some two hundred kilometers distant, despite her uncertainty about where we children would stay and how we would survive. My two older brothers and I were able to board a dilapidated truck for the journey, finding tiny pockets of space as best we could among the others crowding the vehicle. Mother remained behind to assemble the small possessions we had.

She was able to follow in early 1960. By that time in the conflict, there was no public transportation available to her, nor any private parties willing to drive through the danger, and so she was forced to walk the two hundred kilometers with the final group of Baluba refugees. Her strength carried her all the way along that red road, just as she carried our family's remaining wealth atop her head: a few articles of clothing and a black Singer sewing machine, as heavy as it was useful.

So it was that we became a family of refugees. Naturally, I had *seen* refugees before, but that experience had done nothing to prepare me for the grave realities of the situation.

Although we were strangers, a villager in Tshibombo opened his hut to us. It consisted of a single room, no bigger than several meters to a side. With our help, he set up a makeshift divider, allowing him to live on one side and my mother, two brothers, and I to live on the other.

Then we lived as refugees, for better and mostly for worse.

We were safer, yes, than if we had remained within the reach of the Bena Lulua. But we soon learned that safety was relative!

What meager food we received was provided by the United Nations High Commission for Refugees (UNHCR). Every two weeks, or more often if we were lucky, a light blue truck arrived. Twenty-pound sacks of rice and smoked fish would be unloaded and distributed by the UN officials. The rice was palatable. The fish, however, was hard as charcoal and of similar color and flavor. My mother would boil the fish and serve it over the rice. We ate what was served to us because we much preferred the nearly inedible fish to starvation.

Those times, choking down smoked fish in half of a stranger's hut, were the good times.

When the national army soldiers arrived to combat the Baluba rebels, or when the Baluba rebels pushed back against the national soldiers, villages like ours were caught in the cross fire. Everyone was assumed to be a potential rebel or government sympathizer. Anyone could be slaughtered.

Whenever troops approached, we were forced to run into the bush and hide. We could take whatever leftover rice and fish we had, but most forays into the wilderness lasted for a week, or ten days, or more. With branches and grass we would make a kind of camouflaged shelter. At dawn and dusk we would forage for fruit or edible roots, while during the day we would attempt to remain out of sight and safe. Daily scouting trips would reveal the presence of soldiers in the village, and only when they had moved on could we return to the hut.

The rhythm of our lives alternated between terror and hunger, with dislocation and uncertainty always present. Perhaps my reluctance to relive every detail of that period can be forgiven. My family survived. That simple truth may be the best that can be said.

We refer to this time as *anni horribilis,* an expression once uttered by the late monarch of Great Britain, Queen Elizabeth II.

The horrible years.

After the passage of several years, conditions began to improve. Patrice Lumumba, Congo's first prime minister, had been murdered by his enemies in Katanga, with Belgian and CIA connivance, or so I understood. This paved the way for reconciliation between the rebel

Baluba leader, Albert Kalonji Ditunga Mulopwe; his counterpart for the Katanga province, Moïse Tshombe; and the national authorities led by President Joseph Kasa-Vubu.

My mother diversified her economic activity. She sold items outside the shared hut, like sardines and individual cigarettes, which she would display on a blanket. The Singer machine allowed her to create small, hand-sewn items and to mend clothing. The state of political upheaval allowed her to restart her alcohol distillation. All of this allowed her to complete her own hut.

For me, the gifted student, refugee life did not define the entirety of my existence. When I was at home with my mother and brothers, I was a refugee, yes. But something happened to transform my reality.

I was learning that deep beneath the dry and terrible soil of living as a refugee was a seed of hope, and that seed would soon take root.

CHAPTER 4

One More Test

Southern Congo

DESPITE FORCED RELOCATION, DESPITE SOMETIMES LIVING IN fear that roving soldiers or rebels would gun me down, despite a shortage of food, despite *every* hardship of life as a refugee, the first half of the 1960s was also a time of great personal growth and transformation.

Having been enrolled by my brother in the Presbyterian Elementary School of Tshibombo, and having completed sixth grade with flying colors, my attention turned to high school. As it happened, in the whole of our region there was only *one* Presbyterian high school, so naturally it would be *my* Presbyterian high school, regardless of its relative convenience, or lack of it. The boarding school was in Bibanga, a missionary station about sixty-five kilometers from Tshibombo. No small distance, but one I would be forced to travel. Assuming, that is, I achieved a high enough score on the entrance examination.

Because the demand for private high schools far outstripped the available places, each elementary school set its own series of exams, and only the top scorers would be allowed to proceed to take the high school exams. It was a competitive system, to be sure, but my teachers at Presbyterian Elementary School of Tshibombo had been exemplary. Under their tutelage I was drilled, examined, quizzed, and tested until I was ready to face any academic challenge.

Sure enough, when the test results arrived, I had achieved a perfect score. This was enough of an oddity that my instructors asked me to sit a different exam, and with all eyes watching I attained a second perfect score.

In theory my next step was the missionary station of Bibanga. In practice, however, there was the question of payment: forty dollars for the first year.

This was a princely sum for a child like me, even in ordinary times. As refugees, we had virtually nothing. Having no cash at hand, and no ready way to begin earning, I turned to the source of support most common to people in my situation: my family. When word of my academic opportunity spread to siblings, aunts, uncles, and even distant cousins, money began to trickle in, penny by penny. As it turned out, the final dollar would not arrive until after the first day of school, but the high school had informed me that as long as my tuition was paid by the second week of the term, I could join the semester-in-progress—assuming I passed another entrance exam.

There was no question of remaining with my mother and brothers. All agreed on the wisdom of traveling to the high school and enrolling if I could.

"You will be safe there," my mother told me, "and have food."

So, with my recent perfect scores providing confidence in my heart, I packed my suitcase with the few clothes I owned, said goodbye to my family, and began the trek toward my educational future.

Unfortunately, a major obstacle blocked my path. The Lubilanji River stood in my way, sullen and filled with silt. On the other side awaited a truck ride, followed by a hike, to reach the mission station in Bibanga, but on *this* side was a young man feeling suddenly small at the prospect of crossing such a wide expanse of dangerous water. This was not a creek like the one I had slid into as a boy. No, this was a raging *river*, an ominous boundary between me and the brighter future I hoped awaited me on the other side. What could I do except cross it?

I shrugged and began to search the banks for a *pirogue*, a local dugout canoe. When I found one, I climbed inside uncertainly, saying a prayer. I could not swim, at least not against the current of this mud-brown beast. That scarcely mattered, however, given the large population of crocodiles that populated the Lubilanji.

After what seemed like an hour of wobbling through the water, fearing for my life and imagining my imminent death, the canoe scraped onto the dense vegetation on the far shore. Tempted to kneel and kiss the ground in thanks, I instead satisfied myself with a silent prayer of gratitude to be back on firm ground.

From that point my journey became simpler. I asked around until I found a driver with a rusting pickup truck for hire, joining other travelers. My teeth had nearly rattled out of my jaw by the time we arrived at our stop, the town of Katanda, fifteen kilometers from the missionary school. It was as far as my driver would take me. No problem. To reach the school from that town, there were two ways to go: one was a long, curving road that skirted a series of hills, while the other was a steep path that cut directly *over* those hills. The first route was typically driven via truck, which was no longer an option for me, or by moped, which could be hired nearby. The second, much shorter route, was for those on foot.

To my dismay, I learned this information later from a boy at the school. Not knowing about the mopeds, or the length of either route, in the moment I chose to walk the longer road.

At long last I arrived at the missionary school. There had been no signs on the road, but I guessed from the angle of the sun and the heaviness in my legs that I had walked over twenty kilometers. I took my suitcase down from my head and surveyed the campus of Presbyterian High School of Bibanga.

At last, I had arrived.

Entering the school grounds, I shifted my suitcase to my side now. Perhaps it would go some way toward making me appear less of a "country boy," although I suspected the red dirt from the road coating my legs would give away my origins.

After my travels I was so hungry and thirsty that I could scarcely swallow. But first things first. Since the school day had already commenced, I sought out the principal. Perhaps once he had greeted me, he would provide some refreshment and direct me to a dormitory. I was confident that I would be able to pass the entrance exam the following morning, but in my current state, I simply needed to rest.

I soon discovered the principal, a Congolese with a high school diploma, in his office. Francois Katunda immediately took me to a large classroom in the same building, where some fifty kids were already seated. One of the teachers, Benoit Ngoyi, seemed to be overseeing an exam.

I made my way to the front as unobtrusively as possible and introduced myself. The principal studied me for a moment.

"You are very late, and we cannot reschedule your exam. You must sit the exam that is being given right now."

This was not good news. Nevertheless, I squared my shoulders. I had not braved a river full of crocodiles to be intimidated by a mere test. I nodded my acquiescence.

"*This* exam," said the principal, "is for *second*-year math. And we have only *three* open spots." The teacher slid the exam papers across the table to me as if they were poisoned.

I scanned the room again. Yes, there were at least fifty kids sitting for this exam. Those were not good odds, but I had no choice. Taking the papers, I found a spot at the nearest table and opened to page one. The Congolese teacher, Benoit Ngoyi, was patrolling the room. He placed a pencil in front of me and raised his eyebrows as if in pity.

I read the first problem. Could it be? I quickly read through the first dozen or so questions. Could it truly be? Relief coursed through my body. I had done these exact problems on one of my advanced exams back in Tshibombo!

My pencil began to fly across the page. I allowed myself a tiny smile as I furiously scribbled facts and figures.

"Who has reached the end of page two?" asked Professor Ngoyi, the proctor.

I looked up from my papers. Only six hands went up, including mine. I looked down at my papers again. I was already on page *four*. A sense of confidence began to grow in my chest. At least for the moment my hunger and thirst were forgotten as I lost myself in the exam.

I was the first one to stand and carry my papers to Professor Ngoyi. He stared at me for a long moment before shrugging and beginning to grade. I returned to my seat and watched him. Each time he turned a page he shook his head. My confidence began to fade. Had I worked too quickly? Been overconfident? When Professor Ngoyi reached the final page, he stood and rushed out of the room straight to the principal's office. They both returned to the exam room shortly after.

They will kick me out, I thought.

Professor Ngoyi walked back toward me. "The principal would like to see you," he said in a near whisper.

This was it. I was going home. Yet all I could think about was the twisted knot of my stomach, the parched desert of my tongue. Being sent away now seemed inevitable...but I did not want to die on the way, and I surely would if I did not eat and drink.

"Send me back," I wanted to say, if only to end the suspense and my hunger, "but please just give me some food and water first!"

I approached Principal Katunda. I could feel the eyes of the other students on my back, at least from those who had finished the exam. The principal gestured to a wooden chair at the side of his table. I sat. He paged through my exam, and then he looked up at me.

"You know, when we were given the results from the elementary schools last year, we thought perhaps your school had cheated."

I tried to swallow but failed.

"But today, with Professor Ngoyi watching, you have once again earned a perfect score."

He waited. I understood I was expected to say something, but the speech had deserted me. Perhaps sensing I was not in a very conversational mood, Principal Katunda chose to continue. "Your score of 100 percent on this *second-year* exam means you have earned one of the three available places. Welcome to the Presbyterian High School of Bibanga!"

Less than five minutes later, I was perched in a mango tree.

One of the boys who had finished his exam had taken pity on me and whispered the location of the tree as I exited the school building.

Now, my legs swinging below me, I pulled the nearest mango from its branch. Gripping it tightly in my left hand, I twisted off its top with the fingers of my right, exposing the bright flesh. Without a second thought I shoved the end of the fruit into my mouth and sucked greedily. No words could describe how delightful the taste was, how refreshing the juice felt as it coated my tongue and throat.

Three mangoes were what it took. Then I was certain I could last until the evening meal. My first evening meal as an official student at the high school.

CHAPTER 5

High School in Bibanga

Southern Congo

HOW ODD IT WAS TO RESIDE SOMEWHERE SAFE, WITH FOOD AND company, and with so little stress apart from the academic sort. Life at Presbyterian High School of Bibanga could not have been more different from life as a refugee. I remained fatherless, and if not for the care of an incredibly resourceful woman, my mother, and the efforts of my siblings, a refugee is what I would still have been. My entire family had made untold sacrifices to see to it that I had a decent education and the chance of a better, more stable life.

When I arrived, the Presbyterian High School of Bibanga consisted of only two grades, the first and second year, known as the *Cycle d'Orientation* (Orientation Cycle). It was founded in 1960 by Baluba High School graduates who had completed their secondary education at the Protestant High School of Katubue. They were supported in their initiative by a few Presbyterian missionaries from Southern American states such as Georgia and Texas.

After the Orientation Cycle, students were required to choose either the sciences or the humanities. For sciences, one would have to go to Katubue, an impossibility for me since this would mean returning to the Bena Lulua territory. The teachers we had at Bibanga dictated that our high school specialized in humanities (the letters). Since we were limited to two years, the second-year students had to pursue their third year and beyond in other high schools within Kasai Oriental, our new province, or simply return home.

However, when my class advanced to second year, the principal and school leaders decided to progressively add one additional class to the school each year. (My class would become the first one to graduate from the Presbyterian High School of Bibanga six years later. There were eight of us and we all passed the national state exams.)

All the classes were accommodated in one building, which held an office for the principal and a larger room that was used as the library. In front of the building was a large space where we did our morning gymnastics and played basketball. Across the street was our soccer field, and beyond that was our church. This building was the demarcation between the missionary station (where the school building and missionary residences were located) and the rest of the Bibanga village and its inhabitants.

During those first few days at Bibanga, I immediately learned that the instructors presented themselves well. The men wore neat slacks paired with button-down shirts, while the women swished between classes in long, dark skirts or long dresses and conservative blouses.

We students, on the other hand, formed a motley crew. Each student wore what he or she could afford, provided it was modest and studious. For some who were better off, that meant a close approximation of the faculty dress code. For students like me, however, the effect was far less professional. From the ground up, the sum total of my wardrobe was the following: black lace-up shoes, two pairs of black socks, two pairs of shorts (one khaki, one black), and two hand-me-down button-up shirts.

It was also impressed on me that boys and girls were *not* to mix, apart from officially sanctioned times, such as classroom instruction. We slept in separate communities. The girls' dormitories were located close to the main campus, while the boys' dormitories were half a kilometer away. Had I wanted to communicate privately with a certain young woman—which, to be honest, was a pure hypothetical in my early teen years—I would have had to undertake a complicated scheme. After writing a message on a scrap of paper, I would have needed to hide the message inside something innocuous like a corn husk, sneak away from my dormitory, and toss the disguised message over the fence…and then hope it was discovered by a sympathetic girl and delivered to its intended target.

Such potential transgressions call to mind an actual transgression. It was during Orientation Cycle, on a rare visit home, that I discovered my mother had resumed her alcohol distillation. Whereas the Belgians had banned all such activities, forcing her to hide her work in the forest, the nascent and newly independent Congolese government had no such laws on the books. Either that or it had too many other items on its plate to bother. In either case, for all practical purposes the ban on brewing was null and void.

Needing to run some errands, my mother asked me to tend her clay brewing vessel as it warmed on the fire inside the hut. Having observed her using a teaspoon to taste the quality of her work, I decided to do the same while she was gone. Slowly I raised the spoon to my lips and sipped. Swallowed. Coughed! This was interesting. Deciding a second spoonful might be easier to down than the first, I sipped again. Better! And the third sip was even easier.

I never heard my mother return, of course, since I had passed out cold! My punishment was stern, and the following headache felt as if it might divide my skull into two halves. There was no alcohol on our school campus, yet even if there had been, I suspect I would have stayed far away from it.

Certainly, I had plenty of work to keep me busy. Ever since the scarring experience of nearly being named *tshiamsho,* I had been a devoted student.

Some of my elders might have been tempted to equate my reluctance to hoe in the hot sunshine with a more general reluctance to work hard. But that would not have been an accurate conclusion. Already, I was no stranger to hard work in general, and even difficult manual labor. What I objected to was the "busy work." Being forced to do *anything* for no reason raised my hackles.

Perhaps that is why I became so studious. Apart from being spanked for hard-headedness on a single occasion, I had focused on my schoolwork and performed exceedingly well throughout my elementary years. I rightly understood that all my work in the classroom was preparing me for the *next* year's classroom—and all my classrooms were preparing me to make a good livelihood when I was old enough.

So I seldom butted heads with my instructors over my school assignments. But there was another source of conflict.

Early in my time at Presbyterian High School of Bibanga, my instructors began to pressure me to convert to Presbyterianism.

"Athanase," they would say to me, "it's time for you to become Presbyterian. All of us here are Presbyterian. You believe what we believe already, right? Why not make the change from Catholic to Presbyterian?"

With similar words they encouraged me, and with increasing frequency. It was never demanding or rude, but the pressure was consistent.

"Look, I am already baptized and confirmed in the Catholic Church," I told them more than once. "Why do you keep asking me to do this?"

"Well, now it's time to be baptized as a Presbyterian as well!"

Part of me felt attracted to the offer. Like any teenager, I wanted to fit in. I wanted to belong and be accepted. And my instructors were generally kind and well-meaning. I could tell they were sincere believers.

Yet a larger part of me resisted. Of the many lessons I had internalized as a child, loyalty to the church of my baptism was among the most deeply rooted. The church into which I had been baptized, back in Mai Munene, belonged to the worldwide Catholic Church. I belonged to the worldwide Catholic Church. That mother church was the agent of my salvation. To turn my back on my baptism would be to turn my back on God, and surely being baptized into a *different* church would count as turning my back!

My great fear was that such a step would mean spending eternity in hell as a faithless betrayer. The Presbyterians could not hope to save me if I left the Catholic Church.

That, at least, is how the priest's voice in my head presented the issue. I listened to his voice, and believed it, even if that belief was starting to be colored, for the first time, by doubt.

CHAPTER 6

La Gymnastique Tshibakienne

Southern Congo

When the two-year Orientation Cycle finished, students were expected to transition from general instruction to a more focused course of study. Each student was required to select a specialization. Since Bibanga could only offer "the letters" (literature, geography, history, French, Latin, English, writing, and so on), with less emphasis on sciences and math, my choice was largely made for me. I would be exposed to the works of Molière, Voltaire, Victor Hugo, and other French writers. I learned about countries across the globe and could recite their names and capitals and main characteristics from memory. Yet even though I was specializing in "the letters," I was strong in math and various sciences. My longer-term ambition or career aspiration was limited to two areas: a medical doctor or a lawyer. These were two disciplines that would assure me the potential of a paying job after graduating from a Congolese university.

Reaching this grade meant a choice beyond academics, however.

"Athanase, we have been speaking to you about this for years," I was reminded. "Now you *must* decide about baptism, and this is no small matter for you."

It was true. Once a student reached ninth grade, he or she was required to be baptized into the Presbyterian Church to continue attending high school. I had not been at all convinced I needed to convert, but what choice did I truly have? Things were somewhat better back in Tshibombo, certainly, but my family members were still refugees. I was not only safe and well fed at school but was also on the path toward a good job.

As I considered the matter, I realized that baptism was the only option available to me, at least from a practical point of view.

But as I continued to ponder, I observed that my previous misgivings about baptism were fading. Surprisingly, the reason my former religious objections carried less weight was that I had been forming a new set of religious convictions.

I had begun to read the Bible provided to me by the school. And the more I read my Bible, the more I wanted to read my Bible. I hungered for its words. As Saint Peter instructs, so it was true with me: "Like newborn babies, long for the pure milk of the word, so that by it you may grow in respect to salvation" (1 Peter 2:2 NASB). Perhaps in my younger years, the soil of my heart had been too hard to allow spiritual seeds to take root and grow. I had never lacked belief in God, at least as an intellectual truth to which I could assent. And the fear of God had always been something I felt with keenness. But never before had I felt God's words speaking to me personally and beginning to change me from within.

As ninth grade proceeded, I had no real choice about accepting baptism into the Presbyterian Church, yet I discovered myself willing in any case. I wanted more of what I was experiencing and learning about God.

I was baptized into the Presbyterian Church, becoming officially a third-year high school student *and* a convert, at least of a sort.

My younger self would not have assumed high school would be a certainty. Secondary education in my country was not a given, especially for a family like mine. And my younger self would *never* have imagined a turning away from Catholicism. Nevertheless, I found myself a newly minted Presbyterian, likely to finish my educational career at that same school.

On my dormitory bed I devoured chapter after chapter of Scripture. Before long I involved myself with the Youth for Christ club on campus, and I was elected and reelected its president for the rest of my high school years at Bibanga. And my relationship with God continued to deepen.

I grew to appreciate our mandatory school chapels. We met in the church for chapel, which was a full-fledged church on Sundays, providing worship space not only for the students but for the faculty and their families, along with villagers who lived near the mission station. During the week our chapels took place inside this large brick building, which was plain without appearing utilitarian. While the exterior of the church was simply one large and dusty building in the middle of a campus full of such dusty buildings, the interior possessed an entirely different character. An ample number of plain glass windows allowed sunlight to stream into the interior, while behind the altar and choir a slightly more decorated window reflected the light through its several colors and panes. The altar, carved from dark wood, presided over the front of the room, while pews receded back from the altar in orderly rows, built from the same dark wood.

In many ways it reminded me of the church all the way in Mai Munene. It fostered the same sense of respect and decorum, the same sacred space in which to pray and sing.

And sing I did! One of our instructors was an amateur choir director. She translated American songs, usually African American spirituals, into Tshiluba. Our student choir practiced these songs and hymns during the week, then led the congregation each Sunday. I sang bass in the four-part harmony, and the experience was truly glorious. We sang with gusto and full-throated pride, and the music never failed to move me to the core of my being. For me the songs became infinitely more than foreign music. They transported me. Rooted me. Or perhaps both at the same time.

I even took this newfound joy of the Lord public with Youth for Christ. With faculty assistance, we practiced preaching, coordinated discussions and debates, and planned youth meetings on Sunday afternoons.

This was also the time that the Presbyterian Church USA took over the running of the school, strengthening the faculty in numbers and quality. Our new professors had university degrees ranging from bachelor's and master's degrees to doctorates. Professors such as Ann Anderson, John Pritchard, and Emily Boehler significantly enriched our educational experience. They were soon to be joined by professors from Haiti, Holland, and Portugal.

A Texan named Eric Bolton took over as principal, a position that was augmented by other duties. He was also the pilot of the small airplane owned by the mission, and he taught some of the math and physics classes. Principal Eric was a heavily built, strong, and fearsome man. He commanded attention with his mere presence, without having to use his voice, though his voice itself was authoritative and demanded respect, if not obedience.

To this day I am grateful for my teachers. Looking back, I consider them all angels that almighty God placed along my life's journey, to instruct and help shape my character and my destiny.

I do not wish my readers to assume I transformed into some sort of angel, though! I still had a great deal of maturing to do.

Each morning when we completed the kilometer-long trek from the boys' dormitory to the main schoolyard, we performed gymnastics. One of our faculty members would take the role of drill instructor, telling us to march forward, turn left, step right, and so on. This took place in view of the principal's windowed office. Perhaps the idea had been to allow the principal to observe his students drilling, though as far as we knew that did not happen.

One morning, on a whim, I decided to make the instructor miserable. We were lined up according to height, and I was second-from-the-front. Keeping a straight face and appearing to work hard, I performed the opposite of his every command.

"One step forward!"

I stepped backward and bumped into the boy behind me.

"Step right!"

I stepped left and suddenly was standing apart from the rest of the boys.

"I said *right*, Tshibaka!"

I stepped left again. Some of the boys stepped right again, obeying orders, but some took a confused step to the left, thinking of rejoining the line with me.

Soon the whole exercise devolved into utter chaos. I could tell from the furious look on my instructor's face that I had accomplished my mission. I would certainly receive some backslaps and compliments from my classmates later in the day for my shenanigans.

Until my plan collapsed around me.

"*You*... there!"

It was Principal Bolton, shouting from his nearby office window. For an unknown reason he had been watching the entire sad episode. There was no way to pretend I had strayed only briefly or unintentionally.

I froze. Principal Bolton stomped across the schoolyard and stopped mere inches from me. His eyes bulged as his fingers closed around my upper arm. He was not a small man, nor a weak one. I harbored no hope of escaping his strong grasp. Besides, where would I have gone? He held the position of final authority at the school.

He marched me to his office. Without a word he lifted the two wooden chairs in front of his desk and set them down against the wall. He then returned to the open space he had created and faced me. His arms were crossed.

"You will now do gymnastics for me, and you will do them correctly. Do you understand?"

I nodded. In truth I did not understand, or at least not completely. I had not decided whether I would obey my principal's instructions. If I could avoid being kicked out of school *and* avoid complying with this punishment, I would choose that course of action. To buy myself time to think, I muttered an insult in Tshiluba. I stared at Principal Bolton to make sure he understood I was speaking to him, even if he could not understand my dialect. He would be unable to add a punishment for something he could not prove I had done.

He stared back. I swallowed.

Unfortunately, I could tell that he *did* understand my insult. If not the literal meaning, then at least the general sense he was being insulted. He understood and he refused to care. He refused to give me the satisfaction of engaging with my juvenile antics.

"You will begin," he said after an uncomfortable silence. "Hands up! Hands down! Now crouch and hold. Now hands up..."

It took only a few minutes for me to understand that he meant to break me. I began to sweat. My arms became sore. My legs filled with lactic acid and began to shake. Still, Principal Bolton forced me to continue. "Do *not* stop," he scolded, "until we are done."

Eventually I began to cry. And soon thereafter, Principal Bolton thanked me for performing my morning gymnastics so well, and then he dismissed me to class. I fled as fast as my aching legs could carry me.

Why had I antagonized my gymnastics teacher? I had wanted to make him miserable, wanted to frustrate him, but for what possible reason? Yes, he had asked us to perform pointless exercises, but was that sufficient reason for me to aggravate him? Surely not. None of the other students had done what I did.

Something shifted in my heart. I understood that despite the changes in my life, in many ways I remained the same impetuous boy who had thrown down his hoe in a fit of pique and walked away from his school. I no longer wanted to be that boy. And to be completely truthful, I never wanted to get on Principal Bolton's bad side again!

From that day forward I chose to act as a model student, above reproach. And to my general benefit, I became a minor celebrity on campus. The episode entered the collective lore of Presbyterian High School of Bibanga.

"Do you need to perform *la gymnastique Tshibakienne* (Tshibakian gymnastics)?" students would laugh with each other.

And once the soreness wore off, I could laugh at the joke as well.

I continued to visit home when I was able.

The summer before my senior year, I stayed with my sister, Yaya Kayowa, who taught me to roast and sell peanuts. She demonstrated the cumbersome process, step by step, until I could do it on my own.

That summer, most days I would roast two to five pounds of peanuts each morning. In the evenings, I would return home, having sold most or all of what I had taken to the market earlier. The peanuts had to be sold in affordable batches, so the measuring tool we used was a small, empty can of tomato paste. A full can of roasted peanuts would fetch perhaps a couple of Congolese francs. The whole of the purchase could fit in the palm of the buyer's hand, allowing them to munch on the nuts while shopping for other items or going on their way.

This is one way I was of help to my sister during my vacation and visits with her.

On the last day of my visit, my sister took me aside. She placed a few notes of Congolese francs in my hand. "For school," she told me. It was a large sacrifice for her. Selling peanuts did not provide a great deal of income, and she needed every last coin. She was investing in me, from her meager means, because she loved me and wanted me to succeed. To this day, gratitude fills my heart as I remember her loving kindness and generosity.

"And I want to show you something," she then told me. Inside her hut, tucked away in a small box, were several bundles of cash. I looked at her in confusion. "For you to use as dowry, brother, when the time comes."

A dowry? My sister was already thinking about my future family. Not just thinking about it, either, but sacrificing her own comfort to help ensure mine. She had helped support my schooling over the years, yes, but now she was also supporting a wife and children who did not yet exist!

The thought nearly staggered me. Who was I to be loved so deeply by so many? And what might I do in the future to show myself worthy of such love and sacrifice?

CHAPTER 7

Providence and Grace Abound

Southern Congo

ERIC BOLTON SAW SOMETHING IN ME THAT NO ONE ELSE DID, apart from my supportive family.

Certainly, I could not see it myself!

He understood that my stubborn nature, hardheaded and hard-hearted, could be redirected. Not simply toward academic achievement, but toward life, and even toward spiritual growth. I would never have imagined serving as the student body president, for example, but perhaps he suspected such a possibility was in my future on that fateful first day in his office.

This belief crystallized on the day Principal Bolton invited me to his office and told me about the possibility of a university scholarship.

Soon after the inauguration of American President John F. Kennedy in 1961, a new arm of the State Department was created. One of the goals of USAID (United States Agency for International Development) was to reach out to youths in emerging markets and provide opportunities for them to study in the United States. The idea was that the young people would earn degrees, as well as learn American culture, and then return to their home countries to make a positive difference, while hopefully becoming friends and informal "ambassadors" for the United States.

"Students from one hundred and forty-four high schools from across the Congo will be applying for seven of these scholarships," he told me, "and you are going to represent the Presbyterian High School of Bibanga.

We can't guarantee anything, but if you want to apply, we'll do our best to help you."

A chance to study, for *free*? In America?

The possibility was beyond my wildest dreams. But the math did not favor me. I had roughly a one-in-twenty chance…and that was if only one student from each school applied. Two applicants from each school would reduce my odds to 2.5 percent, while three applicants would shrink the likelihood to less than 2 percent.

Still, I had succeeded against unfavorable odds before.

"And listen, Athanase, the tests and interviews are going to be conducted in *Kananga*," Principal Bolton said carefully.

I panicked. Kananga was some 275 kilometers distant. Even if I had the money, which I certainly did not, traveling by road through Mbuji-Mayi would take far too long. I would miss the tests and, assuming I did well, the interviews. Perhaps my hopes were in vain. I could not simply snap my fingers and appear in Kananga. This had all been a waste of…

Snap! Snap! Snap! Eric Bolton snapped his fingers. "Hey, Athanase!"

I looked up, startled. I had drifted into my own thoughts and fears. Had he been telling me something?

"You look like you've just been hit in the head!" he said, half joking. "Listen…there's no way you'll make it to Kananga by truck."

Did he believe that was news to me? I was well aware! And who had revealed to him what I was thinking?

"So, I figure I'll just fly you there and back whenever you need to go. How's that sound?"

My brain had ceased to function. My mouth opened but I was unable to form any words. "Uhhh…"

He smiled and raised his eyebrows.

"I…ummm," I continued, finishing with another eloquent, "uhhh."

"Hey, ease up on the thank-yous," he grinned, "or I'll get a big head. Now let's get started on the application you need to send in."

Principal Bolton was true to his word. Behind the controls of his tiny missionary plane, he piloted me to and from every required appointment in Kananga until the scholarship application process concluded.

All that remained was to wait for the announcement of the winners.

From the vantage point of an older man, I cannot help but wonder why Eric Bolton did this for me, just as I cannot help but calculate what his kindness cost him. Why would he leave his wife and children to fly a kid from the Congo to a series of exams and interviews? Why did he care so much?

Whatever the answers, and reserving the right to keep my readers in suspense as the story continues, I will remark on two things about this time in my life.

First, because of Eric Bolton, I was awarded a USAID scholarship. I would leave behind my family, my country, and everything I knew. I would be educated in an American university.

Second, my family came through for me, collecting money from various relatives for my one-way ticket from Mbuji-Mayi to Kinshasa. My brother Robert came to Kinshasa to help me with my visa application process, and he also arranged for me to stay in the home of his friends, Clement Kanku and his wife, Julienne Mbuyi, during the few weeks I needed to prepare for my trip to the United States. The international travel had already been agreed on as part of the program. The Congolese government would fund my travel to and from the United States, while the US government (USAID) was responsible for my tuition and other costs during my stay in America.

At last, the day of my departure came.

My brother Robert, with several nephews and nieces, came to see me off at Kinshasa's N'djili Airport. My fear of the unknown and my excitement for a new adventure churned within me. Needless to say, embarking on a transcontinental flight was a new experience. I settled into my seat, shed a few tears, and promptly fell asleep.

After months of stress competing for the scholarship, saying goodbye to my mother and family in Mbuji-Mayi, jumping through the hoops of the visa and USAID requirements with the United States embassy…I was exhausted. One thing remained clear in my mind, however: No matter what happened in America, I would strive to rejoin my family as soon as possible.

As I reflect on that transition in my life, I discover one lesson indelibly imprinted on my soul: God's grace is often delivered through unlikely means. Grace may be defined as being given something positive we do not deserve, while mercy is defined as escaping the negative consequences of what we do deserve. If a boy steals a bit of savory goat from his mother's cook pot, he deserves to be punished. A merciful mother may choose to forgo the punishment, and a graceful mother may allow the naughty boy to eat his ill-gotten gains!

So it was that God's grace toward me took the shape of my family, as it often did. And God's grace also took the quite unlikely shape of a white missionary with a Texan drawl—the very same person I had once insulted to his face.

PART TWO

AN IMMIGRANT'S UNEXPECTED JOURNEY

IVY LEAGUER, ACCIDENTAL BANKER, AND A BLESSED ENCOUNTER 1967–1972

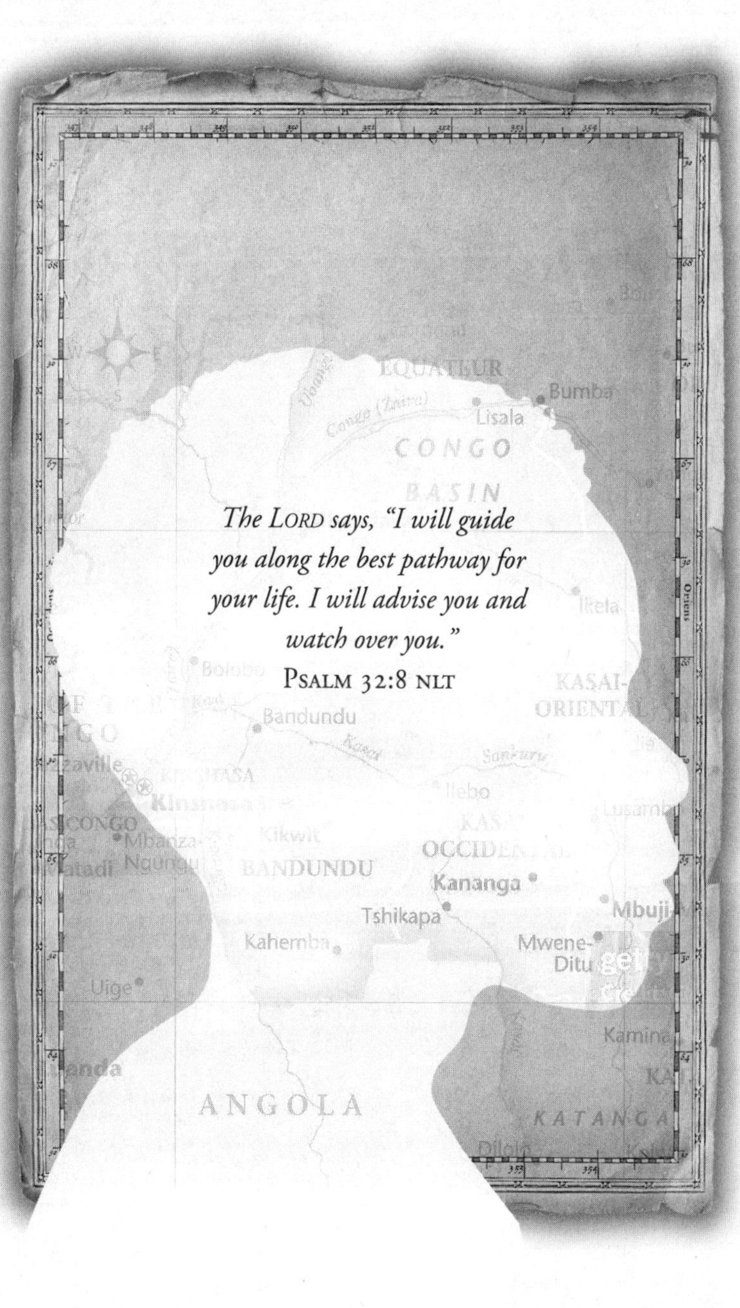

The LORD says, "I will guide you along the best pathway for your life. I will advise you and watch over you."

PSALM 32:8 NLT

CHAPTER 8

From Bibanga to Brattleboro

New York and Vermont

WHAT COULD I EXPECT UPON REACHING THE UNITED STATES of America?

It was a serious question, but one to which my mind could offer a few serious answers.

Eric Bolton had told me to expect many things to be different. Of course, I was familiar with some aspects of American culture because of my voluminous reading. But all such knowledge had been theoretical. Like a scout going into a new land after hearing secondhand reports, many things undoubtedly would challenge and even shock me.

Our Pan Am Boeing 707 touched down at Kennedy Airport and we deplaned down a set of rolling stairs. I followed my fellow passengers across the tarmac and into the curved, concrete terminal. Once inside, before I could get my bearings or discern which direction to walk, I pulled up short and stared. Directly across from me sat a teenage boy and a teenage girl, wrapped in each other's arms and kissing passionately! Although no one else seemed to be paying them any attention, I immediately averted my eyes and walked away.

Perhaps on some level I had known, at least if I had ever bothered to think about it, that the rules of our scholastic society in Bibanga were not necessarily standard in other places. Yet those rules had seemed normal, almost inevitable.

It was as if I had been slapped in the face. In less than twenty-four hours I had gone from a country where sneaking a note to a girl was an act of rebellion to one where public affection was commonplace.

I had anticipated learning many things, but this had not been one of them.

To acclimate to America, and to succeed at university, I would need to work diligently on my language skills. Gaining fluency in a second language, as I had already done, carried with it a certain level of confidence. If I had mastered French, I could certainly master English.

To that end, my first assignment from USAID was a language and cultural institute just outside of Brattleboro, Vermont. The Experiment in International Living was founded in the 1930s, and in the 1960s it became a training institute for Peace Corps volunteers. USAID used it to train foreign students who were entering the United States under its two scholarship programs: ASPAU for undergraduate studies (African Scholarship Program of American Universities), and AFGRAD for graduate (the African Graduate Fellowship Program). For us foreigners, the focus was on mastering the English language and deepening our understanding of and appreciation for American culture. For Peace Corps volunteers, the focus was preparing them for their foreign country assignments. Being on the same campus, sharing the same dormitories, and interacting with American youth gave us an added experiential exposure to American culture.

My academic English far outpaced my practical, day-to-day skills, and I could read nearly anything in English with strong comprehension, from *To Kill a Mockingbird* to the *New York Times*. I had attempted to extend that level of skill to my listening, though comprehending speech depended a great deal on the speed and accent of the speaker.

Conversing with a range of native speakers remained a challenge. This was reinforced early on in my three-month stay. During dinner, a Black American girl across from me locked her eyes on mine. *"Parlez-vous Français?"* she asked me. *Do you speak French?*

I replied in English that I did. What followed was a pleasant conversation in a mix of the two languages. I learned she was preparing to serve as a Peace Corps volunteer in a French-speaking country. Then came the moment when I understood the cultural divide between us was far deeper than I knew.

"I hear that in your country, in the Congo," she said, "you eat people. Is it true there are still cannibals there?"

I was stunned. *Cannibals?!* Then a thought occurred to me: If she believed Congolese still consumed human flesh, what reason would she have to believe a denial from the one Congolese she has only recently met?

I picked up my knife and fork and held them over my plate. Then I widened my eyes and gave what I hoped was a maniacal grin. "We *do* still eat people…and as a matter of fact, I am feeling quite hungry right now!"

That was not the start of a growing friendship between the two of us! The next time she glimpsed me in the hallway, she spun on her heel and nearly sprinted in the opposite direction.

Despite such unplanned interactions—or perhaps because of them—the three months I spent increasing my English proficiency passed quickly.

Classroom learning was not how I spent all my time and energy in Brattleboro. Every student in the USAID program was assigned an American host family to ease the transition into the new culture.

Reverend Keech, a Baptist pastor in nearby Greenfield, Massachusetts, and his wonderful wife welcomed me into their home. Importantly for my assimilation, the Keeches had three daughters, Cyndie, Ruth, and Shirley, who ranged in age from fourteen to eighteen years old. It was through them that I learned some of the finer points of American youth culture. The four of us hit it off immediately.

I soon called Reverend Keech and Mrs. Keech Dad and Mom. And while the four of us "kids" knew Dad as Reverend Keech, we assigned to Mom the honorific title of Most Reverend Mrs. Keech. During my stay, she made me peanut butter cookies, and he spoke with me about life. Both truly cared about me and showed me real love. On Sundays, we attended church service together. I was proud that my "dad" was the preacher.

One day, I was strolling through the neighborhood with the girls, chatting about whatever came to mind, when all three of them stopped simultaneously, as if responding to some secret signal. "Atha..." the eldest daughter began, drawing out my name with enough sweetness for me to suspect she wanted something.

"Listen, Atha, we've got a fun idea," continued the middle daughter. "Will you help us?"

There was little doubt I would help my host family, but I drew out the moment, looking from face to smiling face, as if I might refuse.

"I will help," I said at last, "but with what?"

The youngest piped up. "Booze!"

All three girls laughed.

"Just go into that store across the street and buy vodka and orange juice," I was instructed. "And make sure it costs less than four dollars."

With that, I became an accessory to underage drinking!

It was a far cry from what had passed for bad behavior back in Congo, just as it was a far cry from my mother's *cinq cent*. Yet as the four of us sat beneath a tree in a nearby park, laughing and trying to tell each other jokes, I could not help but appreciate both the companionship and the practicality of the language tutoring.

When we had drained both the orange juice and the vodka, and it was time to return home, the four of us shared an order of onion rings from a nearby restaurant. "That way," declared the youngest daughter, "Mom will never know what happened!" If she did, she didn't say anything.

All too soon, my time with the Keeches drew to a close. At the language institute, the news began to trickle down about which universities our program directors at USAID had selected for us. One of us would be heading to the University of Southern California, one to Purdue, one to Pomona College, and so on. No reasons were given for the selections, leaving us to assume the powers that be knew what was best for us.

For me that would mean studying at Dartmouth College, and I was anxious to begin my academic adventure. But in what field of study?

Had I attended a university back home, my choice would have been law or medicine. During my voyage to the United States, and while attending the Experiment in International Living, I had determined to major in chemical engineering. As I reflect, I am unsure how I came to choose a field of study for which I was least qualified. Fortunately, I discovered my error soon enough. I purchased a chemistry book for American senior high school students to gain a feel for what to expect. The material was so advanced beyond my training and background that I thought, *Forget chemical engineering!* With the benefit of hindsight, that decision, as swift as it was, proved wise.

I was thus ready to leave for Dartmouth with no clue about what my major would be. I was going to be separated from African, Latin American, and American friends I had made at the institute. We were all going our different ways to prepare for our different futures. My family was far distant in the Congo, and we had no idea when we would see each other again.

Perhaps most painfully, I was leaving the wonderful Keech family, including my three American "sisters." My only consolation was knowing that Greenfield was a few hours' drive from Hanover. I would see my American family again during school breaks…or at least that was how Mom Keech tried to console me.

CHAPTER 9

Mission School to Ivy League

New Hampshire

THE ENTIRE KEECH FAMILY DROVE ME TO THE DARTMOUTH campus. A winter storm had blown in and the town was blanketed in snow. The instant I stepped out of their warm car, dressed only in slacks, a button-up shirt, and a sweater, I felt as if I had become frozen to the spot. My constitution was not made for such extreme cold!

A man with spectacles carrying an overcoat ran toward the car. He wrapped it around my shivering shoulders and began to guide me toward a nearby building. I learned he was the foreign students adviser.

"Sir, I think someone made a mistake," I chattered. "A *big* mistake. This is *not* where I'm supposed to be."

I had known I was going to Dartmouth, but I had not imagined what that meant. I was not going to a generic university any longer. I was at this particular university, and as I squinted across the cold distance between the idling car and the building, I suddenly knew what I wanted: warmth.

"Sir, I think I am supposed to be at Stanford!"

"Listen," the official said, injecting just enough force into the word to catch my attention, "all the arrangements have been made for you to be *here*, at Dartmouth. Why don't you try this for one semester? Just one. And if you still aren't happy at the end of the semester, I'll do everything I can to make sure you get into Stanford, okay?"

He waited. I shivered. The Keech family waved to me from inside their warm car.

I nodded.

And so began my first day at Dartmouth.

I was at university for a very specific purpose. As a USAID scholarship winner, I was meant to earn a degree in an important field of study and then secure a good job. My future contributions to wider society would justify the investment being made in me.

I took notice of the students around me. What did they want? What motivated them? The answers were all too obvious. A newer car. A second car. A nicer apartment. A vacation home. A larger bank account. Power and influence.

Should I want those same things? I looked inside my heart and found that I did not. *What is the one thing you want?* I asked myself. The answer came to mind immediately, and I felt no doubt about it.

To give back to the country of my birth.

I did not yet know what that involved, but I understood it was something I must do.

So, to what USAID expected of me, I added an additional purpose: I vowed that whatever job I found would be in the Congo. I was an idealist. I desired to return to the country of my birth to improve it. And the best way to do so would be to graduate from university as rapidly as possible.

To that end I made inquiries about how to speed up my studies. Even if I moved to Stanford, it would not be for at least a semester, so I determined to make the most of the coming months.

I was told about subjects for which incoming students could sit exams: geography, world history, algebra, composition, and so on. Passing those exams would enable me to skip certain classes. Over the next week, I sat exams for four days in a row, supervised by a bored clerk who no doubt wondered why a Congolese student was taking what must have seemed like every exam available.

I passed each test I sat. When the semester began, I was already a sophomore.

•⋊◇◇⋉•

I soon learned that earning a degree required earning money as well. My school funding was provided for me, but I had other expenses that were adding up.

I applied for any available job and was soon rewarded with one: assistant dorm janitor.

The standard janitorial duties were not unpleasant. Cleaning windows, mopping floors, taking out the trash—those tasks did not trouble me. Often, I ran through vocabulary words in my head as I worked or mulled an argument for a paper. The nonstandard duties, however, *were* unpleasant. Drinking was common on campus, which meant cleaning up vomit was all too common as well.

I tried to tackle my work diligently and cheerfully. I wanted to give every task my very best. Yet I could not help but feel pleased when a position in the cafeteria came up. Serving as a waiter was a much better job because, in addition to earning the same few dollars as my janitorial post, I had free food—and sometimes even a nicely cooked steak!

Working diligently at my studies and diligently at my job, my first months at university passed quickly.

So quickly, in fact, that I found myself evolving into a different person, at least regarding the state of my soul.

I had arrived in the United States as a faithful Christian. I went to church each Sunday with the Keech family. I read my Bible. I prayed.

And yet something began to change the moment I stepped off the airplane. That change only accelerated at Dartmouth. If, back in Bibanga, I had been on fire for God, now those flames were being starved of oxygen. A new culture, new peers, and myriad new responsibilities were taking the place of the personal relationship with my Creator I had formerly enjoyed.

Undoubtedly the embers of holy fire remained inside me, but both the practice and the presence of my faith were cooling.

Early in my first year I wrote a term paper for my philosophy of religion course, and the only source I cited was the Bible. My professor, unimpressed with my narrow perspective, awarded me a C+. Rereading my paper, I could not blame him. My term paper had been based entirely on the Bible, yes, but what about my life? My actions? Even I did not believe strongly in what I had written.

Perhaps it was a paradox. Perhaps, looking back, it was providence. But the more time I spent on my studies, the less time I gave to God. My faith was pushed to the margins, and it seemed to me that the tradeoff was fair. Necessary even. There were now aspects of my life, such as my studies, that needed to be emphasized, even at God's expense. Since I would not receive a better grade on an exam if I traded an hour of preparation time for reading the Bible and praying, it seemed wiser to spend my time studying.

Soon, that emphasis on academics paid off in an unexpected way.

The Amos Tuck School of Business at Dartmouth was, I learned, a legendary institution in the world of American business. A master of business administration from Tuck could open many doors to excellent careers. Fortunately, I had opted for economics for my major at Dartmouth. A difficult field of study, to be sure, given my origins, but much less challenging than chemical engineering! Despite having no background in business administration, I believed the MBA was the correct opportunity to pursue.

Acceptance to Tuck relied on a difficult entrance examination, the Graduate Management Admission Test, or GMAT. During my second year, which was already my junior year in terms of progress, I asked to sit the exam, considering it as a practice run for the following year when I would be a senior and need to take the test for real. Taking the test as a junior would provide me with an entire year in which to "bone up" on the content areas in which I was behind.

To my great shock, the subsequent letter from Tuck not only contained my practice score…it also contained a letter of acceptance into the MBA program, along with instructions on how I could combine my first MBA year with my final year at Dartmouth.

> Dear Mr. Tshibaka, I am happy to report that the Committee on Admissions has voted to admit you to the class entering Tuck School in September 1969. Your acceptance is contingent upon completion of all degree requirements, through junior year, of Dartmouth College…

I had just been admitted into Tuck's MBA program after a little over one year on the Dartmouth campus!

This welcome news coincided with another upgrade in my employment. Perhaps my reliability and cheerfulness as a janitorial assistant and cafeteria worker had paid dividends, or perhaps it was the fact that I spoke some of the best French on campus, but either way I was awarded an assistant position with John Rassias, professor of French. My responsibilities included teaching conversational French to first- and second-year students, using the dramatized instruction methodology developed by Professor Rassias, known as the "Rassias Method."

The selection was not automatic. Applicants for the open positions had to undergo training and practice, followed by actual teaching drills under the direct observation of, and subsequent evaluation by, the illustrious professor. I was thrilled to learn I was among several applicants chosen.

Three decades later, I would introduce my son, Niki, to Professor Rassias during a college tour of the Dartmouth campus. Always generous in spirit, Professor Rassias offered to help Niki with his college essay and to advocate for his admission to Dartmouth. My wife, Priscilla, and I visited with him a couple of years later, this time to seek his counsel as our daughter, Mara, was also applying to Dartmouth, in response to her dad's not-so-subtle pressure. Niki was admitted, and Mara was on the waiting list, but both chose Amherst College instead.

Professor Rassias passed away in 2015 at the ripe old age of ninety. Then-Representative Ann McLane Kuster of New Hampshire, also a

Dartmouth graduate, eulogized his life and legacy and led the House of Representatives in a moment of silence in memory of this remarkable man.

How grateful I was to Professor Rassias and to all the instructors who taught and inspired me. It had taken some time, but it appeared as if the academic seeds I had been planting were beginning to bear fruit.

CHAPTER 10

The Green Latrine

New Hampshire

THE KEECH DAUGHTERS HAD TOLD ME CONFIDENTLY THAT American university was not entirely about academics. I would also meet and make new friends, and every now and then it would be important for me to take time away from studies to have fun at mixers or to visit other colleges in the area, especially Smith, Mount Holyoke, and Colby. They also encouraged me to get outside and take a walk when I needed a break.

One day, during the summer of 1969, a Ghanaian friend and I decided to eat lunch at a restaurant located across the street from Hanover Inn. It was known as "the Green Latrine." I never learned how it acquired the name, but in a way it lived up to it. It was far from the most appetizing establishment. It did have one advantage, however: an extremely low-cost menu.

That day, as my friend and I entered, I learned another thing the Green Latrine had going for it: It employed the most beautiful woman I had ever seen. She had blond hair, blue eyes, a sweet face, and a demeanor that stood out among every other person in the room.

I ordered a hamburger and soda for fifty cents and quickly devoured the sandwich, spending the rest of the time sipping on my soda, very slowly. My eyes were desperately (but unsuccessfully) trying to lock on to hers.

I was not going to give up! I still had another trick up my sleeve. If I gave her a large tip, she might notice me. My meal had cost fifty cents. I put one dollar and fifty cents by the bill and waited at the table, still sipping my soda very, very slowly. I needed to be there when she picked up the payment.

When she arrived at last, I don't remember if she said thank you. My ears were decommissioned, and my eyes were doing all the work, following her every move. No eye contact!

Beaten, but still hopeful, I left. Studies and term papers were waiting for me.

Later that week, I attended a party organized by a Nigerian friend, Joe. He had invited twenty of us boys and three girls to celebrate his master of engineering degree with him. To my delightful surprise, Priscilla—the stunning woman from the restaurant—was one of the three girls.

Delight turned to concern, however, and then almost to panic when I considered the boys-to-girls ratio.

The Afro beat of the music was irresistible: James Brown, Aretha Franklin, the Temptations, Marvin Gaye, Ike and Tina Turner, Diana Ross, Maitre Franco, Tabu Ley Rochereau, Nico Kasanda, and Sam Mangwana. As the music played, I sat and observed the lucky guys who were already on the dance floor, staying alert while planning my move.

I did not entirely lack confidence around the fairer sex, but I was wise enough to know that the seven-to-one ratio of boys to girls meant I needed to seize my opportunity. But how?

A thought occurred: Perhaps I could woo Priscilla with French. Yet there was immediately a wrinkle in that plan. If I whispered *actual* "French nothings" in her ear, tempted though I might be, everything could fall apart. If by some chance she spoke French, then it was unlikely she would appreciate a near-stranger whispering, *"Je ne peux pas vivre sans toi."* ("I can't live without you.")

Still, the general idea seemed to be a sound one. I would merely have to "roll the dice" and hope she did not speak French…but I would hedge my bets by whispering something far less romantic. The moment there was an interlude in the music, I approached her and whispered, *"L'habit ne fait pas le moine."* ("The vestment does not make the monk.")

Priscilla looked at me as the music picked up. She frowned ever so slightly, as if trying to understand or process what I had said. Was the jig up? Another few beats of the music…and her face relaxed. I was safe! She did not speak French! To celebrate my good fortune, I whispered to her again, a follow-up to my earlier offering.

"Petit à *petit, l'oiseau fait son nid."* ("Little by little, the bird makes its nest.") I was the bird, in my thinking, and perhaps she and I would someday make a nest together.

I dodged a girl and a boy who danced past. Priscilla now had a half smile on her lips, and her eyebrows lifted the barest amount. I needed to move fast, before any of my competitors interfered. Fortunately, my nerve did not desert me at that crucial moment. My eyes lock on to hers and I held her hand firmly. *You are mine*, I thought.

And loudly I asked, "Would you like to dance?"

By way of answer, she allowed her smile to reach her eyes, and then I found myself dancing with the woman of my dreams. The dream had become reality, and Priscilla was in my arms on the dance floor.

I was not going to let go of her. She was going to be mine for the rest of that evening. I would keep her interested by saying sweet things in her ears, in French, whether she understood them or not. This was one way I thought I could romance this beautiful American girl, against all odds.

Things moved quickly between Priscilla and me. My feelings for her grew stronger by the day, and I could tell she was taking a real liking to me. To think I had met my girlfriend via a chance encounter at the Green Latrine!

One evening that summer, I was walking Priscilla back to the home where she was staying. She was wheeling her bike along on one side, while I was on the other side, holding her hand. The moon was shining bright, and I imagined it reflecting in her beautiful blue eyes. As we strolled through the warm air, we spoke whatever came to our minds.

Then, for a reason I cannot chalk up to anything other than the foolishness of youth, I attempted what I thought was a joke.

"Priscilla," I said. She turned to face me. I continued, in a serious voice, saying, "I applied for renewal of my visa. The US government has turned me down. They are going to deport me. They are going to kick me out of the country."

"Out of the country? For *good?*" she asked. "It can't be true! It can't be true!"

I felt as if someone was squeezing my heart with a fist.

"Priscilla, Priscilla," I interrupted, "it isn't true. I am not being kicked out of the country!"

"What? But..." she began.

"It was a joke," I said lamely. "I was trying to make a joke."

She began to cry. In her face I saw a mixture of emotions. Anger, yes, along with lingering confusion, but something more: heartfelt relief. The same relief I felt that we would not yet be separated.

Her honest reaction seemed to cause my stomach and my heart to switch places momentarily. I understood, at that moment, she *really* liked me! As I look back, I believe that was the moment *I* fell in love with Priscilla Madlyn.

And so, we began to deepen our romance in earnest, meaning that I began to spend every spare moment in her presence.

She continued to work at the Green Latrine, an institution, I learned, whose name matched the quality of its working environment. Priscilla, you see, was a literal head-turner. Performing even the commonest, most mundane tasks, she glowed with vivacious beauty. And it was not only me who noticed.

Her coworkers at the Green Latrine paid attention to her beauty and curves and moves as well. While I was smitten, however, they became jealous, believing she received more customers and larger tips. Blame me! Hoping to annoy her into quitting, Priscilla's coworkers attempted to make nuisances of themselves. They borrowed money from her and hedged on returning it, arranged with the manager to take the best shifts, and turned their backs on her when she approached. When none of that succeeded in ridding them of Priscilla, they reported her to their manager for wearing too short of a uniform skirt. (In this one issue they had a legitimate gripe: The common effect of Priscilla's skirt length, combined with her shapely legs and angelic looks, was dazzling if not outright distracting.)

Eventually, her jealous coworkers achieved their goal. Priscilla had requested a weekend off to attend the wedding of one of her girlfriends. Her coworkers, however, complained to the manager about her "missing work again" and "not giving notice," acting as if they would scarcely be able to keep the lights on at the Green Latrine because of her callous negligence.

The manager fired her, at which point she was immediately hired at a delicatessen down the street for a job that happened to have better hours, higher pay, and a more reasonable working environment. In fact, she had been considering the delicatessen position for some time but had been reluctant to give the required two-week notice at the Green Latrine, suspecting those two weeks would be even more unpleasant than usual. Being fired, however, allowed Priscilla to leave right away.

It became habitual for me to visit her at the delicatessen most evenings, shortly before closing time. I thus had an incentive to complete my schoolwork and any other extracurricular lucrative endeavor of the day.

One night I arrived outside her work to walk her home. She told me that instead of going home, she would be walking to a friend's house within the Dartmouth campus to watch ice hockey on television. We strolled along, chatting amicably, until we reached the front of what she thought was her friend's home. She invited me inside, but I was forced to decline because of my studies.

We hugged. I watched her climb the porch steps, open the front door, go inside...and then race back down the steps toward me.

"Atha, that was the wrong house!" Her face was flushed with embarrassment. "There was a family in there! I..."

And with that utterly unromantic prelude, she rose to her tiptoes and kissed me...right on the mouth.

Lights seemed to explode in my head and heart. I kissed her back, and we kept on kissing, outside a stranger's house.

Everything around us faded into the background, and in that moment, nothing else in the world mattered.

CHAPTER 11

The Dueling Calls of Career and Clan

New Hampshire

To pursue my MBA at Tuck, I worked harder than anyone else I observed. I would often study or write term papers and other assignments until three or four in the morning. Priscilla was caught up in that routine when she and I began dating seriously. She would tell me years later that she received her best grades when we were dating. No wonder—we spent most of our time together studying.

The extra effort required of me made sense. After all, I had joined an accelerated study program in a field that was entirely new to me, all in a language that was mostly new to me. Additionally, most of my classmates at Tuck came from well-to-do families. Many of them had already been in business, whether family owned or general corporate. I had not had the same exposure to economics and business concepts. It seemed to me I was starting out at the bottom of our class.

Nevertheless, I soldiered on.

By that point, my campus employment was in the Tuck School Library. This was a fortunate change because it allowed me to complete assignments while at work, provided I had no remaining library tasks to complete and could keep my eyes open. My classmates would often find me dozing with my head resting on an opened textbook! I was happy to have understanding colleagues, for usually, if they found me asleep at the desk, they would simply help themselves to the materials they needed and check themselves out.

I also benefited from the kindness of Mr. John Albee, the director of admissions and student affairs at Tuck. He was not only instrumental in granting me a scholarship to supplement my USAID funding but also gave me more than I had applied for, knowing I might need some financial cushion.

In June 1970, I simultaneously received my bachelor of arts in economics from Dartmouth and completed the first year of my MBA at Tuck.

That summer I chose to accept temporary employment at Carpenter Technology Corporation as a marketing research analyst, paid at the rate of $825 per month. It was a worthwhile three months, with the excellent compensation being only the least of the reasons. Besides learning valuable job skills and "getting my feet wet" in corporate America, I formed a close relationship with the company's president, Mr. Moxon.

President Moxon took the time to interact with his brash summer intern, and we enjoyed respectful and honorable conversations, despite holding very divergent views on many topics. Like many kids of my generation back then, I was in the anti–Vietnam War camp. At one point, I even dared to send him a letter containing my views on the war, along with magazine and newspaper articles that took the same tack. He had a better appreciation of the issues at stake, while I could only go by the many anti-war demonstrations and negative media accounts. To this day, I remain grateful to him for showing me how to respectfully disagree, even on subjects that are emotionally charged.

That relationship was how, in the fall of 1970, I found myself answering a knock at my dorm room. I opened the door to find Carpenter's president standing in front of me! He was a Tuck alumnus, I recalled, but why had he come to see me unannounced?

Stumbling over my words, I invited him in and provided the sole chair in my room. I perched on the edge of my bed while he turned the chair to face me and sat down. I could hardly comprehend what was happening as he began to speak. He told me that he had driven to the school to offer me a full-time position upon graduation. The company was impressed with the skills and character they had observed in me over the summer and wanted to "lock me in" for the long haul. The VP of marketing had recommended the hire.

I nearly fell off the edge of my bed. Next, he told me my annual salary would begin at $14,000, and I nearly fell off the edge of my bed a second time! The combined income and wealth of my immediate family members back in Congo would not be even a fraction of what I just heard from the mouth of Mr. Moxon. If I accepted the job in Reading, Pennsylvania, where the company was headquartered, I could immediately begin sending money back to my family.

I knew exactly what to do.

"Mr. President," I said, "you have my deepest gratitude for coming to me with this offer. But…I cannot accept it."

Accepting the job was a huge temptation, but one countervailing force inside me was even stronger.

When the president asked if I would share my reasons, I spoke the names of my family. "I miss my mother *very much*," I said, "and I miss my sister and my brothers and my nephews and my nieces and even one or two of my uncles!"

Almost from the moment I set foot on American soil during the summer of 1967, my desire to return to the Congo, to my family, continued to be strong. We had been separated for some four years. During that whole period, our only means of communication was letters. When I could afford to send one, it took at least one month for it to reach Kinshasa.

Mr. Moxon was a true gentleman. He understood my rationale and graciously accepted my decision. "Should you change your mind, Atha, let us know."

With that, we shook hands and parted as friends. When he left, I was once again alone in my dorm room. I returned the chair to my desk and sat down to study. I was determined this offer of a well-paying, respected job would not be the last, just as I was determined to work on the soil of my home country. It would be time to go home….soon. I was also aware that I would be leaving Priscilla behind, as I was keen to follow my family's wishes to find a wife from my tribe.

•◇◇◇•

My determination to return home accounted for a major frustration during my time at Tuck. I was offered a potential postgraduation position with International Business Machines (IBM). At that time, IBM was investing in new or expanded operations in Congo, along with Goodyear, Singer, General Motors, and many other major American companies.

The United States was taking a great interest in Congo. The country had just opened its doors to Western investment, and companies were eager to become players in a country rich with unique and vast mineral deposits. The interest was geopolitical as well. The Congo's leader at the time, Mobutu Sese Seko, was rumored to be a key CIA agent in the fight against communism.

My job offer from IBM was accompanied by a stellar pedigree. Jacques de Maisonrouge, the president of IBM World Trade Corporation, offered me an executive trainee position in my own country. But that offer did not arrive until the final stop on a nearly yearlong path that had been fraught with miscommunication and delay. Then, when the offer finally arrived, my excitement immediately turned to simmering anger.

I digested the details in the letter IBM had sent. Upon graduation, I would train in Kinshasa for three months. Weekly tests would be required, and if I did not maintain a minimum score of 70 percent, I would be fired. During that initial period, I would be paid $180 per month ($2,160 annualized!), followed by a second three-month trial period during which my salary would increase to $230 a month ($2,760 annualized). At the end of those six months, with a favorable recommendation from my training manager, my salary would increase once more, providing me the equivalent of $4,560 annually. Thereafter, promotions and subsequent salary actions would be performance driven and merit based.

I had no issue with merit-based pay increases, but I took serious personal offense at the other conditions. The idea that a Tuck School MBA graduate would be subjected to weekly tests…and especially a graduate who had shaved two years off his university timetable! And yes,

I would be working in the Congo, but the salary was less than one-*third* of what Carpenter had offered me. Who did IBM presume they were dealing with? I fired off a letter that very day.

> Dear Sir,
>
> I acknowledge receipt of your letter of 14th May 1971 offering me a job with IBM-Congo. Thank you.
>
> In view of the neo-colonialist conditions contained in your letter and because of a salary offer too low for somebody of my education level, I find myself with no option but to decline your offer. I hope, however, that you will be able to find other Congolese nationals on the ground ready to accept working under such conditions.
>
> Wishing you all that is progressive and human, receive, dear Sir, my deepest regrets.
>
> Athanase Tshibaka, AB, MBA

There! My letter would ensure Monsieur de Maisonrouge understood the error of his presumptions. His colonial mindset wrongly assumed a Congolese would wish to return to the Congo without regard to the compensation or the potential for future growth and promotion. I was not a pawn.

Once my missive was mailed, I imagined the way Monsieur de Maisonrouge would read it. No doubt an administrative assistant would open and scan it, be shocked by the audacity and weight of my words, and then place it on the president's desk. Having read it, he would, I imagined, turn to stare out the window contemplatively, pondering the error of his assumptions and pledging to chart a new course in his relations with up-and-coming African professionals such as myself.

Having discharged my responsibility to educate the leader of one of the world's largest corporations, I turned my attention to my studies… and to whatever offers would surely arrive next through the mail.

To that end I surveyed other potential employers. I needed a company like IBM that would give me the opportunity to launch my career in my own country. Unlike IBM, however, the company had to recognize my potential and compensate me fairly. Perhaps a bit less than if I opted for a career in the United States, but I had already made peace with that. Returning to my native land after four years away was plan A, and it was plan B…all the way to plan Z.

I will not take the space to list the details of every company I contacted during my search. Suffice to say I cast the net widely. Consumer products, engines, aluminum, chemicals, rubber, sewing machines, advertising, agriculture, oil, mining…any organization with at least a small stake in the Congo, or even a rumored *potential* stake, became a target for me.

My strategy had been to knock on as many doors as possible. Every student had sent out applications for various positions, but as the weeks became months, the status of my own applications could be summed up in a single word: *desperate*. My hope had been to receive several job offers before I graduated, allowing me to choose the best position as well as skip campus interviews entirely.

Yet aside from the IBM offer, which I began to realize I had rejected far too hastily, I experienced radio silence and, when I did receive responses to my applications, they would generally say something like, "We regret that…" and whatever the reasons were for not offering me a position.

Despite the stress of a job search, and amid all the hard work and long hours, I continued to experience a deep gratitude during my two years at Tuck. Toward the end of my time there I received an "Amos Tuck School Notice" from Phyllis Stanton, registrar.

> Your overall two-year exact numerical class standing in a class of 113 graduates places you as follows: 63.

I was ecstatic! I had come a long way since ending first grade fiftieth out of fifty-four and nearly being named *tshiamsho*.

My mission was accomplished, or at least the initial phase of it. I had come to America not in search of a better life but in search of the tools to *make* a better life for myself and for others back home. And I had been given those tools: a quality education and an MBA.

Home.

The word was sweet on my tongue.

I was anxious to put to productive use what I had learned in business school. If only I could find a job that would return my feet to my native soil.

CHAPTER 12

Citibank: God Provides

New Hampshire and New York

I KNEW IN MY HEART THAT THE TWIN DECISIONS ABOUT IBM AND Carpenter Technology had been correct. But that did not make them easy…especially the IBM decision! It was true that IBM had undervalued me as a person and perhaps was undervaluing my whole country and its way of life. Still, that job would have taken me home. But why cry over spilled milk? Certainly, after my letter, Monsieur de Maisonrouge would be in no hurry to speak with me again!

The issue was that my next steps were far from clear. It was a time of anxious anticipation for me.

Every business I contacted had resulted in a dead end, and I had taken no other interviews on campus. All I could do was wait, and if no offer appeared, I would be forced to return to my country and work for two years on my own, without pay, assisting *les femmes commerçantes* (women traders).

It was a strange position in which to find myself. After four years of *busting my butt*, as my American friends were fond of saying, no real options appeared before me. My work ethic and dedication had made me equal to any challenge, and each conquered challenge had led inevitably to a new opportunity. Looking back on my academic career, I felt as if I had been climbing a path into a mountain range. Each lower summit gave me a view of the next higher peak.

Now? Instead of seeing the tallest peak before me, I was trapped in a deep valley. My options had been narrowed to sitting and waiting.

Waiting was exactly what I did, until a classmate passed along surprising news: Citibank had plans to open a branch office in the Congo, in the capital city of Kinshasa.

"I interviewed with Citi for a job in the New York office, Atha," he told me, grinning. "I mentioned to them that I had a friend from the Congo in my class at Tuck School of Business Administration. Here is the HR VP's business card if you are interested. They are eager to talk to you."

I could not help grinning back. This was an unexpected bit of fortune! Was Citibank the next mountain I was meant to climb? Immediately, I called the number my classmate had given me and was invited down to Citi's New York office for an interview the following day.

Packing took almost no time because I had almost nothing to pack. I owned a single suit, navy blue with white stripes, and a single tie. After dressing and placing a few toiletries into a valise, I began my journey.

No one observing me would have concluded the goal of my trip was New York, given that I began by walking several miles in nearly the opposite direction, north from the Dartmouth campus toward the interstate. I did not have enough money even for a Greyhound ticket, so I had no choice but to hitchhike. Once at the interstate, I was soon picked up by another student, rich enough to own a car, who was headed to New York City as I was. The route took us along the western part of Massachusetts, then south through Rhode Island toward the Connecticut coastline. As we motored the two hundred eighty miles, passing through the influential business hubs of New Haven, Bridgeport, and Stamford, I savored the sense of optimism growing in my belly.

How odd to be optimistic about banking. Banking was something I had never considered. But by that point I was enough of a beggar to not be a chooser!

When we reached New York, I asked to be dropped at the International House at Columbia University. I had African friends there, and I knew I would be able to at least eat hot dogs and hamburgers on the cheap, although I hoped there might be some African meal to remind me of home.

The following morning, I took the subway to the headquarters of First National City Bank. It was massive, yet even that high-rise building was dwarfed by the surrounding towers. I was scheduled for interviews with *five* executive VPs of the bank in a single day.

This is it, I told myself.

I straightened my tie using the reflection of a window, and then I walked inside.

Several hours later, I emerged from the last meeting.

Had the executive VPs gone easy on me, or was arrogance taking hold of me? I thought I had done exceedingly well in all the interviews. I had handled all the questions with clarity and reassuring confidence. All my interviewers seemed visibly impressed. Their feedback in word and body language seemed to be conveying that assessment.

I told myself, *Athanase, you can reach the vice chairmanship of this bank within six months.*

I truly believed that.

Immediately after the meetings, I was taken to the office of the VP for Human Resources. He was anxious to know how the interviews had proceeded.

"Excellent!" I proclaimed, exuding confidence. He nodded and then abruptly switched subjects.

"Atha, tell me, how did you get from Hanover to New York City?"

"I hitchhiked."

"You what?" he asked, incredulous.

"I hitchhiked."

He smiled and jotted something down on a notepad.

"And which restaurants did you go to while in New York?"

"I don't go to restaurants," I answered. "My buddies and I make hotdogs or hamburgers at Columbia's International House."

He again jotted something on his notepad.

"And how did you get to the bank from Columbia University? Did you take a taxi?"

I began to worry. Why was this man asking me these detailed questions after I had such great interviews? Was he undermining me? Was he trying to undo what I assumed was a foregone conclusion, that I would be hired and then be promoted to vice chairman within six months? *This HR guy is bad news*, I thought.

"How are you getting back to Hanover from New York City?"

"I will hitchhike," I said grudgingly. My ears were burning.

I wanted to leave. My confidence had deserted me. I could feel perspiration under my clothes, although thankfully not yet on any visible parts of my body.

The man called in his assistant and handed her the piece of paper on which he had been jotting things down. He then switched gears again, asking me questions about my family, my plans for the future, and other personal topics. *Is he now trying to make up for destroying my chances with his last set of questions?* He had dealt a blow to my self-confidence and resown doubts I thought I had overcome after my interviews. There was nowhere I could go, however. I had not been dismissed, and so I sat across from him and gamely answered his queries.

Some thirty minutes later, his assistant returned with an envelope and handed it to the VP of HR. He opened the envelope and looked at its contents.

Disaster, I thought. *Here is the letter telling me the bank is not offering me a position.*

The man then lifted his eyes and handed the envelope to me. "Atha," he said, "open it!"

I did. Inside was a check for $1,200, paid to the order of Athanase Tshibaka!

All that scribbling on the notepad had been his way of estimating how much my visit to New York City would have cost. Citi was reimbursing me for expenses I had not incurred!

Relieved, and with genuine gratitude, I thanked him. I folded the check and put it into my pocket, knowing it was the most money I had received in a single transaction in my whole life.

As I left the Citi building, an overwhelming sense of gratitude impressed itself on me. How in the world had *I* come to such a place? Joy inexpressible overwhelmed me. Was this really happening? Why me, God Almighty? Why me?

I did not choose to move as a refugee from Kananga to Mbuji-Mayi in 1960.

I did not choose to join a Presbyterian school in my village after being kicked out of Catholic school for disobedience.

I did not choose to be the single student from my high school to be awarded a scholarship to attend university in the United States.

I did not choose to attend Dartmouth College.

I did not choose Citicorp.

The train of thought staggered me. No, in all these things I had *been chosen.*

But, chosen by whom? And for what?

And again, why *me*?

There is an old French saying: *"L'homme propose, mais Dieu dispose."* "Man proposes, but God disposes." This echoes Proverbs 16:9, which says, "In their hearts humans plan their course, but the LORD establishes their steps" (NIV). I may have had many dreams growing up. I may have had plans and made gargantuan efforts to see them materialize. I may have made many mistakes in my life, taking a wrong turn on more than one occasion. Through it all, however, it seemed that God my Maker had ordained each and every step on my journey. Thus, I could look to Him with confidence for the rest of the days He would give me on this earth.

God's grace and provision had been burning brighter inside me these last years than I had been willing to notice. The words of Saint Thérèse of Lisieux, also known as the Little Flower, ring real for me: "Everything is grace. Everything is a direct result of the Father's love for us. So, no matter the difficulties you face, however trivial or serious, they're basically all an opportunity."

CHAPTER 13

Determination and Unstoppable Love

New Hampshire and Congo

When I left Congo to study in America, the expectations my family had for me were abundantly clear.

I would travel to the United States for a single purpose: to excel at my studies. Then, upon the completion of my studies, I would return to Congo and put my newfound knowledge to good use in a respectable job. And when I returned, a second expectation would be met as well. The words of my mother captured what was in store for me.

"You will go to America to study, and then you will return, and we will find a wife for you from our tribe."

I had promised my mother that I would honor her wishes, and never had I wavered from that determination. But something happened that complicated my views on the instructions from my family.

I met Priscilla, and we fell in love.

Making the situation even more complicated, Priscilla and I both realized my time in America *would* end at some point, and I would return to Congo without her. It was the summer before I was to begin my job at Citicorp, yet I was determined to return regardless of whether it actually came to pass. Priscilla understood this, of course. We told each other everything. Each of us knew dozens of stories about each other's history and families. I had told her we could never marry. There were far too many reasons we could not be joined together…too many to override either the wishes of my family or the fact that Priscilla and I were in love. I was determined to obey my family.

So it was that I became a storyteller about the Congo. And my stories were calculated to have a particular effect on one particular listener.

"Did you know," I would say, widening my eyes for effect, "the crocodiles in the Congo are some of the largest in the world? Not only that, but they live in both the widest rivers and some of the smallest streams. A person could be leaping across a stream the width of a park bench and *bam!* Another missing tourist."

Or I might say, sadly, "What a shame that the Congo has no ice cream in the entire country. Imagine never enjoying your favorite dessert again! In fact, the Congo has more poisonous snakes than America has ice cream!"

My strategy for discouraging marriage was two-pronged. I not only attempted to scare her with stories about my country but also considered playing matchmaker. "Before I return to the Congo," I told her, "I will work hard to find you a husband." I paused for effect and then continued, half joking, "A white, Anglo-Saxon, blue-eyed man for you to marry!"

It was against this backdrop that Priscilla hatched a plan.

"This summer I want to go as a tourist to the Congo," she told me one night. "I want to see what your country is like. Would you recommend me to your family?"

It was only later I discovered she had outsmarted me. It was true, after all, that she wanted to see what my country was like and meet my family. In a way that *did* make her a tourist. However, as I learned, she *also* wished to convince my family that she would be a suitable wife for me, a game plan she kept close to her chest!

Revealing in myself either a lack of guile or a lack of common sense, I believed she would do nothing more than visit the Congo as a tourist. I did not understand what good could come from her plans. Surely, we were only delaying the inevitable: that I would move back to my home country and marry a woman from the Congo, while Priscilla would remain in her home country and marry someone else, ideally with my help.

Reality proved resistant to such simplifications.

She later told me every detail of her "tourist" visit. At the age of twenty-two, Priscilla had never been outside the United States. Without telling her parents, she applied for a passport and began to research all she would need to travel: vaccinations, travel arrangements, accommodations, and the like.

Eventually the time came for her to leave, and she boarded a Pan Am flight with the letter of introduction I had written tucked safely in her purse, a copy of the original I had sent to my brother weeks before to alert him and the family to the visit, as a tourist, of this special young lady.

"Priscilla is a dear friend," I had written to my brother Robert. "She does not know anyone there, so would you please look after her and keep her safe?" In addition, I had recorded greetings for my mother and my family on a cassette tape, which Priscilla carried inside a small, battery-powered player.

She was pleasantly surprised to find my brother waiting for her at the N'djili International Airport. And not where most other travelers were met either. With his connections in Kinshasa, my older brother, Robert Vianney Kanyiki Mutombo Mpuanya, managed to meet Priscilla on the tarmac. To her even greater delight, Robert, grinning from ear to ear and genuinely happy, greeted Priscilla with, *"Belle soeur, bienvenue chez-nous!"* ("Sister-in-law, welcome home!")

He knows why I'm here, thought Priscilla, *and so does the rest of the family. The man I love is out of the loop!*

She had a further thought. *And I'm not leaving Congo without their consent to marry him.*

In writing my glowing letter of introduction to Robert, I had completely forgotten a tribal practice. Marriages in the village were usually arranged respectively by the families of the boy and the girl. The boy's family would typically take the initiative. If they noticed a beautiful girl, of good character, from a good family, able to bear children, able to fetch water from the river or streams miles away, welcoming, hospitable, and suitable for the boy's family, then the parents of that girl would be approached by the parents of the boy, and a union would be proposed.

Thereafter, the girl would be expected to spend several weeks in a "trial period" with her potential future in-laws. They would observe her every move and interaction, gauging her readiness to help, her strength, and her energy.

At the end of the trial period, the boy's family would finalize their decision-making and, assuming it was positive, dowries would be negotiated before the marriage could be consummated. I had shared such stories with Priscilla, almost without thinking, but she had remembered, and taken them to heart.

Going further in my attempts to dissuade Priscilla from even dreaming of a marriage between us, I had told her she would be *"complètement sous ma commande."* In other words, completely submitted to me. For an American lady growing up in an environment where feminism and independence were important developments within the culture, I assumed such a stance would be a red line Priscilla would never cross. If crocodiles and snakes and the absence of ice cream were not sufficient to discourage her, this one would definitely do the trick.

How naive I was! I soon learned never to underestimate a woman madly in love, a woman who would end up shaping the course of our life together as eternally committed loving partners. Of her own accord, she ended up on a mission to convince my family she was suitable for me and for the Ngandu clan. And she left both me and her parents completely out of the loop!

Still, despite her planning, her trip to Congo soon took an unpleasant turn. The government had commandeered the airplane she needed for the next leg of her journey, and she was forced to spend a couple of unplanned weeks in Kinshasa.

Priscilla, undeterred, took up residence in Kinshasa with the Kankus, a family who were dear friends of Robert, the same Kanku family who opened their home to me during the time I was preparing for my trip to the US four years earlier. She studied French, using the grammar book and dictionaries she had brought along. This was also a time she productively used to observe and learn about my culture. She watched how other women dressed and, more specifically, how her hostess, Madame Julienne Kanku, interacted with her husband and children.

Priscilla learned to use the pit toilet, a hole in the ground sheltered in an outhouse, sharing the moment with flies and mosquitoes, depending on the time of the day. Washing involved water in a pail in the outhouse, located by the side of the pit toilet.

At last, after two weeks, she was able to find another airplane and fly two thousand kilometers east to Bukavu, on Lake Kivu, to rendezvous with my brother's family.

Robert had two wives, and his family lived in Uvira, a distance from Bukavu. Their home had intermittent electricity but no hot water. This time around, the toilet was indoors, though Priscilla had to learn the art of using buckets to flush. Robert's house had another luxury: a bathtub. But, again, one had to use a bucket of water to wash. Kerosene lamps provided a warm glow at night. And thankfully, given the altitude of Uvira and its cold nights, a wood fireplace provided some degree of comfort.

One of the first things Priscilla noticed was the generosity of my extended family. Like the men, Priscilla was served goat (including the entrails), chicken (including the feet), or beef every day, while the women and children did not receive any meat. The generosity of my family and friends she met wherever she traveled in the Congo (Kinshasa, Bukavu, Uvira, Kananga, Mbuji-Mayi, Tshibombo, and Miabi) became one of her most consequential takeaways, an experience of such impact that it shaped her approach to dealing with other people's hunger and physical needs later in her life, as we've often hosted guests in our own home throughout our lives together.

One Saturday night in Uvira, Priscilla woke to the sound of a rainstorm and the much louder sound of pained groaning.

Robert had left for the weekend on business. His first wife, Marthe Tshiela, being eight-and-a-half months pregnant, had stayed behind. By this time Robert had already divorced the wife of his youth, Jeanne Mulanga, who was the mother of his first five children. Robert had told

Marthe that he would be home in time for the birth, but considering the sounds she was making, Priscilla knew that would not be the case.

"Someone, boil water!" Priscilla shouted in French, springing to her feet and turning her head this way and that to assess her resources. "And you," she continued, pointing at the nearest teenager, "please get me the cleanest sheets you have!"

Her instructions sounded authoritative, even though she had no idea what she was doing, and most of her knowledge was based on what she remembered characters shouting in television dramas.

The previous week, Priscilla had met the local postman, a gentleman who had eight children and, more importantly, a Volkswagen bug. With Marthe continuing to groan in pain, Priscilla ran to the postman's house and knocked and knocked and knocked. It took her *forever* to wake him, but she persisted, suspecting that Marthe's only hope was to get to the hospital in time for delivery. Eventually, the postman, Marthe, and Priscilla were bouncing toward town, swerving and sliding on the muddy, rain-slicked roads, slowing down only long enough to pick up a local nun who would help deliver the baby at the tiny local clinic. They made it with only twenty minutes to spare.

By the time Robert arrived home on Monday morning, his wife and new child were back home, along with Priscilla.

"Congratulations," Priscilla told Robert in French as he approached his house, "you have a baby boy!"

Assisting with the delivery of Robert's son was not the only propitious event of Priscilla's supposedly "tourist" visit to Congo. In another test of her suitability as a potential wife, she found an opportunity to cook her signature corn beef casserole. It was one of my favorites whenever she would make it for me while in college, and she knew my brother would enjoy it. After Robert took one bite, the look on his face told her she was right. He *loved* it, just as he loved knowing that his younger brother would get to enjoy it many times in the future.

The situation grew a bit trickier when Priscilla decided to impress my family by cooking *kaleji* (also known as *matamba* or *saka saka*), the leaves of the manioc plant, which are a staple in the Congolese diet. Cooking them properly involves boiling the leaves and draining the water once or twice. The leaves are then pounded and readied for cooking, which itself requires patience, since *kaleji* must be cooked for a long time, with water added along the way. The other ingredients are usually palm oil, salt, and, at times, *pili pili* (hot peppers). Where Priscilla had grown up, vegetables were cooked for a few minutes before eating, the better to preserve their nutrients, digestive benefits, textures, and flavors. Often, they would be eaten raw and called salad. I called salad "goat food"!

"*Belle soeur*," Robert queried upon tasting Priscilla's offering, "how long did you cook the *kaleji?*"

The dish in front of him was bright green rather than the olive green it ought to have been.

"Oh, about fifteen minutes or so," replied Priscilla confidently. "You know, vegetables must not be on the fire too long or they lose their nutritional benefit."

Imagine her shock when she learned that some *kaleji* varieties could have cyanide in them, the whole reason for boiling and throwing water away several times followed by hours of cooking. My wife-to-be had nearly put her life and the lives of my brother and his family in deadly danger!

Still, Priscilla had successfully passed the unexpected test of midwifery, and learned from her *kaleji* mistake, so Robert decided that she, along with his second wife, Marie Muadi Tshiala, would visit my mother and extended family in Mbuji-Mayi. The initial flight would take the two women from Robert's home to Kananga, and from there a smaller plane would shuttle them to Mbuji-Mayi.

While waiting for their connecting flight in Kananga, Priscilla ate a few *beignets*, popular local donuts usually fried in palm oil. She had purchased them from a nearby small marketplace. She instantaneously fell sick with stomach problems. She and Marie went looking for a pharmacy and, on the way, they popped into an English-language bookstore and began chatting with the white lady behind the counter.

Before long, Priscilla had shared the whole story of her visit.

"So that's why I'm here," she finished with a weary smile, "because I'm in love with a *Muluba.*" (*Muluba* is singular for someone from the Baluba tribe).

The lady leaned forward, curious. "Really? A *Muluba*? What's his name?"

"Athanase Tshibaka," Priscilla replied.

"My baby!" the lady exclaimed.

She gave a shocked laugh and explained, "Athanase is a former student of mine. My name is Ann Anderson, missionary from Augusta, Georgia. I taught your boyfriend at the Protestant High School of Bibanga until 1966."

Ann kindly took Priscilla and Marie into her home for three days, nursing Priscilla back to full health before a second plane was eventually found to take them to Mbuji-Mayi.

Priscilla had reached the final stage of her quest to convince my family she would make a good wife for me.

In Mbuji-Mayi, two of my older brothers met Priscilla at the airport in a hired jeep, then drove her twenty kilometers to the village of Tshibombo. They arrived at sunset.

As she climbed out of the jeep, a nicely dressed woman in her late fifties approached her. It was my mother. Dressed for the special occasion, she was holding a live chicken, waving it back and forth at Priscilla's feet. As the rest of the family and others from the village approached, my mother began to ululate, welcoming Priscilla as an honored guest. Then she killed the chicken and offered it with *fufu* and rice to Priscilla, a special treat befitting a special guest.

From that moment on, Priscilla was welcomed into the inner circle of the family women. Mom's village friends lingered to see Tshibaka's American "wife."

After the meal, Priscilla brought out something special from her bag: a cassette player. "I have something for you to listen to," she told my mother in French, interpreted in Tshiluba by one of my brothers.

A small wooden table was set up outside my mother's hut, along with four chairs. Priscilla sat down, joined by my two older brothers and my mother. Dozens of people from our village ringed the table, watching. Someone placed a small kerosene lamp on the table, beside the tape recorder, so that Priscilla could see the buttons. A hush fell. Light flickered on every expectant face. "This is a message from your son," she said in French, "because he couldn't come himself."

When Priscilla pushed Play, the effect on my mother was instantaneous. My voice emerged from the speakers, and from my mother's throat erupted *kasala,* a mournful, ear-piercing ululation. She cried inconsolably, with tears flowing down her cheeks and dampening her *pagne*. Relatives and friends stepped forward to comfort her, placing hands on her shoulders and head. She had not heard her son's voice in four years, nor touched him, nor cooked *fufu* and *biteteku* (the spinach variety) and smoked fish for him. To hear me, even through the tinny speaker of the cassette player, overwhelmed her with longing and love.

Eventually, she asked Priscilla if she could record a message back to me. Priscilla flipped over the cassette to the blank side and hit Record. She expected my mother to talk about all the ways she had missed me.

Instead, my mother began to sing. It was once again the *kasala*, a traditional ode of praise. She sang about me, retelling the unlikely story of my life, and wishing for me all the good things that a mother could wish for her son. "We will see each other again," she sang, "we will see each other again, my great and wonderful son, Athanase Tshibaka Lumbala Kadita Baya Bakaji Wa Ngandu, Mukala wanyi." (The latter expression meant "my baby.")

Priscilla was awed by my mother's song. When the *kasala* was finished, Priscilla put the tape recorder safely back in her bag. And then it was time for *kamulangu*, a communal dance involving the women. Priscilla jumped right into the circle, stepping back and forth in time to clapping and goatskin drums. She was inside the heart of my culture, the heart of my family, and they were welcoming her with open, waving arms. She was winning their approval.

The next morning, Priscilla woke at 5:00 a.m., intending to walk the two-kilometer path to the nearest spring to fetch water. My family would not hear of it. Instead, a breakfast of bread, jam, and tea was prepared for her, an extra luxury because my family did not normally eat breakfast. We simply could not afford bread, butter, and jam every morning.

As Priscilla was finishing her tea outside the hut, several men from the village led a goat to her. My mother had bought it for Priscilla's next meals since, in her mind, Tshibaka's "wife" must be well fed. After presenting the animal as a gift, the men tied it to a nearby lemon tree that I had planted before leaving the village. With no preamble, they slit the goat's throat, spraying blood across the dirt and nearly causing Priscilla to spray tea out of her mouth! *How do I savor this breakfast while watching a goat being slaughtered?* she wondered. Still, she understood the staggering generosity of the gift, and she determined that she would be worthy of my family's opinion of her.

There remained one final visit for Priscilla to undertake.

Using the same jeep that had been hired to bring her to Tshibombo, she was driven another fifteen kilometers to meet Ntumba Wa Katshinga, my grandmother, known as *Kaku* in Tshiluba. When Priscilla arrived, my grandmother sat ramrod straight, dressed in an impeccable *pagne*. All five meters of the Dutch wax fabric, colored orange and blue, patterned with leaves, were wrapped tightly around her torso. Kaku Ntumba Wa Katshinga not only had all her teeth at some eighty years of age, but she also had all her wits! She spoke in Tshiluba to Priscilla, with my brothers translating into French. "I need to feel your belly," she told Priscilla. "I want to make sure you will be a good wife."

"But I'm not pregnant!" protested Priscilla.

Yet Kaku Wa Katshinga's wiry fingers were already touching Priscilla's belly, though not for the reason Priscilla had suspected. Rather, she was examining her pelvic bones to ascertain her childbearing capabilities. This was followed by an examination of her legs, to determine whether they were strong enough for her to fetch water from the river or carry wood or a bag of manioc from the bush.

Satisfied that Priscilla would be a good wife for Tshibaka *Mukala* (the youngest of Ngandu Alphonse's children), Grandmother sat down and served water and boiled fresh peanuts to her guest, thus ending the visit.

Mission accomplished! thought Priscilla as she drove away. *The family and everyone I have met so far have welcomed me. This has been a worthwhile adventure.*

The loss of fifteen pounds did not seem to matter to her. She had come to win my family over, and she felt and hoped she had achieved her objective. Or at least 90 percent of it. In her mind, the remaining 10 percent represented my say (as if I had any) in the decision-making.

But there was still the matter of whether I was going to propose marriage to her.

CHAPTER 14

She Is the One!

New Hampshire and Boston, Massachusetts

When Priscilla returned from Congo, she visited me in my small apartment in Boston. During the summer of 1971, immediately after my MBA from Tuck, I had moved to that city to work for the consultancy firm Arthur D. Little. I led a team of African graduates who, like me, were doing summer training at the firm. The only difference between them and me was that I had rejected the couple of offers I had received. (The Citibank opportunity had not yet materialized.)

I wondered about what Priscilla had brought back. I was curious and anxious to hear the story of her trip, the whole of it, yes, but especially news about my mother and the rest of my family. I had not spoken to my mother in four years. In *four* years! Our village was too remote for telephones and too far for my mother to make the trek to a larger, more connected community.

First came a stack of letters from my brothers, sister, grandmother, and extended relatives. "Let's see what your family thinks of my tourist visit," she said, half joking.

I smiled, then devoured letter after letter. As I did so, one common theme became clear: I was *not* to go back to the Congo without Priscilla! She had left such a good impression on every member of the family that they had decided I must marry her.

Not once had I acted counter to the instructions given to me by my family. When I left the Congo in 1967, my family was clear that I was to focus on my studies, while for their part they would find a young woman for me to marry, one from my tribe. That message had now drastically changed.

The same love I had before Priscilla's adventure remained intact. Now, I was in awe of her courage and the clear manifestation of the depth of her love for me. Her determination to "get" me was unquestionable. My family urging me to marry her came as a huge relief. I was now free to propose to the love of my life—something I wouldn't have done if they had told me to return for the wife they had selected from our tribe.

"Are you ready for the cassette?" Priscilla asked me.

As she set it on the table, I could not help but notice how thin her arms and fingers were. She had indeed lost a great deal of weight on her trip.

I nodded. Priscilla pressed the Play button.

The first notes of my mother's *kasala* triggered uncontrollable sobbing. Not only because I was missing my mother and my family but also because of the unexpected joy Priscilla's return had brought.

She had visited my family. She had sat across the table from my mother. And she had returned with the best news imaginable. With my head in my hands, I cried and cried, shoulders heaving, feeling like a weight was being lifted from my body with every sob. Relief flooded me.

The next time I saw my family, it would be with Priscilla at my side.

When I was able, I looked up at her. She had a sweet, shy smile on her face. "You know, I went to your country, and everything you told me was true," she said, "except for snakes and crocodiles everywhere, that is."

We laughed. But I detected weariness in her eyes as well as her body language. The trip had taken a toll on her.

"Athanase, I don't think we should make any rushed decisions."

Priscilla was right, of course. There was no wisdom in rushed decisions.

But I could not deny being over the moon about the way events had transpired. All along I had been determined to obey my family and return to my country to marry a Congolese woman, but now I could obey my family by marrying Priscilla. From the sound of things, I would be disobeying my family if I did not marry her!

Thus, I determined it was time to set the wheels of marriage in motion, knowing everything would take additional time in our particular situation. If I was going to propose to Priscilla, I wanted to do things the correct way and respect her culture. With that in mind, I wrote to her father, asking for permission to marry his daughter.

What I received from him was a five-page letter consisting entirely of reasons why marrying his daughter was a bad idea. Chief among them were matters of cultural differences, Priscilla's expectation of a "certain standard of living," and my race, as contrasted with hers. This was 1970s America, where most frowned on interracial marriages.

I could not help but respect his thoroughness, and I understood that I was reading the words of a man concerned about his daughter. He was thoughtful and quite objective in his articulation of the problems, all of which were real, at least as he saw them.

So, respectfully, I composed a letter in return, addressing his concerns. I began by reiterating my deep commitment to Priscilla, and I assured him we would do everything possible to overcome whatever obstacles would undoubtedly arise between a happy married life and us. As to the issue of cultural differences, I could not argue with the challenge that it presented. Still, I wrote, Priscilla's visit to the Congo, combined with my time in America, had provided us both with exposure to our respective cultural backgrounds. As to the issue of my (and my family's) poverty, I assured him that my intention was to work hard and be able to provide for Priscilla.

With a master's in music pedagogy from Columbia University following her BA at Smith College, Priscilla could work as a music or piano teacher in my country. She could also do administrative work at the US embassy or within a subsidiary of a multinational company. We were committed to each other and determined to make it work despite the incredible odds against a successful marriage for the very reasons so well articulated by my (future) father-in-law.

Finally came the predominant issue, the racial question. To put it crudely, Priscilla was a blond Caucasian with beautiful blue eyes. She was as white as a Minnesotan of German and Swedish heritage could be. I, on the other hand, was black. African black. And while attitudes about race in the United States were certainly changing, there was still widespread opposition to interracial marriage. I knew, however, that at least one side of the cultural and racial divide had been won over following Priscilla's daring Congo visit: My family was "all in" on Priscilla and would be supportive, at least emotionally. Indeed, they had now demanded I marry her and return to the Congo with her!

I closed the letter with a plea to Priscilla's father. "I am not giving up on marrying your daughter," I wrote, "but I need your blessing. Please, sir, give me your blessing. I will be committed to Priscilla, I promise."

Unfortunately, Priscilla's father wrote back with a compromise I could not accept. He suggested that I should take Priscilla to the Congo, but not as my wife. Then, if we were still together after two years, he would give me his blessing to marry his daughter.

He had no way of knowing, but his idea was a nonstarter for me. Living with a woman in the Congo, unmarried, carried very different connotations than it did in the United States. People would view Priscilla as my concubine (*mukaji wa ndumba*) and thus fail to respect her as they would a married woman. Not only that, I reasoned with my future father-in-law, but if we ran into any thorny issues in our relationship, we would be far more likely to split up if we were *not* married. The commitment of marriage would be an asset in the hard times, a guarantor of our union.

He ultimately did not agree to our marriage, but at least we were able to speak about the issues. Unfortunately, that sense of reasonableness exhibited by Priscilla's father was not mirrored by her mother. Her disagreement with our relationship was adamant and visceral.

She had long disapproved of us being together, which had been part of the reason Priscilla had undertaken such a sly trip to the Congo. When Priscilla's mother learned we wished to wed, she became overtly hostile. She informed Priscilla that she was no longer considered a daughter. She had no wish to see her again, and if we had any children, she did not wish to have any contact with them.

For her part, Priscilla did not slam the door closed on a future relationship with her mother. She occasionally sent her mother letters and left open the possibility of reconciliation.

By God's grace, one day that possibility came one step closer to reality.

After our son, Niki, was born, Priscilla took him to visit her family in the United States. She stayed with her aunt, Elizabeth Holmer, known to us as Aunt Betty. Priscilla used the opportunity to reconnect with other relatives in the Chicago area.

Her mother came too, for reasons known only to herself. She was still adamant that Priscilla was no longer her daughter. Yet we learned later that during that visit, Priscilla's mother accidentally entered a bedroom where Niki was taking a nap. Glimpsing her grandson tore at her heart, and this providential interaction may have planted the seed of future reconciliation.

For my part, I wished for the blessing of Priscilla's father, yes, but his opinion was not the only one that counted. And we wanted, of course, Priscilla's mother to be part of our relationship, but that was something outside our control.

What *was* in my control was the choice to ask Priscilla to marry me.

As an ambitious young man, my self-confidence had no bounds. My hopes and aspirations were limitless. What couldn't I do with a BA from Dartmouth College and an MBA from the Amos Tuck School of Business Administration? My future wife, Priscilla, was an accomplished classical pianist with a master's in music pedagogy from Columbia Teachers College to boot. Together, we would not only survive but would aim to thrive.

So it was that we decided to proceed with our plans to marry, without the blessing of Priscilla's father. With a modest ring that had cost me nearly all my savings from that summer's internship at Arthur D. Little, I asked Priscilla to marry me.

She said yes.

CHAPTER 15

The Birth of a Banker

Congo and Lebanon

THE NEXT YEAR PROVED TO BE A DIFFICULT ONE FOR PRISCILLA and me. Her mission to the Congo had worked, and upon her return she had accepted my marriage proposal. This was something to celebrate, certainly.

At the same time, the reality of what we proposed to do began to set in. From her trip to the Congo, Priscilla had realized the extent to which my immediate and extended family would be dependent on me. By extension, that meant they would be dependent on her as well. The Congolese culture would certainly impose ongoing hardships on her, just as it would demand sacrifices of us. And we had to admit her father had been correct in his assessment: Moving to a country so very different in terms of material comforts would present many complications and ongoing stresses.

From her personal point of view, there were other concerns. On her visit to the Congo, she had learned from my future boss at Citibank, Kim Abbott, what my salary would be. It was so low, in her mind, that she negotiated an increase in my compensation package. Kim was sympathetic and agreed to a 10 percent raise for me on the spot. As for the car and appliances, Kim assured her that the bank would consider a low-interest loan to help us set up a home when we eventually moved to Kinshasa as a couple. He wisely omitted telling her that granting the loan would be conditional: Her future husband would need to successfully complete his probation period of six months before such benefits could accrue to him.

There had also been her bouts with illness while touring the Congo. Would she acclimate to the environment and the food, or would she continue to be plagued with ill health?

All those factors swirled in her mind and heart. It was as if she were asking herself, I love this man with all my heart, but is marrying him and moving to the Congo really the right thing to do? She also confessed that if we moved to the Congo as husband and wife, she feared being a burden to me.

These concerns combined to make the other offers of overseas work I had received (and turned down) more attractive. I could work in Kinshasa, until the following summer, while Priscilla remained in America and continued to study. "If it was to be, it would be." That was the theory we were operating on, after a great deal of prayer, thought, and heart-to-heart conversations. Additionally, Priscilla encouraged me to date Congolese women, as part of our experiment. Perhaps I would find someone from my country whom I preferred to Priscilla. If this truly was God's plan for us, we knew that only He could make it happen.

We arrived on a tentative path forward in our relationship. It did not appear to be a fairy tale to us, true, but at least it would allow us to write our own story. That September, in 1971, I said goodbye to Priscilla and flew to Kinshasa, to begin working for Citibank. My role would be to contribute to the opening and setup of Citibank in Kinshasa, especially in the areas of local staff training and implementation of policies, procedures, and systems. I was back home, where I belonged and wanted to be, and I completely immersed myself in my work.

As Priscilla had graciously and selflessly encouraged me to do, I went on a few dates. Each date confirmed instantly that Priscilla was the one for me. She had taken a huge risk in giving me permission to date other women. Thankfully, God had His plans for us that no one could counter. My dating experiments back home came to nothing.

To increase my knowledge of banking operations, Kim decided to send me to Beirut, Lebanon, in December that year, after we had successfully launched Citibank Congo. Lebanon was politically stable, affordable, and Francophone, and Beirut was then known as "the Paris of the Middle East." It was a booming, buzzing city, known for its business climate and reputation for salesmanship. The Lebanese were renowned traders and merchants. Attending the training center in Beirut would further hone my grasp of the basics of banking, from bookkeeping to treasury and credit analysis. There, I would also meet participants from Europe, America, and Asia, all of us recent hires within Citibank. In addition to cross-cultural exposure, this was an opportunity for me to work hard and excel. Even while competing with others, I would learn the need for teamwork and, just as important, I would develop enduring new friendships.

Besides receiving classroom instruction in auditing, commercial credits, documentary collections, local and foreign currency transfers, foreign exchange operations, and credit routines, we were inserted into Citibank Beirut for practical application, working alongside experienced bankers.

I quite enjoyed the training in risk assessment and treasury operations. In very general terms, risk assessment sounds a lot like what it involved: ensuring that our banking transactions, especially loans, didn't involve risks that could jeopardize our business. And treasury operations, as we defined them back then, dealt with the noncustomer aspects of the business, such as interbank transactions and buying and selling foreign currencies.

Our hosts set up a simulation game for us, wherein each of us was given "capital" and took the role of a one-man bank. We competed, we traded, we lent and borrowed, and we engaged in all kinds of interbank dealings within self-established strategies and tactics. Each end of day, we would close the books and file a report to the "central bank" (a role played by the training center director), briefly summarizing our actions and achievements. Our report included confirmation that we had played within the rules. I learned to write tickets, set exchange rates, borrow, lend, and negotiate with other bank counterparties…all the while being supervised by the "central bank." I did not know it at the time, but these skills would shape my professional life.

At the end of the simulation, I was top of my class, winning awards for generating the best analyses, the most profits, and the best reports for the "central bank."

On the personal side, I was set up in a fine little apartment and soon made friends with others who were training. In the evenings, we would stroll the city, eat fresh lamb kebabs and chatting, and sometimes go to movies.

That Christmas, Priscilla came to visit me. On one memorable day, we swam in the Mediterranean and hiked through snow atop the mountains in a single twelve-hour period. This trip exacerbated tensions with Priscilla's relatives, however, who could not understand why she was deserting the family at Christmas to travel to the Middle East. Her mom had even wondered if Priscilla was marrying an Arab!

No, Mom, she thought, *your daughter is marrying someone very special. She is marrying an African from the very heart of that continent.*

Overall, our separation proved to be a Godsend…literally. Our time apart provided Priscilla the time and space to ponder her decision to marry me. She was able to sit with her feelings and process them. She truly understood the challenges of marrying me, just as she came to truly understand she did wish to marry me. For my part, I came to realize I had no other choice, and wanted no other choice, than the woman God had brought into my life.

Both of us agreed. We had been together and then been apart. Now it was time to be together once again…for good. We began to plan our wedding while I was still in Lebanon.

When I flew from Beirut to New York, it was to marry Priscilla.

CHAPTER 16

The Triumph of Love

New York and Congo

PRISCILLA AND I WERE MARRIED ON JUNE 25, 1972, AT COLUMBIA University Chapel.

The wedding was a small affair, and the reception even smaller. Priscilla's family was represented by her sister, an aunt, and several cousins, while my family, of course, was represented only by myself. A few of my friends were also present. The university chapel was decorated in unconventional colors for a wedding: pink and yellow. Because we could not afford flowers, we had called a florist, pretending to be a local theater company in search of cheap or free flowers for a "performance." The ruse worked, although the colors (and the fact that the flowers were carnations) were less than ideal. Still, it was a wedding—*our wedding*.

Before the marriage ceremony in the chapel, we had gathered with a few of the family members and friends to address an important question. Who would take the place of Priscilla's father to walk her down the aisle? She was disappointed that her father wouldn't be there, but by then, she was reconciled to the situation. We settled on one of her cousins, but my Congolese friend Constantin Nsekela was not happy with the decision. He found it inadequate.

"What is the matter, Constantin?" I asked.

"I am going to be on the *other* side of Priscilla. Her cousin and I will walk her down the aisle together and present her to you," Constantin explained.

It was clear from his tone that this was not a negotiable request. After consultation, Priscilla and I accepted the proposal, unusual as it was. Constantin, who loved being the center of attention, was going to insist.

We both loved him and were used to his ways, and besides, we did not have time or energy to spend debating the matter. Soon the ceremony began. As I watched Priscilla walk down the aisle toward me, a decidedly unromantic thought struck me: *Too late to change now!* Truthfully, I did not have any doubts. I knew that we were meant to be together, whatever the future held. "Too late to change" was not regret but rather expectation for what was to come.

The ceremony was brief. Constantin spoke a bit in English, then switched to French, and finally recited a love poem in Latin. I could tell that my bride did not fully approve, but I was struggling to contain laughter.

When the university chaplain pronounced us man and wife, Priscilla and I exited the chapel and posed for several snapshots on the front steps. From there, it was a short walk to her dormitory building on campus, where we had reserved a small room for our reception. Priscilla's friend had made a cake that was only large enough for each guest to have a single bite. There were also slices of watermelon and a plate of small sandwiches. It was unconventional but had the advantage of being affordable and, even more importantly, simple. Priscilla had spent the week before the wedding sitting for final exams, packing, planning, and even making her own veil.

A friend from Tuck School, Roland Heinz, lent us his apartment in New York for our first night together as a married couple. He was an executive at an advertising company. Compared to Priscilla's room at Columbia Teachers College, Roland's apartment was a luxury, a gift we gratefully remember to this date.

The days before we left for our honeymoon were filled to the brim, at least for my new bride.

Priscilla was still finishing her final exams at Columbia, and she was also receiving vaccinations, getting blood tests, and sorting out all manner of other last-minute details.

But finally, the moment arrived.

We did not have much money, so we purchased the cheapest tickets we could find from Alitalia Airlines.

Leaving the United States of America for a new life back in my native Congo proved deeply emotional for both Priscilla and me. We had grown used to student life on college campuses, eating in cafeterias, and sleeping in dorm rooms with no other cares than studies, homework, term papers, quizzes, and exams. We were now headed to the unknown as a married couple, to fend for ourselves.

We had located a tiny *pension* or room in Rome where we could just about afford to stay. It was located at the intersection of six bustling streets, and even inside our room, with the windows fastened, we could clearly hear the racket of cars, scooters, and Italians sharing their opinions about each other's driving abilities. To make matters worse, the woman who ran the *pension* was tightfisted. On our first night, Priscilla and I approached the desk to pay fifty *centesimos* for a shower…which of course we would be enjoying together! However, when the woman understood our plan, she insisted that because there were *two* showers being taken in total, we would have to pay her one *lira* instead.

Still, we enjoyed Italian cuisine at restaurants we could afford. We walked everywhere in Rome, seeing as much as we could of this romantic and historic city. We visited Saint Peter's Square, the Sistine Chapel, the Colosseum, and as many tourist sites as we possibly could.

When our time in Rome came to an end, we prepared to leave for Kinshasa, the Democratic Republic of Congo. We expected the flight to be an uncomfortable one, given that it took off at midnight, but at least we would be landing in the country where we would start to build a new life together during the day. Priscilla had come down with an illness during our final day in Rome, so she was anxious to get the flight over with and begin recuperating. A taxi dropped us at the airport, and we gave the last of our money to the driver. Then, with a weakening Priscilla leaning on my arm, we navigated through the terminal until we reached the Alitalia Airlines counter.

I presented the airline agent with our tickets to Kinshasa, only to be met by a confused stare. The words she spoke next were like a slap to the face. "Sir, your ticket was for a midnight flight…*yesterday*."

Immediately I understood how we had mistaken the dates, just as I understood there was nothing that could be done about it. We had missed our flight by an entire day. We had no money to our names. No credit. No place to stay. And the next flight?

"I'm sorry, sir," reported the airline agent, "but the next flight to Kinshasa isn't for six days."

"Please," Priscilla said weakly. "Please. We…"

The airline agent looked at her. Between her sickness and the news of our missed flight, Priscilla was in a pitiable state.

"Maybe there is a cargo flight," the agent said at last, picking up the phone. "*Maybe.* I still need to check. Don't get your hopes up."

But hope we did. With our spirits at their nadir, we clung to even the tiniest amount of good news.

Eventually, the agent replaced the handset and looked at us. "Alitalia has a cargo flight leaving for Johannesburg soon, and it will be stopping in Kinshasa. They've offered you two seats."

Priscilla nearly collapsed with relief. Soon we found ourselves strapping into metal seats mounted on the side of the cargo hold and then powering into the air. My wife was still in poor shape, and she slumped against the wall of the plane, clutching a thin blanket. A sheen of sweat marked her feverish forehead.

It seems I will be bringing my wife into my country as if she were cargo! I thought. Then another thought, this time comforting and funny, hit me. *At least I will not be paying import duties for her!* Since she was not in a mood to appreciate jokes of that kind, I quietly chuckled to myself.

Looking past her through the small window, I knew that soon we would be flying above the Sahara Desert as we headed south. Soon I would be back in Africa, back in Congo, for the second time since I left Kinshasa as a high school graduate. How much had changed!

Taking one last look at Priscilla, who had fallen into a fitful sleep, I closed my eyes and allowed the roar of the engines to lull me to sleep as well.

•◇◇•

Citibank, in the person of my Kinshasa boss, Kim Abbott, had already kicked into action before Priscilla and I left Rome. Knowing I would not have a salary until my first month on the job, he had reserved a hotel for Priscilla and myself until we could find a place to rent.

I held my bride's arm as we made our way out of the cargo plane and toward a row of taxis. The scent hit me…the scent of home. Charcoal, kerosene, cassava roots drying on roofs, and everywhere the sand and red earth.

The road from the airport to our hotel took us past vendors of all kinds, selling cassava, raw and roasted peanuts, hot peppers, and mangoes. I had been gone for so long, yet everything was instantly familiar.

Eventually we reached the hotel and collapsed into bed. Priscilla was still ill, and both of us were exhausted. I kissed Priscilla and said, "Welcome home, sweetie!" We then fell right asleep.

When we first opened our eyes, we were greeted by the sight of the rising sun—rising over the city of Kinshasa, our new home!

It was an inspiring sight, seeming to suggest that new opportunities awaited us. But it did not take many minutes for us to discover something odd about the dawn: The sun was actually setting lower in the sky.

"So, we slept…" began my wife.

"Yes," I finished with a laugh, "we slept for nearly twenty-one hours straight!"

PART THREE

THE INDOMITABLE BANKER

PERSEVERING THROUGH POLITICAL IMPRISONMENT, PROFESSIONAL BETRAYALS, AND COUPS D'ÉTAT 1972–2007

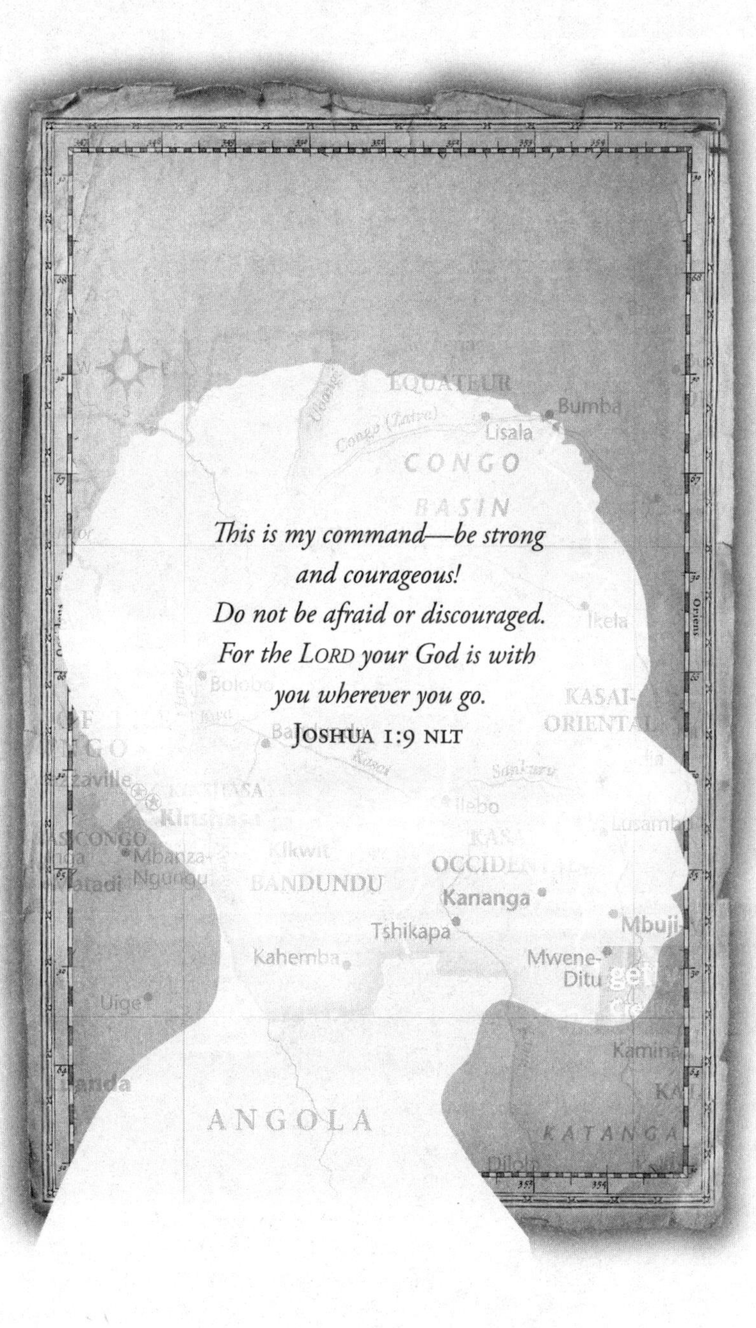

This is my command—be strong
and courageous!
Do not be afraid or discouraged.
For the Lord *your God is with*
you wherever you go.

Joshua 1:9 NLT

CHAPTER 17

The Consequences of Doing Right

Congo

When it came to my banking career, I was thrown, as the saying goes, into the deep end of the pool.

Those first few years were ones of difficulty and growth in equal parts. I was never afraid of learning the expected complexities of the job, such as trade finance, exchange rates, and the like. What was more challenging were the unexpected hazards of personal relationships.

For example, at one point, Citibank auditors from New York came to inspect our books. It did not take them long to discover a series of transactions that had been incorrectly accounted for, under the approval of a new managing director, who had replaced Kim Abbott after his transfer back to New York. Naturally, I had expected this, for my new boss and I had argued about this very issue several months earlier. I had insisted on what I had learned in Beirut during my training, and he had insisted on what he thought to be the correct accounting. And because he was the boss, he prevailed.

After the audit, my managing director had the grace to apologize and admit that he should have listened to me earlier. That was well and good. But in the time between our argument and the audit, I had been given my annual evaluation, and because of the argument, the managing director had decided not to promote me that year. I thought I had performed very well and that I deserved a good merit increase and commensurate bonus. But there was no bonus for me, and the merit increase ended up being a token allowable minimum.

This was the sort of experience that no amount of banking training could have prepared me for. It was only in the trenches of daily life that I could learn such lessons. I began to understand that there are moments in life when you know what is right and what is wrong, and that doing the right thing has consequences that are not always positive. The critical thing for me was to realize that I did what I knew was right, going by the book as I had been trained. My conscience was at peace. Others may not have had such training or knowledge, and if they did, other considerations may have clouded their judgment. I had decided to focus on my job and continue to perform to the very best of my ability. I could only control my work ethic and behavior. I could not control the thoughts or actions of my boss.

In this particular case, all ended well. At my subsequent annual evaluation, I was promoted two positions, from pro-manager to senior assistant manager, with a decent merit increase and a bonus. My altercation with the managing director did not affect my approach to work and to my responsibilities. I continued to work as hard as anyone, if not harder.

Another time, after my appointment as corporate bank head years later, I was tasked with a full review of the bank's loan portfolio. Not all my findings were pleasant. Among the borrowers was one start-up project, a company owned by a man from my tribe. Muamba Beya happened to be a friend of my brother Robert Kanyiki, the same Robert who had met Priscilla at the N'djili Airport with, "Welcome, sister-in-law!"

In its efforts to contribute to the development of the Congolese economy, Citibank included in its target market a few local companies meeting preset risk acceptance criteria. Under the bank's three initial credit approvals process, the credit committee had decided to extend a very large project finance loan to Muamba Beya's company, Levurerie du Zaire (LEZA). It was arguably the largest loan in the portfolio, financing a new yeast manufacturing plant in Kinshasa. Muamba Beya boasted that the yeast plant would become the largest manufacturing facility in Central Africa.

Or at least that is what the documents told me. The trouble was that I did not *know* if any of this was true and could not afford to take information of that magnitude on faith. Since the project was significant, I would be in significant trouble if it were discovered that any of the funds had been misspent.

I communicated with Mr. Muamba Beya that I would need to see all the receipts and other paperwork that justified the money that had been dispersed up to that point, and that going forward I would need to track every expenditure.

To my surprise, he refused. This only lent credence to my suspicions. "If you do not provide me the documents I require," I informed him, "then I will freeze your credit and I will not disperse any more loans to you."

Still, he refused. I was left with no choice but to stop the disbursements.

It was several days later that I was called into the office of my director at Citibank. I was not the only one sitting in the office: Mr. Muamba Beya and his chief financial officer (CFO) were there as well. He had with him a letter that detailed my supposed misbehavior. By appealing to my boss, he intended to have me fired. And if that could not be done, he wanted his account to be transferred to another banker who would be more understanding and less demanding about how he spent project funds.

My managing director beckoned me to sit and read the letter. I did so, then handed the letter back to him. In a calm voice, my director asked Mr. Muamba Beya, "What else?"

His eyes widened. "What *else?*" he repeated incredulously. "Our project is stalled because of this man! We want your bank to resume disbursing funds to us again! Shouldn't Tshibaka be fired for hiring his girlfriend as a teller?"

It so happened that the girl in question was a distant cousin of mine. The decision to hire her had been made by the personnel committee of the bank, consistent with Citibank policies, and the managing director knew the facts of the case. The employee in question was also one of our top performers.

The director looked at Mr. Muamba Beya, then at me, then back at Mr. Muamba Beya. "Athanase oversees your account. All the decisions of your account, he will make!"

The men were extremely disappointed, and their expressions as they looked at me were the very definition of "staring daggers." The following day, they returned to my office with carton after carton of boxes filled with documents. It was clear they wished to intimidate me and that they guessed I would not bother to check so many papers.

They were wrong on both counts. I spent the next four days with my team, reviewing every single receipt. By the second day I understood enough to know they had been misusing the funds, and by the end of the fourth day we had clear proof of exactly what they had been doing.

I arranged an appointment with them in my office.

"There is a massive gap between what we have disbursed to you and what you can account for," I began. "A massive gap."

I paused briefly to let the information sink in. I was determined we would begin with the truth as our foundation and build on that.

"However," I continued, keeping control of the conversation, "I am not going to go back to the past. I am not going to ask you to repay what you have...*misspent.* From now on, your vendors and other service providers will deliver their invoices to the bank, and the bank will pay *them* directly!"

They stared at me, incredulous and defeated.

"We will also pay the salaries of your employees directly," I continued. "And if you need petty cash, you will come to the bank and request it."

I had watched the anger rising in Mr. Muamba Beya's face throughout the encounter. Not even a tiny amount of gratitude that we were allowing the project to continue! He had imagined he could command and control a lowly bank official, but I had other ideas.

As it turned out, Mr. Muamba Beya had other ideas as well.

My brother Robert arrived in Kinshasa for a visit, but it wasn't just for pleasure. "Listen," he said, putting one hand on my shoulder, "you and I need to go visit with Muamba Beya. It is a matter of life and death."

The following night after work, I found myself inside Muamba Beya's home. Robert and I sat on one side of his living room, while facing us were Muamba Beya and his CFO. Robert and his friend began to converse about me, and I could scarcely believe what I was hearing: that if it weren't for their friendship, Muamba Beya would have already framed me for diamond smuggling and sent to prison under the dictatorship of Mobutu Sese Seko, the ruthless ruler of the country at the time. Even worse, he revealed his fallback plan, which was to hire assassins to kill me if his smuggling trap failed!

Robert was able to reason with him. "Listen to me, Muamba Beya! Calm down. My brother was simply following the rules, policies, and procedures of his bank, like a good employee."

"Maybe," allowed Muamba Beya, "but we have lost both money and reputation. How will this be made right?"

In the end, the situation reached a satisfactory conclusion, though not without a great deal of effort on my part. Muamba Beya agreed not to pursue me, while I was able to negotiate a complicated settlement among him, our bank, and Congo's finance minister. The latter's involvement, of dubious justification, was required since the project was guaranteed by the government of the Congo. Over time, Citibank recovered every penny of the project funds, and I rid myself of the prospect of encounters with Muamba Beya and his CFO.

As I later reflected on the experience, I had risked many things, including my reputation and, as it turned out, my life. Had it been worth it? I believed so. If I were to be a successful banker, I would likely be faced with difficult decisions. In addition to hard work, my mother had taught me to carry myself with honesty in my dealings, personal and professional. I would continue to do the right thing, I resolved, and in so doing, make my country a better place.

CHAPTER 18

Divine Intervention

Congo

DESPITE THE LESSONS I HAD LEARNED AS A BANKER, SOON BEGAN one of the strangest, most trying seasons of my life to that point, although even at the time I had not the slightest inkling of what would soon occur.

Our branch, and indeed our entire corporation, had clear "Know Your Customer" or "KYC" policies and procedures regarding daily operations. If someone wished to open an account, for example, we had several questionnaires to help us establish that person's fitness to bank with us.

One day, a gentleman entered the bank wanting to open an account. I walked through each step of our protocol with this gentleman, but with each step, he grew more agitated. Comments like, "Don't you know who I am?" and "How dare you?" punctuated our proceedings.

I was not the kind of banker who wished to rely on reputation or anyone's political connections. Nor, as a junior banker, could I afford to do so. The bank's rules were sound, and they were to be followed in letter and in spirit. "Unless we have all the information we need," I told him in what I hoped was a patient voice, "I cannot open an account for you."

I could tell by his frown and angry mannerisms that this was not what he wanted to hear. Eventually, however, he cooperated, and we completed the required paperwork. I was able to open the gentleman's account. The moment everything was formalized, he spun on his heel and left the bank in a huff.

A few weeks later, on a Wednesday, a colleague and I decided to leave for a bite of lunch around noon. Our branch locked its doors at 11:30 a.m. sharp for any transactions involving cash. As we approached the front door, we could hear an argument. The bank guard, on the inside, was being shouted at by an irate man outside.

"Tell me who your boss is!" came an angry shout from the other side of the door.

Unfortunately, I recognized the voice of the man, and then I saw him through the glass doors. Even more unfortunately, the guard turned around at that moment and pointed to me, the head of domestic banking operations, as his boss.

"Mister Tshibaka is my boss, and he is right here!" yelled the guard through the door.

I was left with no choice but to interact with Mr. Mwenenge. How could I forget his name? And it didn't take long to understand that he was, once again, demanding special treatment. He insisted that he needed to make a withdrawal from our cash boxes *immediately.* I could have butted heads with him and insisted on bank procedures. After all, our cash boxes were locked for the day, just as the front door had been. Who was he to think he could barge into our bank and inconvenience the staff?

Still, my previous interactions with him convinced me that honey might work better than vinegar. I instructed the guard to allow the gentleman inside, and once he had entered, I gestured toward the tellers with my arm. "Come, let's get your money," I said in a soothing voice, "and along the way you can tell me about your family and the new decrees President Mobutu has just promulgated."

Mobutu had just banished Christian names for all Congolese. I had gone from being known as Athanase Tshibaka (or A. T.) to my self-chosen new name of Kadita Tshibaka Wa Ngandu. And that was not all. The name of the country was changed officially from the Democratic Republic of the Congo to Zaire. The currency became the zaire from the Congolese franc, with an initial exchange rate of two US dollars to one zaire. The Congo River became the Zaire River. Of concern to me was the requirement that Western-style clothing be banished. Specifically, Zairians were not to wear ties and suits. The latter were to be replaced with Indian and Chinese style suits called *abacos.* (I learned much later that *abacos* stood for *"A bas le costume"* or "Down with suits.")

Once he had his withdrawal, I assumed we could move on with the day. As we proceeded to the teller, and as he received his cash, he became less agitated and even began to smile.

I apologized to the teller and thanked her once the man was gone. "Hopefully this will be a onetime occurrence and not a precedent-setting accommodation," I said. By the time the gentleman exited the building and climbed into his waiting car, I felt as if I were a great banker. I had handled a potentially explosive situation with tact, "the ability to tell someone to go to hell in such a way that they look forward to the trip," as the saying goes. Well, I had not exactly sent Mwenenge to hell, but I had sent him away satisfied and, hopefully, pleased with his banking experience and with the young officer who went out of his way to accommodate his unreasonable expectations.

The following Saturday I was working in the bank, catching up on paperwork from the week. A few tellers had come in to help me, and we were deep in the ledgers when a commotion outside demanded our attention.

First came the sound of expensive cars making rapid stops, and then came the sound of screaming and slamming car doors. Most ominously, this was followed by the unmistakable sound of gunstocks pounding on the bank doors.

"Where is *Citoyen* Tshibaka? *Where is Tshibaka!?*" Among his decrees that year, Mobutu had also banished the use of Mr., Mrs., and Miss. We were all now *Citoyen* and *Citoyenne* (feminine for *Citoyen*). I had become Citizen Tshibaka overnight, no longer Mr. Tshibaka.

One of my colleagues looked at me, wide-eyed, then hurried to the front door. He cracked it open and authoritatively asked, "Why are you asking for Tshibaka?"

I could not hear the response from the other side of the door, but my colleague practically raced back into the room, shutting the door behind him.

"What?" I asked. "Who is it?"

"A. T., I think it is Mobutu's gorillas," as Mobutu's secret service agents were known. "They threatened me…" my colleague stammered. "Unless…"

I understood even though I did not yet appreciate what the visitation portended at the time.

I was the one they wanted.

Without another thought, I walked toward the door, opened it, and announced, "I am Tshibaka."

The words were still on my lips when the wrongness of the scene struck me. I noticed several black Mercedes-Benz sedans parked at odd angles. Standing beside them were men who were clearly with the secret police: no uniforms per se, but well-muscled, dressed impeccably in *abacos*, and carrying themselves with an air of authority and barely restrained violence. They well deserved what everyone called them: *gorillas*.

I was seized and forced into the back seat of one of the cars. To my dismay, I watched several of the gorillas enter the bank and drag out the tellers as well, forcing them into the cars.

As we raced away from the bank, it became clear that our destination was a military camp, "Camp Tshatshi," near a state-of-the-art "village" Mobutu had built for the Organization of African Unity, not far from his own residence. It was infamous as a place where his political enemies were interrogated, and many eventually disappeared.

A feeling of dread began to fill me. What had I done to deserve such treatment? I was a low-level officer of the bank, carrying responsibilities beyond my age. I was determined to tell them the truth and give them facts as I knew them firsthand. The other silent prayer I had was that they had mistaken me for someone else. Perhaps upon realizing their error, they would simply apologize and bring me back to the bank to catch up on my work.

When we arrived at the compound, I was led to the interrogation room. There was a wooden table in the center with two chairs on either side. At the far end of the room, against the wall, was another table in mahogany wood with a leather chair behind. Four men, one in military uniform, were standing around that table. They briefly took notice of my entrance, secured between two gorillas. The four men continued their conversation in hushed voices, as if strategizing on the approach to take with my case.

I immediately recognized my accuser, Mwenenge. I did not know the other three gentlemen but was to learn later that the four were members of Mobutu's security apparatus. One was the country's attorney general (AG), the one in uniform was the head of Mobutu's security, and a senior prosecutor in the AG's office.

I was led to one of the chairs and forced to sit down, bewildered and in shock. The AG approached the center table and sat across from me. Behind him stood the top prosecutor. Their demeanor conveyed to me they meant business.

The AG started by asking, "Why did you act the way you did at the bank?"

I told them the story, recounting the facts as they happened, exactly. I concluded by emphasizing that I had simply been following the policies of Citibank, and that I had treated Mr. Mwenenge the same way I had dealt with all my customers...politely and courteously but also uncompromisingly regarding bank policies and procedures.

My questioners were clearly unsatisfied with what I told them.

The AG called in one of the gorillas and ordered that I be taken to an adjacent room. Other than a large picture of Mobutu on the wall, a king-size bed, and a lone wooden chair at the foot of the bed, the room was bland and austere. The walls were painted white. The imposing picture of Mobutu on one of the walls and the whole decor of the room seemed intended to instill fear. And yes, I was afraid. But I was not hopeless. I was convinced the whole situation was all a misunderstanding and that the gentlemen would soon realize that their accusation was baseless. As a result, I hoped they would soon present their apologies and let me return to my catch-up work at the bank.

My hopeful thoughts were interrupted by the same gorilla who had shown me to the isolation room. He came in and, grabbing me by the arm, took me back to the interrogation room. What followed was the same questioning from them, and the same story and facts in response from me. Back and forth, from isolation room to interrogation room, with what seemed like hours of intervals in between.

By late afternoon, I was exhausted and upset. I had not had any food or drink. Worse, it did not seem like my interrogators cared about my answers. *Why in the world would they put a diligent junior bank officer through such treatment?*

"Look, I've told you the truth!" I snapped. "You've asked the same questions repeatedly. It seems to me that you've been given instructions about what to do with me. If nothing I say will make a difference, then why don't you just carry out your orders?"

The AG stared at me, surprised and shocked by my outburst. "*What* did you say?" he asked.

Perhaps unwisely, I took his question as genuine, and I repeated what I had just said to him, staring back at him, defiant.

"Okay," the AG growled, standing up and bringing his face closer to mine. "We will show you what we can do. Believe me, we *will* show you!"

Documents were brought into the room for me to sign. I was so angry that I did not bother to read what they had put in front of me. Besides, even if I read a single word…what would that gain me? Enough was enough! I signed everything they instructed me to sign, then sat back to see what they would decide next.

I did not have to wait long. I was marched outside and put in a military jeep secured by two armed soldiers. The gorillas had accomplished their mission. Mobutu's top security men had concluded their sham interrogation. I was now at the mercy of the military, with an uncertain fate.

The soldiers soon took me to Camp Tshatshi. Upon arrival, I allowed myself to feel a glimmer of hope. The so-called prison appeared to be a house from the outside, which seemed better than what I had been imagining.

Priscilla did not know where I was, but perhaps there would be a way to contact her once I entered the building. The managing director and other bank staff did not know my whereabouts either. I determined to contact them as soon as I could.

Minutes later, my hope plummeted. Inside the house, I was taken to a cell that was roughly eight feet by fifteen feet in size. There were twenty-two of us in the cell, crammed into that cramped space. The corner of the cell had a pit that my nose told me was the only toilet, the one place where twenty-two men were made to do their "relief business."

"This place is for political prisoners. And there is a basement here," one of the prisoners told me. "If you are taken down there, that's it for you. You're done. Either disappeared or found floating in the river."

I thought about his words. "And what about this cell?" I asked.

He looked around it and shrugged. "People come, people go," he said, "but not all go to the basement."

That meant there was hope. Slim hope, but hope nevertheless.

Further inquiries with the men in the cell revealed that all of them had been educated abroad, in Europe or North America. None of them knew exactly why they were there, and all, like me, were waiting for their fate. We were all young lads in our twenties.

The prisoners had organized shifts for sleeping: one-third of us could lie down and sleep, elbow to elbow, while the rest of us stood, shoulder to shoulder. I was not given food or water during the time I was there.

Priscilla, in the meantime, was desperately asking Kim Abbott and other bank staff where her husband was. They only knew, through the tellers who were taken with me to Camp Tshatshi and later returned to the bank, that they had last seen me there, being interrogated by Mobutu's agents.

Kim said to my wife, "A. T. seems to have gotten himself into a little bit of trouble with the Congolese authorities. We don't know where he is now, but we will do all we can to find out. Go home. I will get back to you as soon as we have news."

I was to learn later that Kim was frantically calling everyone he knew who might be able to help. He contacted Bill Spencer, who at the time was president of Citicorp and, coincidently, a hunting buddy and personal friend of Bill Rogers, the American secretary of state. Kim had also reached out to the American ambassador to Congo, Sheldon B. Vance.

The US secretary of state thus learned of my arrest through diplomatic channels and from the president of Citicorp. (A couple of decades later, I learned that President Nixon had also been informed that an officer of Citibank was imprisoned by Congo's dictator and held in one of his infamous cells in Kinshasa.)

Soon, official word reached Mobutu: The government of the United States of America knew that an officer of Citibank was being held in an infamous prison. And, the US stressed, that officer was not to "disappear." If he had committed crimes, he *must* be put through the normal judicial process, or else there would be consequences.

Looking back on that episode in my life, I am grateful for how President John F. Kennedy launched a program that provided me a scholarship opportunity and for how President Nixon's administration intervened to save my life.

Because Mobutu was an anticommunist and received support from the United States, the call for my protection carried actual weight. So it was that on the third day of my confinement, a Tuesday, an armed soldier took me in a jeep from the Camp Tshatshi cell and transferred me to the office of the attorney general of the Congo.

Inside the office, along with a guard and the attorney general, were Kim Abbott and Priscilla.

Kim shook my hand, and Priscilla embraced me, even though I smelled like a corpse. She handed me a baguette sandwich. I took a bite, but I had to spit it out because my mouth was so dry, and my throat hurt very badly. She handed me a thermos of water. I took a sip, but I couldn't even swallow the water.

I learned that because Kim had involved the United States government, I would be transferred to the main prison in Kinshasa.

Going to Makala Prison was scarcely something to be pleased about, given its reputation as the holding pen for some of the most violent criminals in the Congo. The only bit of good news was that prisoners could not be disappeared from Makala, as they could from the hellhole I had just left.

As it turned out, the troublesome bank customer was a cousin of Mobutu, and he expected to be always treated with deference. My trouble was that I had bowed to bank policies rather than to his identity. I was to be taught a lesson I would never forget, assuming I survived the ordeal. I had dared treat him like any other person entering Citibank premises, *lèse-majesté*! In anger, he had reported me to his cousin, the dictator, as someone who was questioning his newly proclaimed decrees. Now that the United States government had intervened, the AG had acquiesced to send me to Makala Prison, without any formal charges.

"But what have I done *wrong*?" I asked. "What were they going to charge me with?"

No one could tell me. And so, I thanked Kim for his intervention and told Priscilla that I would see her as soon as possible, still optimistic that justice would prevail in the end. Then, regretfully, I was taken away, leaving Priscilla in tears in the AG's office.

I steeled myself to begin a new season of life as a prisoner.

At Makala Prison, there was an intake point where all new prisoners were to be registered. We stood in an antechamber between metal doors, waiting our turn to be entered into the prison ledger. The soldier handling the duties was small and rude. I thought of half a dozen ways of improving his attitude and his bookkeeping within minutes of observing him. Unwisely, I reprimanded him. "Why are you behaving like this? You should be treating us with respect!"

The slap I received was hard enough to make me gasp and taught me a lesson about prison: Holding my tongue would sometimes be the wisest course of action.

Once I entered the main courtyard, I must have looked like easy prey to the men who filled it. My shirt and pants, though reeking to high heaven, were of good quality. I also wore a gold watch and a leather belt.

I knew that I was surrounded by a mix of men, from people like me to petty thieves to murderers. Just as I began to edge my way toward a guard, a hulking prisoner spotted me.

"Hey!" he yelled, pointing at me and then looking at his fellow prisoners. "This is *my* boss! No one play games with him, understood? Stay away from him!"

Relief flooded me, but also confusion. Why was this man being protective of me?

He arranged for me to get a sleeping mat in a large room with more than one hundred prisoners, the majority of whom were newcomers like me. He ushered me to a spot against a wall that looked better than many of the other options. After saying he would see me soon, my protector disappeared in the crowd.

The following day, I was assigned to a particular section of the prison. They called the different buildings in the prison *pavilions*. I learned that the prisoners were segregated by occupation and offense. One section was filled with political prisoners who had run afoul of Mobutu. The next section, where I was placed, was filled with so-called intellectuals, such as businessmen and teachers. The third section was a catch-all for every other prisoner, from forgers to rapists to murderers, and everything in between.

At that point, my protector explained that he wanted me to hire him as my "houseboy." Young men from the third section often hired themselves out to prisoners in the first two sections, most of whom had small amounts of disposable cash. In exchange for a fee, he would not only keep other prisoners from harming me but would also perform various tasks such as washing and ironing my clothes.

I was assigned a small room with two cement platforms. Both my roommate and I could afford thin mattresses, though not everyone could. Small holes in the wall allowed fresh air to enter the room, along with mosquitoes. One electric bulb hung from the ceiling, and it could be turned on and off only by our guards.

•✕◇✕•

And so began my prison career.

Each Sunday, Kim Abbott and Priscilla arrived to visit me. He would pick up my wife at seven in the morning, then drive her to Makala Prison. There they would wait in line, together with all the other Congolese who had come to visit their relatives. Sometimes, Kim would bring his eleven-year-old son, George, to visit me as well.

"I'll throw a rope over the wall," George whispered to me once, "and you can just climb out!"

Kim was like an angel watching over me. He had not only secured my release from Mobutu's deadly prison camp but also made the decision to pay my salary while I was in prison, ensuring that Priscilla would be able to pay rent and buy food. He did not owe these things to me because I was special or held some unique role at the bank. In fact, I was replaceable. Rather, he did these things because he was a fundamentally good and godly man.

If Kim was my angel, my archangel would be Priscilla. She brought food to me every single day, without fail. This was important because the prison food lacked both nutrition and taste. She would also bring frozen water, and I would sip it sparingly throughout the day, thankful for her thoughtfulness.

Most conversations involved me attempting to discover how my beloved was coping. During one such conversation, she shared with me about a horrific dinner she had attended. At the party, the wife of Congo's ambassador to one of the North African countries surprised Priscilla by introducing her to an Italian diplomat.

"Priscilla, that handsome Italian gentleman you see there is interested in you," the wife said. "Why should you deprive yourself of some pleasure? You are still a young, beautiful woman, with all your future ahead. Be sensible now and take advantage of this opportunity."

My archangel was shocked and, disgusted, declined decisively. How thankful I was to God Almighty for the blessing of this special woman!

Priscilla brought me food and conversation, but there was another worry. Diseases ran rampant in the prison, so Priscilla taught herself how to give cholera injections by practicing on oranges at home. She then hid a syringe inside some bread, and when no one was looking during one of her visits, she administered a preventive shot to me. Another time, my roommate had infectious hepatitis. As his condition worsened, I became concerned. The next day, Priscilla snuck in an immunization for hepatitis inside *fufu*, our staple food, but this time she was caught. The prison director was furious and ordered that I be transferred to solitary confinement. I would have been had Kim Abbott not intervened once again. He pleaded with the prison director, explaining the hell my young American wife was enduring. He prevailed. Not only that but Kim also managed to arrange for me to be given the hepatitis shot by the prison nurse.

One day, after Priscilla had returned home, a thought occurred to me. *I have literally nothing to do while in this prison…so how can I be fruitful?*

I proposed to the prison director that I could give English lessons to my fellow prisoners, and he agreed. By the time I had my first round of classes planned out, I discovered that more than 150 men had registered to attend.

Then a far better thought occurred to me, and I approached the prison director a second time.

"My wife is American, sir. She is a native English speaker, educated in the finest schools in America. She can advise me on how to teach an excellent English class for the men who have registered. Will you allow me private times with my wife to get her advice on the lessons?"

To my shock, he agreed to this idea as well. Additionally, he provided us with an office where Priscilla and I could talk, plan lessons, store our books, and kiss whenever safe.

Still, despite making the best of my situation, the daily slog of prison was miserable. One of the sources of comfort for me was reading *Papillon*, a French novel about a prisoner in truly atrocious conditions on an isolated island, who survived by eating cockroaches and mice he caught in his solitary cell. *At least*, I reflected, *I have food and water brought to me daily by Priscilla!*

It took two full months to learn why I had been incarcerated, perhaps because the authorities were struggling to invent a charge that could pass muster in court.

Eventually I was accused of inciting my fellow bank employees to armed rebellion against Mobutu's regime…a strange charge given that I had never owned or fired a weapon!

Three months after my arrival in Makala Prison, I was taken to my first court appearance. The government had been given strict expectations by the United States that I was not to be disappeared, true, but there were no expectations about how long the legal process might take or even if it would be fair. I was assigned a corporate bank lawyer, Maitre Nkuba, but he seemed (perhaps understandably) more focused on his other cases than on mine. I prepared my own defense, laying out the facts in such a way as to show that I was the victim of a witch hunt.

In court, I showed my lawyer what I had prepared. Seeing that it was much more thorough than his own material, he decided to read it. As he did, I watched the three judges. Dressed in black and looking quite stern, I suspected they had no real interest in the particulars of my case. One kept glancing out the window, while another fidgeted with his robe. The presiding judge, for his part, seemed attracted to something on the ceiling.

Perhaps they have already been instructed and know what to do with me, I thought.

As the judges dismissed me from that first hearing, the presiding judge informed me that the prosecution had asked for a three-year sentence. "You will have to await our judgment in prison," he said.

One week later, I was brought back to the same courtroom. One of the judges informed me that I had been found guilty but that my sentence had been reduced based on the generosity of the court. Instead of three years, I was sentenced to eighteen months' jail time.

The sentence did not surprise me. I was expecting much worse. Having been spared from death, anything that allowed me to live a little longer was still welcome. Nonetheless, how could I allow injustice to prevail?

With the help of Maitre Nkuba, I appealed my sentence but was forced to remain in prison during the process. After three additional months, I was brought to the court of appeals and received yet more bad news: The presiding judge was a member of Mobutu's tribe. Needless to say, this did not bode well for me. To make matters worse, my lawyer was on very bad terms with the presiding judge.

Perhaps I can consider what happened next as a moment of divine intervention. Despite having every reason to reject my appeal, the head judge chose not to. This was because his personality, like mine, preferred to follow procedures exactly. And he was upset that my accuser was not in court to testify, as would have been expected.

"I won't hear this case unless the accuser is present," he intoned to the prosecutor.

The prosecutor shrugged, having no idea where the man was. Immediately, the judge ordered soldiers to find my accuser. Several hours passed, and then the soldiers returned. They reported to the judge that they had found the man at the International Fair of Kinshasa. When contacted and asked to come to court, Mwenenge refused to come back with them.

The judge slapped his palm on the table. "Go back!" he declared. "If he doesn't come immediately, tell him that the maximum sentence that Mr. Tshibaka would have been given will instead be given to *him*!"

Again, we waited. At last, the soldiers returned, escorting my nemesis, Mr. Mwenenge, the troublesome bank customer and cousin of Mobutu. He was dressed for the fair in a garish outfit, complete with gold chains to show his wealth and platform shoes that were in vogue those years. As I viewed him from a utilitarian perspective, Mwenenge was a short man indeed, and his platform shoes certainly could *not* lift him anywhere close to my height!

The judge addressed him. "What has the defendant done to you that you have put him through this legal process?"

I prepared to hear about my role as a so-called armed leader who had incited bank employees to rebel against Mobutu's regime.

Instead, Mwenenge shuffled back and forth, frowning. He scratched his chin. He shrugged. "I...don't know."

"Do you even know what he is charged with?" demanded the judge.

Mwenenge shrugged again. I was fuming inside. Of course, he'd trumped up the charges against me, but even now, when he could have used his family connections to make me suffer, all the man seemed to care about was returning to the fair to party. He did not seem prepared to even recollect the facts of our encounters.

The judge sized up the situation and dismissed Mr. Mwenenge.

Now, however, the judge was left with a dilemma. He knew I was not a rebel. He knew I was innocent and had been set up by Mwenenge. But if he let me go immediately, he would be likely to face trouble from the Mobutu regime, which, despite the fecklessness of Mwenenge, kept a close eye on the judiciary. A not-guilty verdict would not have pleased Mobutu.

After considering the matter, the judge decided that five months was more than enough punishment for someone who did not deserve even one day in prison. Further, he announced he would be including the time I had already spent in prison. Therefore, he sentenced me to four months in jail, which was his way of letting me out since I had already served five months.

The judge had played it safe with the Mobutu regime. He gave me a jail term, yes, but one that allowed me immediate freedom. At the same time, he managed to avoid provoking the ire of the regime by throwing out my case altogether. I would be returned to jail after the court proceedings and, I was informed, would be allowed to pack up my things and leave prison that same day.

I learned that when you are powerless, when there is truly nothing you can do to change your situation, you are faced with two choices: despair or trust.

For me that meant trusting that God had His reasons and plan for my imprisonment, though I am ashamed to say that I did not actively pray as much as I would have liked during my prison time. Yet even amid my despair and hopelessness, God provided helpers. How much worse my stay in prison would have been without Priscilla, Kim Abbott, and even my burly protector.

CHAPTER 19

Love Tested, Commitment Unshaken

Congo

PRISCILLA'S FIRST YEARS IN CONGO AS MY WIFE WERE FAR MORE difficult than even her father had warned. My unexpected and unjust stint in prison showed Priscilla how isolated she truly was. For example, our neighbors, an American-Congolese couple just as we were, did not invite Priscilla to dinner even once while I was behind bars.

Additionally, her employment situation was not ideal, both in quality and compensation. She taught English as a second language at the American School of Kinshasa (ASK), and she also organized the music and drama performances. The children in her classes could range in age from kindergarten to middle school, and it seemed every child spoke a different native language. The classroom itself was a primitive affair. The school was without air conditioning, and the windows were covered in metal grills rather than glass. When the weather was hot, classes were conducted early in the day. But the window grills meant it was possible for rain to blow directly into the classroom, causing Priscilla to seek shelter beneath her desk!

Other teachers were paid in US dollars because they were hired directly from the United States. Even though she had been promised she would be treated the same way, the school administration decided to switch her pay to the local currency, the zaire, which was losing value quickly because of inflation. The school's line was that she was married to a local and a permanent resident of the country, so she would be paid as a local. There was nowhere to appeal the decision and no other viable employment opportunities we could find.

Compensation in dollars would have meant she could comfortably buy a plane ticket to the United States occasionally, while compensation in zaires meant extreme scrimping and saving to visit her family.

There was another factor complicating our lives: my relatives. Because we lived in Kinshasa, our home was a welcome waypoint for any relatives traveling to, or through, or residing in the city. Entertaining kin was a given, across the Congo. If a second cousin thrice removed wished to have dinner with us, we would say yes…just as we would be welcome at that cousin's home if we were ever in his or her neighborhood.

But requests for our hospitality outstripped our ability to fulfill them. Perhaps we were seen as having more largesse than most in my family, owing to my banking job. Additionally, my being married to a *mundele* (white woman), and an American to boot, carried an erroneous projection of wealth in the eyes of my family and acquaintances. In truth, however, Priscilla and I were nearly living hand-to-mouth.

One of these visits, while I was still in prison, was from my older brother Antoine Tshiyombo Muka. He told Priscilla he could use witchcraft to free me, and she was ready to try anything to get me out of my imprisonment. He performed his rituals, and that night, my wife woke to the presence of what she perceived as evil spirits in the room. She saw garish colors swirling around and around her. *What does this mean for my husband in prison?* she thought. *Is he going to be killed? What does it mean for our future?* She decided not to linger on such thoughts. Terrified, she repeated the name of Jesus, over and over, until the presence departed.

I was oblivious to such traumatic experiences at the time, of course. In hindsight, I am thankful my wife chose to stay and support me, notwithstanding the many challenges she was facing, alone in a foreign country. I must also admit that I am glad I was not in the apartment to witness evil spirits swirling around!

Although the timing of my relations' visits varied from week to week, and from month to month, over the course of a single year innumerable extended family members visited our home in Kinshasa. One cousin might request money to pay for medicine, while another might ask (unsuccessfully) for cash to cover three months of salary. Usually, they would tell us they needed money for the *fula fula* (truck transport) back to wherever they may have been staying.

My brother Honore Ngandu once told me he had lost a large sum of money and that he needed my help. On another of his visits, Honore half-jokingly made it known to us that if Priscilla and I did not have a child in a year's time, the family was going to curse us! Even as a half-baked joke, this announcement did not go over well with my wife.

I must confess, however, the most serious factor in Priscilla's difficulties was me.

Upon my release from prison, work at Citibank began at seven o'clock in the morning, and technically it ended at three in the afternoon. I was a bank officer with ambitions to rise through the ranks, so I would work until six o'clock in the evening. On the nights I came straight home, it was with the traditional expectations of any Congolese man: to put my feet up, to be handed a beer, and then to be fed.

On the nights I did not come straight home, perhaps because I was enjoying drinks with my work colleagues, Priscilla would be alone, wondering where I was. On weekends, I chose to do whatever I wanted, with no regard for Priscilla's feelings or desires. I might, for example, take the car to the tennis courts and play several matches with friends. That would be followed by a stop at the bar and capped off with a three-hour daytime nap at home. Other nights I would stay out late and come home drunk, keeping my wife wide awake with worry.

Some of my colleagues enjoyed clandestine "work girlfriends" (referred to as *deuxième bureau* in French) with whom they would drink and carouse after hours. I was committed to one woman and never considered having a *deuxième bureau.* Nonetheless, I will admit to being caught by the company I kept and the culture of irresponsible habits prevailing in the city. I always had a plausible story to tell Priscilla upon returning home.

To cap off my egregious shortcomings, I had also increased my smoking habit to a level that could fairly be described as chimney-like.

Since kick-starting smoking in Beirut in 1972, I had progressively moved to more than a pack of twenty-four cigarettes a day.

In short, it would be an understatement to say Priscilla was unimpressed with my choices.

The charitable explanation is that I was enjoying my freedom post-prison or that my behavior and habits were caused by the intense work-related stress associated with my responsibilities at the bank. Or I could blame my shortcomings on the circle of friends I kept.

In truth, I was merely living selfishly, concerned only with my career and personal pleasure. Our marriage was falling apart, and the responsibility was mine. Increasingly, I was engaging in activities that were splitting our relationship further and further apart.

I was not surprised, therefore, when my wife informed me she would be heading to the United States as soon as she could make arrangements.

CHAPTER 20

A Deal with God

United States and Congo

It was no wonder Priscilla needed a break from, well, everything in Kinshasa. When she arrived in the United States, two events occurred that would change not only her life but my life and the shape of our entire marriage.

The first event took place in the guest bedroom of her aunt's home in River Forest, a suburb of Chicago, Illinois. Priscilla made a deal with God.

If You are really there, God, she prayed, *save my marriage. Save my marriage, and I'll commit my life to You.* At the time she could not have known the result of that prayer or even the full meaning of the terms of the deal. Nevertheless, it was a cry from the depths of her heart.

A few weeks later, she traveled to the St. Paul, Minnesota, area to visit her brother and his family as well as her father. It was there that the second event took place in a high school gym. Priscilla was attending a worship service with her father one Wednesday evening and, during the singing, she noticed that everyone around her was experiencing a genuine connection with God. They were not merely mouthing words. Rather, they were praising someone with whom they were in a genuine, faithful relationship. Their worship of the Creator of heaven and earth, God Almighty, was real and heartfelt!

I want this, Priscilla thought. After the service, she asked her father, "I want what you have, but how do I get it?" Her father led her to the priest who was leading the worship that day. The three of them opened the Bible, and Priscilla learned about being "born again of the Spirit," as Jesus explains to Nicodemus in the third chapter of John's Gospel. She acknowledged and confessed her sins and invited Jesus Christ to be Lord and Sovereign in her heart and life.

My wife was officially born again, and she began speaking in tongues (as mentioned in the twelfth chapter of 1 Corinthians), praying fervently, and reading the Bible and books by Christian authors. Everything she learned and experienced confirmed she was on a path the Lord had traced for her. Each time she prayed, for example, she would listen, then write down what she heard. "A. T.," she told me later, "I just can't believe *how much* Jesus loves me!" She developed the habit of journaling to record messages she was receiving from the Lord through her Bible reading. At other times, she simply jotted down prayers to God during her reading and meditation.

She had become a new woman. And then?

Then she returned to her husband in Congo. Specifically, to her husband who believed himself to be a Christian already and who saw no need to change his own behaviors. As I witnessed her new life, such as constantly reading her Bible, one of the first things I told her was, "I know my Bible better than you do." This may have been true at an academic level, but it was untrue, I came to learn, at a spiritual level. I was still puffed up by the biblical familiarity I had acquired as president of the Youth for Christ at the Presbyterian High School of Bibanga.

My wife's newfound interest in Jesus did nothing to change my life. "Good for you, but not for me," that was my motto. I was quite happy for her to choose how to fill her free time, leaving me to do what I chose to do.

Priscilla began attending a women's Bible study. She learned she could find a home at an English-speaking Protestant church in Kinshasa, which believed in the Holy Trinity and the works of the Holy Spirit in the lives of Christ's followers. At home, she spent more and more of her time in Scripture. Outside the home, she soon acquired an entirely new social life. It seemed she was always being asked to attend a meeting, pray with someone, or take a walk to discuss a new book. In less than a year, she read the entire Bible, using the recently published Living Bible.

Whenever Priscilla's new Christian friends came to visit or share a meal, it was all too easy for me to hide behind an arrogant facade. I had grown up Catholic, then attended a Presbyterian high school. While there, I had joined Youth for Christ, taught Bible studies, sung in the church choir, and preached sermons in nearby villages. What could Priscilla and her friends possibly have to offer me?

Her newfound friends would not give up trying to get me to join their Bible studies or read the newest Christian books. I shared with them my Christian credentials. I was attending the International Protestant Church of Kinshasa and was chairman of its finance committee. I was very clearly a Christian! What else did they, and Priscilla, want from me?

The more they tried to persuade me, the further away I tried to get from them, convinced I was right in my misguided arrogance and intransigence.

I did not understand at the time, but I was echoing (and wrongly applying) the apostle Paul's message where he says, "Indeed, if others have reason for confidence in their own efforts, I have even more!" (Philippians 3:4 NLT). I was blissfully ignoring the preceding verses, which make it clear that born-again Christians "worship by the Spirit of God" and that they rely on what Christ Jesus has done, putting no confidence in their own human efforts. I was continuing to boast in my own accomplishments and had not yet considered them "worthless" compared to the infinite value of knowing Christ Jesus and receiving Him as my Lord and Savior.

I had refused to attend Priscilla's church regularly since she returned from the United States, and I turned a cold shoulder to any spiritual books she kept in the house…or even any spiritual conversations! But it was not long before she began to play piano for the church. Next she became choir director and helped organize one of the Bible studies. As if the gravity of Priscilla's commitment to the church was pulling me into its orbit, I began to attend sporadically, and then more regularly. I still believed our missionary friends had nothing new to offer me, yet I could not deny the changes I was seeing in my wife.

For example, one night I came home inebriated (again), expecting to receive another stern lecture. I must have fumbled with the front door because I was not yet inside when I heard Priscilla call out, "Are you okay? Honey, please come in."

I managed to open the door. Stepping inside, I saw Priscilla looking at me with concern. "Do you need an aspirin?" she asked. She was smiling kindly.

I shook my head, unwisely, then recovered my balance and found a chair. "No, I'm fine," I insisted. After a moment I stood, again unwisely, but managed to make it to the bedroom. Priscilla brought me a glass of water. After making sure I drank it, she tucked me in and wished me a good night's sleep.

Why is she acting so kindly? I wondered. *It is like she has become a different person, a better person*, my fogged brain managed. But *how?*

The answer was obvious to me, even in my inebriated state: God.

The following day, I asked her about her compassion for me the night before. She told me that in the time before I returned home, she had prayed and read her Bible. She knew there was nothing she could do to chide me into changing and that God would need to move in my heart.

The same proved true of my smoking habit. One evening, despite a clear prohibition on smoking in our bedroom, I lit up a cigarette. Priscilla did not react in the slightest. When I asked her about it later, her face showed a moment of surprise. "To be honest," she said, "I hardly noticed. I asked the Lord to take away my frustrations with your smoking, and now He has!"

Her actions and attitude were certainly making me think. *If she can change, and change for the better*, I wondered, *perhaps I can as well. Perhaps there is something she has that I am missing.*

CHAPTER 21

Irresistible Pursuit

Congo

ONE YEAR AFTER PRISCILLA RETURNED FROM THE UNITED STATES a spiritually transformed woman, we decided to take our annual vacation. I was entitled to annual leave of one month from the bank, and that year we decided to vacation with another mixed-race couple. Albert Mupenda was a gynecologist obstetrician and Priscilla's doctor. Originally from the northeastern part of the Congo, he had returned from Canada to serve at Mama Yemo Hospital (named after President Mobutu's mother). Carolle, his Canadian wife, was a nurse.

Carolle, as a foreigner, was paid more than her husband, who was a full medical doctor specialized in his field and well respected. Understandably, this did not sit well with Albert. He was happy for his wife but distressed at the injustice he was living through. As for me, I had understood from Kim Abbott that my MBA degree did not mean much as far as compensation structures were concerned. Citibank's policy was to pay locals according to local market practice, and the local market practice was to pay locals substantially less than expatriates, even those performing the same or lower jobs. I tried to help Albert understand this, but to no avail. They'd ultimately return to Canada, where Albert could be paid a wage consistent with his position as a specialized medical doctor.

We decided to vacation together in a missionary village called Nsiamfumu to the southwest of Kinshasa, where the Congo River meets the Atlantic Ocean. The thatched-roof homes, quite nice and well kept by local standards, were two of several dozen missionary vacation homes that overlooked the meeting of the mighty waters.

Nearby was the main town of Muanda, a proper beach town that included a tourist-friendly hotel, a nice restaurant, and other amenities. In Nsiamfumu, however, the pace of life was far slower. The missionaries who owned the houses would rent them out to make extra money, yet the cost was a mere three dollars a week. There was a nearby street market, where Priscilla and I purchased simple, cheap food such as fresh fish and vegetables.

Besides fishing, which I was hopeless at, and staring at the confluence of the ocean and river, which I grew bored with, there was very little to do. The only entertainment in our house was a shelf of worn paperback books. Sitting beneath a baobab tree outside the home, I read through the Ludlum thrillers and Agatha Christie mysteries all too quickly and was dismayed to discover that the only remaining reading material consisted of Christian books, among which was a Campus Crusade for Christ manuscript, *Ten Basic Steps Toward Christian Maturity*. I tried ignoring it for half a morning, but my boredom eventually caught up with me. I was not a person who could sit comfortably in silence in his own company… not even with a view of the Atlantic!

I walked to the reading bench outside the house, which sat beneath a baobab tree. I opened the pamphlet, which promised to teach me a verse each day, along with some spiritually edifying content. I sighed and began reading. I was not looking forward to beginning my remaining days of vacation in such a way.

Priscilla was more content with the contours of our trip. She relished the time to pray and journal in the peace and quiet of our coastal retreat.

But conflict found us. One night we decided to splurge on a fancy dinner at the hotel in Muanda. No sooner had we taken our places at our table than a man approached, showing more interest in the beautiful, blond-haired lady accompanying me than in the nonsensical pleasantries he was uttering. That provoked suspicions and anger in me. The German man and Priscilla had met previously, when Priscilla had traveled to the coast with some missionary friends. She and the German had hit it off and ended up chatting for hours about music and gardening. However, he had tried to kiss Priscilla, which she did not reciprocate. Knowing the situation was not right, she had cut her trip short and returned to Kinshasa.

Perhaps because we were in different places spiritually, running into the German caused an argument between Priscilla and me when we returned to our vacation home. Both of us said hurtful things, although I am sure I was the greater offender. That night, back in our rented missionary home, I fell asleep with my head in my wife's lap.

She stayed awake, continuing to pray and cry.

Later, when she finally went to sleep, she dreamed that Jesus was walking toward her, and He invited her to walk with Him. Eventually they came upon me, though I did not notice them. In the dream, Priscilla invited me to come meet Jesus, but I did not respond. She grew angry and castigated me for all the bad things I had done. Surely I could see I needed to meet Christ! There was no response from me.

Still in the dream, she cried out to Jesus, and He washed away her tears and lifted the weight of my bad decisions from her. Soon she felt clean and relieved. She then understood that her attitude would determine if I would ever decide to receive Jesus Christ as Lord and Savior, or else continue in my obstinacy.

At that point, the dream remained between Priscilla and the Lord. I did not yet know it had taken place.

The next morning, I found my typical spot beneath the baobab tree. I opened the Campus Crusade for Christ pamphlet, discovered the day's verse, and opened my Bible to read the chapter from which the verse had come.

Before I could begin reading, I distinctly heard a quiet but clear voice inside me.

Today is your day of decision. Will you accept Me as your Lord and Savior?

I shook my head to dismiss the thought.

Again, I heard it. *Today is your day of decision. Will you accept Me as your Lord and Savior?*

"This is real!" I whispered to myself. I understood, somehow, I could not postpone the decision. Perhaps, however, I could argue my way out. In my heart, I "reminded" God I had already been baptized Catholic as a child, then baptized and confirmed as a Presbyterian as a teenager. If I wasn't a Christian, what was I?

Today is your day of decision. Will you accept Me as your Lord and Savior?

There was both persistence and urgency in the question. It felt as if God was not simply knocking on the door of my heart but battering it down!

I was certain that this was indeed my moment of acceptance or, alternatively, continued resistance and denial. I could not be sure another opportunity would be offered to me. God, Creator of all things, the seen and the invisible, was pursuing me, a fallen and undeserving human, through His Holy Spirit. Amazing!

At last, I relented. There was nothing else I could do.

Yes, I prayed, *I am a sinner! I need forgiveness. I need Jesus to come into my heart and be the Lord of my life!*

I opened my eyes. I felt…peace. No, I felt *peace!* Ultimate, undeserved peace.

I looked out at the waters spread wide in front of me. My soul seemed to swell. Turning, I ran inside. I do not know how much sense my jumbled flow of words made to my wife, but she understood the important part. We hugged, pulled apart, grinned at each other's tear-stained faces, and hugged again. The tears were filled with joy, yes, and also relief. We understood it was a new beginning for us. After years of difficult striving, like the majestic Congo River tumbling through canyons and over rocks, we had reached something good, something God-ordained.

We looked at each other with true love. An ocean of possibilities stretched before us.

Priscilla and I soon returned to Kinshasa. Two weeks later, the University of Kinshasa campus hosted a charismatic Christian retreat. We counted quite a few friends and acquaintances planning to attend, and we decided to go as a couple. Catholic priests, Protestant pastors, and missionaries were in attendance, outnumbering those of us from secular occupations.

During the Saturday evening session, the leader invited some in the audience to share about their walk with God. I was not pleased when I felt the same prompting in my heart that I had felt back at the seaside in Nsiamfumu. While others took turns standing and sharing, I argued internally. Another fierce battle raged inside me. It was not my first argument with the Holy Spirit, nor would it be my last!

Stand and share.

But what can I share that is of value?

Stand and share.

I have only just become a Christian!

Stand and share.

I feel that I am like mud, while these others are clean.

Stand and share.

I was sweating because of the intensity of the argument within my soul.

Stand and share!

Stand and share!

Stand and share about your own encounter with Jesus!

I was reminded of Romans 10:8–10. "'The message is very close at hand; it is on your lips and in your heart.' And that message is the very message about faith that we preach: If you openly declare that Jesus is Lord and believe in your heart that God raised him from the dead, you will be saved. *For it is by believing in your heart that you are made right with God, and it is by openly declaring your faith that you are saved*" (NLT, emphasis added).

I *had* to obey. Reluctantly, cautiously, I raised my hand, but only to just above my shoulder. My hand was technically in the air. I had plausible deniability. *God, I tried. I obeyed by raising my hand, but no one saw me.*

Except someone did see me.

"Yes, you there in the back, who just raised your hand," came the amplified voice. "Go ahead and stand up."

I had no choice. I stood and confessed that I continued to feel unworthy, surrounded by so many saints, and that all I could ask was the privilege of being prayed for by so many of my brothers and sisters. My words lasted for less than a minute, but they seemed to take hours. By the time I closed my mouth, I was sweating and crying at the same time. Tears ran from my eyes and snot from my nose. I was a mess! People came to my side, laid hands on my shoulders, and prayed over me. I knew which hand was Priscilla's, and I grasped it, as if holding on for life. The love of my Savior surrounded me, expressed through His faithful servants.

How much time passed in that holy space of prayer? I do not know, other than to say it felt as if I was finally living, for the first time, the way my Creator had designed me to live.

Driving into Kinshasa for work the following day, I saw the city spread out before me, lit by the morning sun. Everything was the same in my life, yet everything felt different. I was driving to the same bank, and yet I felt I was beginning a new career, with a fresh mission. I was the same man, and yet I had a new vision of who I was and what I was meant to do. I had been cleansed inside, but even my eyes seemed to have had scales removed from them.

From that day forward, gentleness and a sense of purpose were placed in my soul. Duties became privileges. People became more than their job titles or pawns to be utilized. Priscilla became a trusted partner with whom I could pray. Gratitude became a way of seeing everything in my life. None of this happened overnight, of course, and I made (and continue to make) countless mistakes. But the trajectory of my life had been changed for good, and forever.

I had formerly been my own boss, but I had been fired and replaced by a new Boss: one infinite in loving mercy and grace, indescribable, unimpeachable in character, faithful in all words and promises, trustworthy, King of kings and Lord of lords, God Almighty!

As had happened with Priscilla, my transformation involved new habits. I read through the Bible on my own, and we began attending weekly Bible studies together. We met many couples, some of whom brought their infant children. We all brought meals and enjoyed potluck dinners. The babies would be put to sleep and the adults would pray, study Scripture, and share about life.

In due course, our group prayed that I would stop smoking, and I did so the very next day. Only God could do that!

At times I have pondered: What would have happened in my life had I not said yes to God on that seaside bench in Nsiamfumu?

I think it is safe to say that when it came to my professional life, I would have continued to seize any opportunity for personal advancement. Self would have trumped others. I shudder to consider my personal life, and the likely dissolution of my marriage to Priscilla, to whom I have been married for more than fifty years as of this writing.

Looking back on my life, I can see clearly what happened that morning in Nsiamfumu and that evening at the retreat in Kinshasa: the beginning of God really getting to work in (and with) me.

Those were the first two steps on my Christian walk.

And, I would like to add, those first steps came at a God-ordained time in my life. Priscilla and I wanted children. Actually, it would be more accurate to say that Priscilla wanted children, and I wanted *many* children. Yet what would have happened if we had welcomed our first child while our relationship was struggling? I shuddered to consider the home environment: smoking, drinking, arguing, and, worst of all, parents uncommitted to serving the Lord.

Instead, God's goodness and provision prevailed. He made a way for Priscilla, and then for me, to truly meet His Son, Jesus Christ our Savior, before we became parents. After my conversion, my awareness of my own sinfulness was dramatically heightened. I had a greater understanding of

God's path for me, at home and at work, as well as a sensitivity to when I strayed from it. I sought forgiveness more often and more willingly. My relationship with my wife grew stronger and more loving by the day.

God was exceedingly good to us! At His appointed time following my conversion, Priscilla informed me she was pregnant. I had hoped for a son as our first child and told her we would have a boy born in January, and on a Sunday like me. In my own planning, I thought if we had boys first, my desire for a large family would be realized. I knew Priscilla would stop at two if one were a girl. I already had a name chosen for my first child. Our first born would be named after my brother Robert Kanyiki, who was a surrogate father to me and whose love and caring I always felt growing up. As I've shared, names in my family are significant. Naming my firstborn son after my brother was the highest level of honor and expression of gratitude I could give to him.

Jean Christian Kanyiki Wa Tshibaka (Niki) was born late January 1977, on a Sunday. The Lord and I were on the same wavelength. What a blessing!

CHAPTER 22

Times of Testing

Congo, Angola, and South Africa

AFTER MY CONVERSION, I WORKED HARDER THAN EVER AT THE BANK, aiming to excel in all tasks and exceed all goals set for me. Within the following years, I was promoted multiple times: first to senior assistant manager (from pro-manager), then to manager, and finally to resident vice president and general manager of Citibank Congo. With each promotion, my responsibilities increased, as did my sense of satisfaction with my banking career. I could imagine banking the rest of my life, despite, or perhaps because of, the difficulties Priscilla and I experienced in our first few years in Kinshasa.

Soon, my developing banking skills were subjected to a series of tests. Citibank had invested capital in a bank in Angola but had withdrawn its activities following a communist takeover and the ensuing instability in the country. Angola had, for several years, been run as a communist state, with direct help from both Cuba and the Soviet Union. My assignment would be to travel to Luanda and negotiate for the return of as much of Citibank's investment as possible.

However, Angola was in the throes of a civil war at that time, so it was recommended that I visit the Angolan ambassador in Kinshasa. From him, I learned that to enter the country, I would need to go through a demanding bureaucratic process. Five different ministries, such as security, immigration, finance, central bank, and so on, needed to approve any trips to Angola, given the security concerns of the dictatorial communist regime there.

My confidence, and my experience traveling internationally, made me skeptical all those hoops needed to be jumped through. "They are African, I am African," I told the ambassador. "I can handle this!"

The ambassador strongly disagreed, but when I asked him point-blank if it was legal for me to enter his country with only a basic visa, he allowed I was correct, technically.

Armed with only a basic visa, I soon boarded a flight for Angola. As near as I could tell, the economy section of my flight consisted of Angolan refugees returning to their country, while the first-class section consisted of diplomats, along with me, a banker. When we arrived at the airport in Luanda, the immigration officials unfortunately assumed I was one of the refugees, owing to my black skin and African last name. They spoke only Portuguese, rendering my French, English, and Tshiluba useless. This was the first time I wished I had brought along better documentation, as the ambassador had recommended.

Despite the language barrier, it soon became clear that the officials wished to load me onto a truck that would take me to a refugee camp.

To avoid that fate, I parked myself on a bench by the immigration counters in the airport until a translator could be found. By now we were close to midnight, so I slept on the bench. The next morning, a translator arrived, and at long last my passport was stamped. I fled the airport, eager to move on with my trip.

Eventually, I made my way to the best hotel in town, Hotel Panorama, located right on the ocean. I was wearing my *abacos*, which drew the attention of three fellow Congolese in the lobby.

"Citoyen!" they hailed me. "What are you doing here?"

I introduced myself and summarized my mission with Citibank, along with my trip up to that point. I learned they worked for the Congolese intelligence service. When I told them I wished to go check in, their leader responded, "But they will not let you stay in this hotel!"

I asked why, only to hear some familiar advice: I should have obtained permission from additional ministries. The leader asked one of his men to speak with the hotel staff on my behalf, but I was still turned away. Then the leader had an idea. There was an empty room next door to them because a Congolese diplomat had flown back to Kinshasa. With a bit of subterfuge, I was able to pass as the missing diplomat, ensuring I would have a place to stay.

The actual conditions inside the supposedly high-class hotel were dreadful. The only thing the restaurant served, three meals a day, was boiled potatoes with salted fish, and every fabric in my room was threadbare and stained. Each night at ten, my phone would ring, and when I picked it up and said hello, there would be no one on the other end. My Congolese friends told me it was simply the authorities making sure I was "at home" and not out making trouble.

Several days later, after an incredibly inefficient back-and-forth process, I was finally allowed to meet with the appropriate bank official, the governor of the central bank of Angola, *and* with his minder from the communist party. (She actually outranked him, and he was required to have his replies to me approved by her.) Despite the situation up to that point, we had a productive negotiation.

After a similar meeting at the Ministry of Finance, I was able to fly back to Kinshasa. On my flight home, I wondered, *Is Citibank testing me?* If they were, I was certainly learning a great deal while taking on reckless risks at a personal level!

My visit planted the seed for the eventual reimbursement of Citibank's investment. I was delighted when, several years later, I learned of the outcome from the new managing director of Citibank Congo, that the bank had gotten some of its investment back.

•><><•

My next test came when Citibank coordinated a cultural exchange between its offices in Kinshasa and Johannesburg.

The idea was to send a black African to South Africa (where apartheid still held sway) and to welcome a white Afrikaner to Congo. Citi hoped to introduce a level of person-to-person understanding, at least among their bank leadership. I was chosen as the Congolese representative or, perhaps more aptly, the bank's experimental guinea pig.

At the time, the proposal did not sound too difficult for me. Besides enjoying a stay at the well-regarded Hotel Conrad, I was sure I would benefit from the banking challenge. I had also spent enough time with white people to be unworried by the cultural differences. Until, that is, I learned the particulars of my brief. My task in Johannesburg was to conduct an *audit* of a department led and staffed by white Afrikaners. That was a much thornier cultural scenario than I had anticipated.

In the apartheid era, South Africa was considered by most other nations to be a pariah state, unworthy of inclusion in the international community. As my trip to South Africa would prove, merely spending time in a pariah country did not make a person into a pariah. But that did not mean I could ignore the potential consequences of visiting South Africa. As a Citibank employee hoping to rise through the ranks, there was no doubt I would be called on to travel even more extensively than I had up to that point. I could not afford to be stopped, and potentially detained, at every international airport. Therefore, I needed my interactions with any officials in South Africa to be as bland and boring as possible.

When I reached the immigration kiosks, I noticed all the officials were white. That was not ideal, but it was not a surprise either. Immigration lines were very long at that hour of the day, so I chose a line at random. When I finally reached the counter, the official took a long, intimidating look at me and then at my passport. The visa was not stamped in the passport but rather on a separate piece of paper. A South African visa in my passport would have caused problems with travel to other countries opposed to the apartheid regime. After studying my documents for what seemed like an intentionally lengthy period, he lifted his head again and informed me in no uncertain terms that I would need to pay the equivalent of three dollars in the local currency, the rand. I only had US dollars on me.

"Officer, there is no bank in this arrival hall. Where can I exchange my dollars into rands?" I asked.

"At a bank, behind me," he responded curtly.

"Will you please let me through to do the exchange and bring the rands to you?" I pleaded.

"No!" was the answer, emphatically delivered.

He directed me to find agents of the airline that had brought me into the country. My Lufthansa stewardesses were nowhere to be seen, so I approached the South African Airlines agents at the only service counter in the hall. They seemed offended that I would dare interrupt their conversation. If I needed help, I would have to wait for a Lufthansa agent. It was not their job to assist me. They ordered me to go sit and wait.

Banishment to the bench proved to be a boon, because it gave me time to consider my options. After waiting for at least thirty minutes, I thought of going back to the immigration line and trying to convince the official to let me through. That carried the risk of creating an even worse situation with the official. Or perhaps I could appeal to the kindness of the South African Airlines hostesses, pleading with them once again to take pity on a tired traveler. That could create an awkward scene, however. I determined that neither option was advisable and opted to stay put on the bench, waiting for the appearance of anyone working for Lufthansa.

Almost instantaneously, I saw a Lufthansa stewardess passing through, and I leaped up and ran after her. I explained my predicament and asked her for help.

"Okay, I have another pressing task to attend to right now. Wait here and I will return to see how I can help," she said.

"No, please. I have been waiting a long time since my arrival. Please take these three dollars with you and exchange them into rands for me."

She took the dollars and asked me to wait for her return. She disappeared once again for a long time. When she reappeared, she put a hand into her pocket and gave me a few rand notes and coins. Before she could disappear again, I asked her to wait for a moment to allow me to verify that I had the exact change required by the immigration official.

"Ma'am, I am missing one cent."

She checked again in her pocket and found the missing cent. With that, I headed back to my original immigration line, choosing to deal with the man who had sent me on a pointless errand. He had treated me poorly, yes, but he had also given me specific conditions to fulfill. I knew that if I chose a new official there was a *chance* I would be treated more fairly…but there was an even greater chance I would encounter *new* "issues" that might be even harder to resolve.

When I reached the window, we went through exactly the same process. I wondered, *Are we done? Has he attempted to humiliate me sufficiently?*

No. Not yet. Without a word, the official pulled out a pipe from his pocket. From a drawer he withdrew a tin of shredded tobacco and packed the bowl. His preparations complete, the man stood and sauntered away from his kiosk, then lit his pipe. I watched from the other side of the window while blue-white smoke wreathed his head before reaching toward the airport ceiling.

I glanced over my shoulder. The line behind me was now among the longest, and the travelers in it were not enthusiastic about the lack of movement. I was the reason for the delay!

This is going nowhere, I fumed inside. *Who does he think he is to treat me like this?*

More smoking by him led to more fuming by me. Then, just as I was about to pound on the window, my thoughts took a different turn. *He is trying to provoke you. He* wants *you to lose your temper. Do not give him an excuse to keep you out. Thus far you have handled yourself well, exercising considerable patience.* I folded my hands behind my back and resolved to look patient and calm.

A final wisp of smoke unfurled from his pipe, and then the agent removed it from his mouth. He seemed to be studying me as he strolled back to his kiosk.

"Mister Tshibaka?" he asked.

"Yes?" I replied.

Bam-bam-bam-bam. He stamped every necessary paper. "Welcome to South Africa!"

An Englishman, an officer of Citibank Johannesburg, had been sent to drive me to the hotel. He had assumed my lateness was due to problems with immigration but could not imagine half the frustrating ordeal I had been subjected to.

When I arrived at the Citi office in Johannesburg the next day, I discovered its facade looked like nearly every other bank building in the world. I was unprepared, however, for the shock of seeing its employees. Most black Africans were employed below bank officer level. As Citibank worked to project a progressive image, one black South African had just been promoted to pro-manager, the first official rank within the bank. No Afrikaners worked as janitors, guards, cleaners, or service staff. The entire operation resembled a pyramid with a dark foundation and a white peak.

I was taken to the office of the bank's most senior official, an American who carried the functional title of country corporate officer, the equivalent to CEO of Citibank South Africa in today's title structures. He in turn took me to the office of the vice president responsible for national corporate banking (NCB), the most important client-facing department of the bank, which managed all local corporate relationships. It would be here that I would audit and rate the work of an Afrikaner.

I began the audit, uncertain how long it would take and how the vice president for NCB and his staff would interact with me.

The local black South Africans I met at the bank were impressed and genuinely pleased to see another black African in a senior position visiting, and, to boot, one with the task of auditing an area of the bank run by an Afrikaner. They had not known such a thing was possible, given the state of apartheid under which they were forced to operate. In fact, I was invited to spend time with them in Soweto, or the South Western Townships, just outside Johannesburg. I learned that only three years previously, riots there had resulted in the deaths of hundreds.

Taking an afternoon away Sunday, I was able to spend time with a wonderful cross section of residents. My new friends at the bank had invited teachers, artists, entrepreneurs, and other members of the community to meet with me. We shared lunch and eye-opening conversations. They took turns sharing about their lives in apartheid-era South Africa, and I in turn shared my story and told them what I could about living under Mobutu's corrupt dictatorship. But most of my time was spent sharing about my work at Citibank Zaire and the bank's efforts at positively influencing the status quo in South Africa. They attentively listened to the hopeful message I shared. Throughout the whole afternoon, the informative conversations were fueled with a generous flow of beer and whiskey.

Time went so fast that before I realized it, the dinner table was set and ready. My brothers and sisters had gone through the trouble of preparing representative dishes that they had discreetly kept in the kitchen. We ate, and after dinner, how could I say no to music and dancing? They eventually brought me back to my hotel around nine o'clock at night.

Since I had enjoyed my time in Soweto immensely, I decided to reciprocate and proposed another gathering the following Sunday, this time with a handful of the people I had met. I asked them to join me for dinner, my treat, at the Hotel Conrad.

As it happened, the entire front-of-house staff at the hotel restaurant was white, and our dinner party caused a stir. We sat at a high table, on stools, and from my perch I could see expressions on the staff that ranged from shock to disgust to hostility. I chose to pretend everything was normal, because in a sense it was: We were simply enjoying dinner together, that I was going to pay for!

My social life included senior bank staff as well. One of the senior vice presidents at Citibank Johannesburg was an American, and he did not share the obvious prejudices of the Afrikaners at the bank. As head of the corporate bank, he was the boss of the relationship management team, including the department run by my Afrikaner colleague.

One night, he invited me to attend the Johannesburg Civic Theatre with him. Opened the previous decade, the theater held nearly one thousand people. According to my host, we had "the best seats in the house," but I did not discover how literal that was until I met him on the sidewalk outside the theater and he handed me my ticket. We had front-row aisle seats.

I raised an eyebrow and confirmed, asking, "Row A…as in the front row?"

He laughed. "You got it, A. T. Like I said, the best seats in the house!"

We crossed the lobby and approached the center doors, where a staff member took an inordinate amount of time to examine my ticket, my face, and my companion. When we were finally admitted, I discovered the house lights were still on, though most of the seats were already filled, exclusively by white Afrikaners.

That meant, to reach my seat, I had to walk the center aisle all the way to the front. With every step I took, I noticed a growing number of eyes tracking my progress. Nothing was said or done to me, but nevertheless it was a harrowing journey. I slumped in relief when the house lights were turned down. To this day I can still recall the feeling of all those eyes boring into my back.

Several weeks later, I completed my audit of the national corporate banking department. We used a four-point rating scale at Citibank back then, marked in tenth-of-a-point increments. I had identified a handful of minor issues that could be remedied in a short period. The department was in good shape overall. I believed the score of 3.5 I awarded was both accurate and relatively generous. It was well above average by Citibank standards.

My Afrikaner colleague believed otherwise. Upon reading my report, his face grew livid. "Point *five*, Tshibaka?" he fumed. "Are you serious? Citibank's professional auditors have never given us a score below 3.8, and usually give us a 3.9. But we're not good enough for you, are we?" He asked this last question while gesturing to the other bankers in the room, all of whom were white, mostly Afrikaners.

I had remained calm throughout his tirade. I was confident in the accuracy of my report.

He was not finished, however. With a snort of disgust, he folded the report and tossed it back across the desk toward me. "I don't accept it!" he fumed.

I quickly learned that his unwillingness to accept my audit rating guaranteed both of us an emergency meeting with the CEO of Citibank South Africa. I felt some trepidation about this. The National Corporate Bank head was not contesting any of my findings per se, but he took issue with the rating I had given to his business. The CEO of Citibank South Africa would judge me as a *line auditor*. While I believed in the quality of my audit, I was uncertain about the CEO's position.

Would my audit crash on the rocks of apartheid-fueled prejudice, or would it be evaluated solely on its merits?

At the meeting, the NCB department head and I sat across the desk from the CEO, while he read my report. The tension in the room was palpable. After what seemed far too long, he closed the report and looked up. He studied me. I remained calm on the outside, while inside my stomach was twisting. After a long moment, he turned his attention to his staff member.

"This," he said, tapping the report, "is a simple matter."

From the corner of my eye, I saw the NCB department head allow himself a small smile.

"The report seems objective and well-supported by factual findings. Take corrective action," he instructed the NCB head. "Address the issues raised by A. T. within the stipulated target dates. What is all the fuss about?"

My Afrikaner colleague stammered something I could not make out, then stood quickly and left. I allowed myself a cordial goodbye with the CEO before leaving as well.

My final test had already happened, though I did not learn I had passed it until a providential encounter during that trip to Johannesburg.

By the end of the decade, the value of our currency had plummeted. Under Mobutu's rule and monetary policies, inflation was out of control. The saying "this money isn't worth the paper it's printed on" became very nearly literal. A small sack of printed currency was needed to buy a loaf of bread.

At a personal level, the buying power of my salary was greatly diminished. After eight years, and many promotions at the bank, my take-home pay was a fraction of the compensation I had earned as an executive trainee at hiring! Without Kim Abbott, I do not know how Priscilla and I would have survived. Kim arranged for part of my annual salary to be paid in US dollars, which made a tangible difference. The additional five hundred dollars in monthly pay helped compensate for the depreciation of our currency, the zaire.

At a national level, anyone being paid in our national currency was suffering. To solve this crisis, Mobutu chose to introduce entirely new currency notes. Each citizen would be allowed to exchange up to three thousand dollars, although the well-to-do found ways around that, such as paying line-sitters. No matter how the transition was managed, people would lose money. The only question was how much the loss could be reduced.

In anticipation of the demonetization, we had diligently trained our staff from both technical and ethical angles of the operation. We had insisted on delivering excellent service to the masses who were expected at our counters, showing courtesy and patience, especially given the distress that people were under. We had also put in place processes to avoid fraud and minimize temptation for staff to engage in bribery schemes with desperate customers. It was thus critical for me to redirect my focus to personally overseeing the whole process from start to finish, often managing from behind the counters.

On the day of the changeover, Zaire's national TV station had dispatched crews to film and report on the demonetization operations at the various banking institutions. Banks were given amounts of new currency notes commensurate with their customer count. Throughout the days allowed for the exchange of notes, breaking evening news showed images of what was happening at bank counters in Kinshasa and, at the end of the exercise, Citibank's very organized, orderly performance stood out.

Other banks had turned into virtual circuses. When each bank submitted its official accounting to the central bank, the difference between Citibank and other banks became even more stark. Most banks showed massive discrepancies, while we showed far and away the best results. As the face of Citibank throughout the demonetization process, I became a reluctant overnight sensation.

Although I was very pleased with the outcome of the exercise, and the public recognition sounded like good news, the accolades precipitated unexpected limelight and triggered a personal crisis for us. *Radio trottoir* (rumors in the street) had it that Mobutu was considering me for governor of the Central Bank of Zaire (CBZ). Mobutu. The one who had me thrown in prison unjustly!

It was a terrifying proposition. No amount of pay or prestige could make up for the danger of that inherently political position. The person who filled that vacancy would truly be gambling with his life. On the one hand, refusing to accept the governorship of the central bank would be interpreted as another act of rebelliousness against the regime. On the other hand, saying yes, which would require a public expression of deep gratitude to the *président-fondateur*, would lead to a potential death sentence.

It was known that Mobutu could use a simple phone call to ask for money from the governor of the central bank, and it was estimated a third of a billion dollars were annually demanded by, and disbursed to, the president. This was on top of his salary and whatever had been set as the budget for the presidency. The central bank was thus effectively Mobutu's personal petty cash box. The options open to the governor were stark: Comply with the president's demands, no questions asked, or be found floating face-down in the Zaire River. Given my earlier altercations with the regime, and my moral stance against misusing public funds, the dead man's float would have been a real possibility for me.

Blessedly, God had already prepared a way out for me. Citibank EVP Jack Clark was coincidentally visiting Johannesburg when I was there for my cultural exchange audit assignment. He happened to be staying at the same hotel, the sole international chain where blacks were allowed. Standing outside the hotel one evening while waiting for the bank car to take us to dinner with the executive team of Citibank Johannesburg, he confided that Citibank New York had decided to promote me to managing director or country corporate officer (CEO) for Citibank's business in Liberia. The only pending issue was the timing of the move.

The relief Priscilla and I felt was immense. Now we could depart Zaire and Mobutu's regime for calmer waters. I felt as if I had fought the good fight in the Congo. I had been with Citibank from the very beginning, in 1971, when I (and others) helped Kim Abbott launch Citibank's banking operations in Kinshasa. In the nine years since, I had helped manage the bank through national crises, assisted with the opening of Citibank in Côte d'Ivoire, fended off hostile and jealous coworkers who wished me to be fired, and proved my banking credentials.

And when the time came for our flight to Monrovia, in March 1980, Priscilla had another blessing for me, one she could no longer hide from the public. She was five months pregnant with our second child, our darling girl, Mara Julienne.

CHAPTER 23
From Unrest to Peace

Congo and Liberia

LIBERIA WAS AMONG THE MOST PEACEFUL, STABLE COUNTRIES ON the entire continent of Africa. Founded by freed black slaves with funding from the United States, Liberia declared its independence in 1847. James Monroe, the fifth president of the United States, played a prominent role in resettling the slaves and so was recognized in the name of Liberia's capital, Monrovia.

By the time we moved to our new posting, Liberia had been independent and at peace for more than one hundred and thirty years. In addition to the expectation of peace and better living conditions when compared to Zaire, I looked forward to fulfilling the CEO position for a Citibank subsidiary that enjoyed a nearly one-third share of Liberia's banking market.

You can go and relax a little, Tshibaka, I told myself. *You will love the job in Liberia.* After all, we had endured many hard times in Zaire. Did we not deserve to enjoy a stable environment? Niki was three, Priscilla was pregnant with our second child, and I enjoyed imagining what it would be like to live and work in a place where the government could not arrest and detain me for no reason.

Unfortunately, the process of securing my passport was far from simple. Because of my previous "issues" with Mobutu's government, I could not exactly walk into a ministry office and exit with a passport in hand. Thus, I had begun applying for my passport as soon as the move to Liberia was agreed on with Citi, hoping to allow plenty of time to resolve the matter. Each time I was unable to secure it, I became a bit more worried. I could chalk up some of the delay to typical bureaucratic incompetence, but not, I suspected, all the delay.

Passports were kept by the security services of Zaire. Whenever Zairians needed to travel abroad, they had to apply to the relevant agency for the release of their passports. The background checks carried out included verifying that the individual had no criminal record. The real reason for this procedure was controlling the citizenry and ensuring potential opponents would not be allowed to leave the country and cause headaches for the regime.

The restrictions did not apply only to me. My wife's passport was also retained by the government and, in her case, she had two obstacles to overcome. First, she needed a written authorization from me as her husband that she could leave the country. Second, the security and immigration services had to conduct their own background checks before releasing her travel documents.

This explained part of our predicament, but it was not the full story. If I were to be generous, these services were known to be inefficient or incompetent. To put it less generously, they were very corrupt.

To complicate things even more, I had debts that needed to be settled before leaving. Owing to the disastrous financial situation in the country, we had to sell most of our possessions to generate the necessary liquidity. Thankfully, we were able to settle all our debts and retain some cash. We used the money to purchase a pickup truck for the extended family we were leaving behind. Priscilla and I would eventually leave Zaire with no credit balance in a bank account.

As our departure date grew closer, my anxiety increased greatly. I was helpless, as I could not leave the country without a passport, although Priscilla's passport had finally been released to us. The night before our flight, the responsible Citibank general services officer had informed me that I would probably see mine the following morning. *Probably?* Well, it would have to do.

Priscilla and I put Niki to bed, and then ourselves, for what we hoped was our final night in Kinshasa.

The next morning came. We were all packed and ready. No passport. The general services officer was nowhere to be seen. We presumed he was still negotiating the release of my passport with the immigration and security people. Or had they dug up my past troubles with Mobutu and decided to complicate life for me? Kim and Alice Abbott were with us, both to encourage and to make phone calls they deemed pertinent. We waited…and waited…and waited. We were running the risk of missing our flight.

I called one of our executive secretaries. Her husband, Mushobekwa Kalimba Wa Katana, was then the minister of transport and communications. We got word back that we were to head for the airport without further delay. Our personal effects had preceded us to the airport and were already loaded. Yet I still did not have my passport! We got in the car and raced to N'djili International Airport. Heavy traffic and crowded streets added to our anxieties.

No passport.

No news as to the whereabouts of the bank agent charged with procuring it.

No assurance that the airplane would still be there.

O God, I prayed, *are You going to leave me in Mobutu's den, to be devoured? Have mercy!*

We arrived at the airport almost at the same time as the general services agent. He had my passport with him. There was not one minute to waste. The Air France plane had been waiting for us on the tarmac. Mr. Mushobekwa had called the airport officials to detain the flight just a little longer for us. Rather than going through the main departure area of the airport, a side gate was opened for us and our car was allowed to drop us right by the stairs of the plane.

There were many quick hugs, handshakes, and shouts of "Goodbye!" and "Good luck!" Then Priscilla, Niki, and I raced up the stairs, ducked through the aircraft door, and walked as quickly as we could to our seats in the first-class cabin. No doubt the other passengers wondered about this unusual—and unusually sweaty—family, but no one dared to complain, at least not loudly. Before we had even buckled our seatbelts, the plane began to taxi. I looked out the window, half-expecting to see government cars pulling onto the tarmac to detain me.

Liftoff! We had made it!

I allowed myself to anticipate a new and calmer season of life.

Our route to Liberia took us through Lagos, Nigeria, and while our family transitioned smoothly to our next flight, our personal effects did not. Our clothing, record player, sewing machine, and all my files, including my diplomas, were lost to the elements as they sat for three months on the tarmac, soaking in tropical rains and torched by the sun.

CHAPTER 24

Navigating a Coup d'état

Congo and Liberia

BACK IN KINSHASA, I WAS THE DE FACTO LEADER OF CITI'S BUSINESS as resident vice president (RVP) and general manager. Kim Abbott, however, remained my superior. I did not mind this arrangement at all. Kim was not only a wonderful person to work with; I also valued him as a genuine friend. The saying that "a friend in need is a friend indeed" was true of our relationship, especially considering his support during my prison episode and the sound, objective advice he would give me whenever needed. The fact that he was an American, as I have recounted, carried great weight when it came to interacting with the Congolese government.

By contrast, I would be the highest-ranking Citi officer in Liberia. Yet the potential lack of a powerful ally did not trouble me. As I mentioned, Liberia was the safest, most stable country on the continent. Additionally, the internal culture of Citibank was similar to what I had left behind in Zaire. Policies and procedures were the same, the daily tasks would be largely the same, and business was conducted in English. I would also be the incoming president of the Liberia Bankers' Association.

During the first few days and weeks in my Liberian office, I breathed many sighs of relief. Besides benefiting from my own professional stability, I was looking forward to my family enjoying a season of peace and hopefully prosperity. There would certainly be new challenges to which we would need to adapt. Priscilla would need to find new places to shop, new parks, and new taxi routes. We would need to find a church and make new friends.

If we pulled together for half a year, I reckoned we would be golden. Yes, the transition would be harder on Priscilla than it would be on me. Still, the Tshibaka clan would make it through with flying colors.

Three weeks after we arrived in Liberia, a bloody coup d'état was successfully executed.

We were living in the official Citibank compound, which sat atop a small hill near a river. The half dozen houses were built close together, and a cement wall delineated the compound. A single gate made of iron bars provided the only entry point. Every family in the compound included an expat senior executive at one of the foreign businesses operating in Liberia at the time.

The coup began with no warning, as gunfire erupted across the city around 5:00 a.m. one morning.

"A. T., wake up! I hear gunfire," Priscilla said, "and it is getting closer and closer to the compound."

"Go to sleep, Priscilla," I retorted. "It is okay." As I was turning to resume my sleep, the telephone rang. It was my operations manager, Ben Torres, who was an experienced Filipino banker. He and his family had joined Citibank Liberia around about the same time as we did.

"A. T.," he exclaimed, "there's been a coup d'état!"

Radio and television news reports soon confirmed that a new man had taken over the country with a group of soldiers. He was a former sergeant in the army, Samuel Kanyon Doe. We soon learned that he had only an eighth-grade education and, as we discovered, even that meager accomplishment placed him far above his uneducated thugs and triggermen.

Very early the following day, the jangling of the phone snapped my eyes open. When I answered, it was my operations manager once again. His voice was cracking, conveying great fear.

"Yes?" I asked, dreading the bad news I knew would follow.

"Rebel soldiers paid a visit to the bank during the night. They have forced our guards to stand back, then fired into the vault door, attempting to open it. The guards called me to ask if they could go home…"

I waited to see if he had more to say.

"What do we do?" he finally asked.

"Ben, please send them home to be with their families," I told him, confirming what he likely already knew I'd say.

The situation was spiraling out of control. There was no reason to risk the life of even a single Citibank employee. My primary responsibility was to protect my family and Citibank staff members. Protecting bank assets would come later, but we all needed to be alive for that phase of the crisis.

Even as I was speaking to Ben, the unmistakable *kak-kak-kak-kak* sound of AK-47s could be heard, this time drawing closer and closer to our compound. It was not difficult to guess what was happening: A group of rebels was going door to door, asking for protection money from residents. From the sound of things, no one was being attacked, but that did not mean the situation was safe.

Knock…knock…knock.

I checked through the window and saw a jeep full of soldiers. I hesitated, but only briefly. "Priscilla, please stay in the house."

I decided to meet the lead soldier at the front door entrance, closing the door behind me. The fewer bullets sprayed wantonly into the city air, the better, and besides, perhaps they could be reasoned with. As I exited, the sound of the door opening caused me to glance behind, only to see Priscilla waddling after me, pregnant with our baby girl. She told me later her reasoning was that Africans love children and their families, so perhaps the rebels would spare me if they saw a pregnant woman. At that moment, I did not know if her presence with me was terrifying, useful, comforting, or a mixture of all three, just as I did not know whether to be thankful or angry.

Except for the lead soldier, the rebels stayed in the jeep, all dressed in loosely matching "uniforms." Their eyes were bloodshot, whether from a lack of sleep or an excess of adrenaline or narcotics, I had no idea. Perhaps I had been rash to think I could confront them.

They stared at me. I stared back, hoping that was the correct decision. Being the first to speak felt as if it would put me at a disadvantage, so I swallowed my fear and continued to stare at them. After a long moment of silence, the lead rebel shifted his gun and cleared his throat.

"What we want is money!" he snarled. "For your protection," he clarified.

I relaxed fractionally. Perhaps this whole situation could be resolved peacefully. After a pause, I took from my pocket a roll of bills, which I held out toward the soldiers. I allowed them all to glimpse the money, but as soon as their leader soldier reached forward, I stopped my hand.

"This is fifty," I said. Then I dared to wait again, continuing to maintain eye contact. I was offering a decent amount of money. More than decent, in fact. Then came the rest of the plan I had just formulated in my mind. Then, audibly to the lead soldier, I said, "There are other houses on this compound. I am responsible for them. If I give you this money, it is with the understanding that you will not disturb any other family here. I am sure you appreciate that even revolutions need bankers and foreign investors to function."

He nodded. I was not convinced his nod signified any real understanding, but a nod was better than a fist or a gun barrel.

"Additionally," I continued, "now that you know the importance of this compound, we would appreciate it if you and your armed comrades would keep its safety in mind. No more disturbances is a good beginning, but we would also like you to promise to patrol this compound regularly on our behalf."

He nodded again. "We will do better than that, Mr. Manager. We will station soldiers at the entrance to the compound for your protection."

I handed fifty US dollars to the lead soldier.

I looked back at Priscilla. She gave a small, private sort of shrug which I interpreted to mean, *You've gotten away with something, Tshibaka.*

When the rebels turned and departed, I supposed she was right.

Surprising exactly no one, the soldiers never returned to "guard" our compound. Which was the point—they had learned our compound was not "easy picking." This was undoubtedly a good thing, because in the following days of the coup d'état, we learned that not every rebel soldier was as restrained and harmless as the ones who had visited us. We also learned they had gone house to house asking for money before showing up at our home.

Meanwhile, Samuel Kanyon Doe had established his Revolutionary Council, consolidating the takeover. The coming days would witness him inviting television crews to a nearby beach to see and report on the gruesome public executions of more than a dozen former government ministers, many of whom were descendants of American freed slaves and who had constituted Liberia's ruling class up to that point. Bankers did not seem to be on the chopping block yet. We prayed fervently that we never would be.

Priscilla and I could scarcely believe the unfortunate timing of our move. In the near term, however, there was nothing for us to do. We knew that leaving the country was not an option, owing to the chaos and violence.

Because of the coup, none of the compound residents felt safe, including us. Since there appeared to be nothing productive to do, all the foreigners living within the Citibank compound convened at our home during those early days of the coup. Our house guests would bring blankets, whiskey, gin and tonic, vodka, cases of beer, snacks, games, and decks of cards. Priscilla and I would turn on all the lights in our home, play "high life" African music, and generally attempt to buoy everyone's spirits, including our own.

Several weeks later, I was visited at my Citibank office by one member of the Revolutionary Council. The man, a captain, arrived at the bank surrounded by four armed soldiers. He ordered two to remain outside the door to my office, then entered with the remaining two guards at his side. He sat down in a manner that suggested he owned the place.

There was no preamble to his approach. "Mr. Manager," he said sternly, "your bank fired my cousin a few years ago, in 1978 to be precise. I want you to compensate him for the unjust dismissal and the suffering he and his family have endured."

I glanced at the guards, buying myself a moment to take a breath and say a short, silent prayer. "What is the name of your nephew, sir?" I asked.

He told me and I wrote the name on a notepad. It was not familiar, so I had no way to judge whether the captain's complaint had any merit. I suspected it did not, but that was not an opinion I was prepared to share with the captain and his armed guards.

"Sir," I said calmly, "I must investigate the circumstances of your cousin's firing. Can you give me some time to do so?"

The captain thought for a moment before responding. "Of course, you must investigate it, Mr. Manager, but I am sure you will discover we are correct. You must do the wise thing in this case, eh?"

With that veiled threat he nodded to his soldiers and strode from the building.

I soon located the appropriate file, and when I opened it, I discovered a double surprise. The captain had indeed told the truth about his cousin. He had certainly been fired by Citi. Also, his cousin had been fired from the bank for an extremely good reason. He was fired for cause—namely, the theft of six thousand dollars!

This was a crossroads. I knew I could choose to simply acquiesce to the captain's demand. If I "compensated" his family, Citibank would not hold me liable. We were facing a continuing situation that was, legally, a war. I did not want to die, nor did I want harm to come to any of our staff members.

On the other hand, his demand did not sit well with my sense of justice, nor with my conscience. I knew I could not live with myself unless I did the right thing, so I decided to thoroughly investigate the circumstances and handling of the man's firing. Over the next several days, I prepared myself to meet the captain. When he called to follow up,

I explained I had carefully examined the case, that his cousin was fired for cause, and that he had irrefutably stolen six thousand dollars from the bank. I assured him I had all the evidentiary documentation with me.

That week, a Friday afternoon, the captain showed up at my office again, accompanied by four armed soldiers. This time, however, he also brought along a young man, a university graduate, another relative. His task was to interpret the captain's message to me. The captain did not want there to exist any doubt whatsoever that I fully grasped what he was saying in his limited English.

The captain's appearance was even more imposing than the first time he visited. His guards were with him, of course, and his uniform was the same. What had changed was his scowl. If before his face had appeared as a thunderstorm, now it was a full-blown hurricane. I briefly second-guessed myself. There was still time for me to change course and "compensate" the man's cousin. But I steeled myself to do what I knew to be right.

As calmly and professionally as I was able, I recounted the facts. The takeaway was that yes, Citibank had fired his nephew; and yes, his nephew had stolen six thousand dollars; and no, we did not owe the cousin, nor the captain, anything. I thought my message was very tactful.

However, I was not successful. The captain was livid. He stood up, looking down at me. He had come with a letter that he asked the young man to give me. He continued standing there, still looking down at me, waiting for me to read and take in his message. It was going to be clear, self-explanatory.

According to its contents, I was commanded to bring a check to the captain's office by ten o'clock in the morning the following Monday. If I did not comply, I would have only myself to blame. And the amount of "compensation" had increased dramatically: Instead of six thousand dollars, the captain was demanding *eighty*-six thousand dollars! I have no clue how he had come to that precise figure.

He stormed from my office, leaving me with a sense of dread.

I called my superiors in New York and explained the developments of that day in detail. I was told that my life was of much greater value than eighty-six thousand dollars and instructed to pay the sum to the captain. As much as I appreciated the value placed on human life by the bank, that course of action left me uncomfortable. I certainly did not wish to be thrown into prison or physically harmed, but it made my stomach clench with anger when I thought about the bully of a captain profiting from his corrupt scheme.

Unfortunately, there was nothing I could do except obey my superiors' directive. I had a bank draft prepared for eighty-six thousand dollars and placed it inside my desk drawer, just in case I had a surprise visit that weekend before the Monday morning deadline. I was not at peace with myself. What New York directed made sense. Paying the captain's cousin would certainly spare me and my team troubles, at least in the short term.

But consequential questions were coursing through my mind. Would paying the captain really solve that sort of problem once and for all? Wouldn't he and his colleagues on the Revolutionary Council be incentivized to present all kinds of unjustified claims for the bank to settle? How about the other foreign banks in the country? Would they be spared?

I decided to reach out to my counterparts at Chase Manhattan Bank, Bank of Liberia (a subsidiary of Chemical Bank), and Tradevco (a subsidiary of an Italian bank).

"Listen, I need your support. If Citibank is forced to succumb to this extortion, word will get around. Other members of the Revolutionary Council will come to my bank and yours to make similar demands. It won't stop with Citibank. How could it? When word gets out, *every* bank in town will be extorted."

They all understood and agreed. Emboldened, I asked, "Will you support me if I decided to close my bank?" I put the question to them because I was going to use the threat of all foreign banks closing their operations in Liberia to force Revolutionary Council members and the head of state, Samuel Kanyon Doe, to rethink their actions.

They once again agreed.

Having secured the support of these three foreign banks, I called the governor of the National Bank of Liberia. He was an ex-Citibank man. I told him everything that had happened with the captain. "Listen," I told the governor, "If I am forced to pay on Monday, I will close Citibank, and my colleagues at other foreign banks will do the same!"

"I beg you, do not close Citibank!" he exclaimed.

"If I need to, I will," I responded.

I proceeded to have similar conversations with the minister of finance, the minister of planning, and the minister of state for presidential affairs. I had come to know some of these government officials through the various special committee meetings at which I had been invited to discuss ways and means the government could stabilize the economic and financial situation of the country. All this took me until dinnertime, at which point I went home, exhausted and fearful.

Later that same night, the minister of finance called me at home. "Mr. Tshibaka, would you come to the executive mansion tomorrow morning at 9:00 a.m.?" he asked. "The president would like to see you."

His tone made it very clear that he was not actually asking. I told him that I would arrive first thing.

I knew that I needed, as the Americans were fond of saying, "some backup." I was not going to venture to the executive mansion on my own. Accordingly, I contacted the CEOs of Chase, Tradevco, and Bank of Liberia (Chemical Bank), and each agreed to accompany me.

Bright and early Saturday morning, the four of us rendezvoused outside the mansion. We were ushered in, shown where to sit, and made to wait. Finally, three hours later, the minister of finance emerged from a door. "I am sorry," he informed us, "but the president is quite busy. He cannot see you today after all. But go back to your homes, and he will take care of this problem himself."

We departed, but my emotions were roiling. How did the president hope to "solve" the situation by Monday morning? I doubted that even he could solve it!

It was a difficult weekend. The uncertainty weighed heavily on me each hour I was awake. My dreams were troubled. What if the captain decided to come to my residence and harm me or my family? Priscilla, as always, was supportive through the whole ordeal. And thankfully, Niki was then too young to fully grasp what his parents were going through.

Monday morning, at eight o'clock, I said hello to Gwen, my executive secretary. Gwen was in her fifties and protective, like a mother to me. She knew of female staff members who were determined to "have me." I recall instances when one of them would come to my office with a document for me to sign or a case for me to resolve and, if she closed the door, it would never take more than a minute for Gwen to open my door to ask if I needed coffee or tea. She would usually make sure to leave the office door open.

Skipping our usual pleasantries, she exclaimed, "What are you doing *here*?"

"What do you mean, Gwen?" I asked.

She replied, "Didn't you hear on the radio? The Revolutionary Council met last night, and the president instructed the minister of labor to deal with the situation. You're supposed to be in the minister's office right now!"

My heart began to beat at roughly double its normal speed. What was the minister of labor going to say or do? He was a soldier, after all, a lieutenant in the army. I called my counterparts at the other banks to update them on the development. The CEO of Tradevco was brave enough to come with me to the ministry of labor. Better to be accompanied by another senior executive than going alone to some unpredictable encounter.

Upon our arrival, the minister stopped a meeting he was in so that he could speak with me. "Mr. Manager, the president is very sorry," he said, getting directly to the business at hand. "He's asked me to ask you for forgiveness. He regrets that one of his officers has harassed you. He has dealt with this captain and is begging you not to close the bank! The president has instructed me to assure you that this situation will not happen again. Please don't close Citibank."

I knew the correct decision to make at once. I was very polite, very by-the-book, in my reply to him. I thanked him a great deal, reminded him that of course our bank strove to be a fair institution, and gave my view that the court system, rather than intimidation and threats, was the right way to handle disputes. We parted on what I hoped were good terms, and after thanking my Tradevco colleague, I returned to my office.

No sooner had I sat at my desk than the phone rang. It was the captain.

He was angry enough to shout at me for several minutes!

I learned that the president had chewed him out during a Revolutionary Council meeting. "All I wanted was a little money for my cousin, Mr. Manager, but *you* had to make everything difficult! Now will you come to my office so that I can apologize to you in person?"

I had no intention of going anywhere near his office, so I attempted to take the high road. I told him there was no need for an in-person encounter and that I appreciated his call and accepted his apology. He continued to insist that I go to his office, and I continued to accept his apology long-distance, until at last he hung up in fury.

Early that afternoon, the captain barged into my office with his usual accompaniment of four soldiers. After rehashing his feud with me, he swore, "You will *never* see me step foot in your office again!" With that he left.

I collapsed into my desk chair. If he had meant that final line as a punishment of some kind, I viewed it as a wonderful denouement.

So the incident with the captain reached a satisfactory conclusion. I did not burn any bridges with government officials, apart from the captain. The bank was not forced to pay a ransom, and no similar extortion attempts were made against any of the other banks in town. Most satisfying to me, I emerged from the whole affair with the bank's reputation, and my own, intact.

I was thereafter invited to join various committees set up by the Revolutionary Council to tackle the many challenges faced by the new government: stabilizing the country's finances; new tax/import duty policies; how to go about restoring confidence in the country and attracting foreign direct investment; and the difficult decision to close a struggling foreign bank, Bank of Liberia (the Chemical Bank subsidiary).

A special task force was set up to review and recommend an appropriate course of action for the Bank of Liberia. Its members insisted that I assume the role of president of the task force. I thought it over and determined that the optics would not look good. The idea of the CEO of Citibank and president of the Liberia Bankers Association presiding over the closure (or not) of another foreign bank would be misinterpreted. Rightly or wrongly, I feared that it was not going to pass the smell test in the court of public opinion. Accordingly, I convinced task force members to appoint a Liberian, president of a local bank, to the position. I then offered to serve as secretary for the group. This meant that I would be the one writing the report and summarizing our conclusions and recommendations to the government.

I was also proactive in my zeal to help, writing and publishing newspaper articles advocating for the lowering of taxation rates, my argument being that such a move would allow for more liquidity in the system for the private sector to do its job of fueling economic growth and job creation.

At the micro level, we put Citibank Liberia on a sound profitable trajectory, having cleaned up our balance sheet and shown loyal support and service to our select customer target market during the crisis.

CHAPTER 25

Déjà Vu

Liberia and Kenya

WE SPENT TWO AND A HALF PRODUCTIVE YEARS IN LIBERIA, and welcomed Mara into our family, but Citi had plans for me that required relocation.

"A. T., all of these conflicts and dangers are the last thing we expected when we asked you to transfer to the Monrovia office!" my bosses in New York told me. "That's why we want you to accept a position in Nairobi. Kenya is peaceful. No more coups. No more dangers. You'll be responsible for Citibank's business in Central and Eastern Africa."

As before, we agreed as a family to relocate, but this time there were *four* of us agreeing. Theoretically agreeing, at least, because our daughter Mara was merely a toddler and did not have a strong opinion about the move.

The history of Mara's unusual name is worth mentioning here. When she was born, I wanted to give her the name of Wa Katshinga, after my paternal grandmother. This caused a serious disagreement with Priscilla as she was recovering from a C-section operation in the hospital.

"You want to call our daughter *what*?" my wife exclaimed. "No way she will take on the name Wa Katshinga! I can just see people giving her the nickname 'Wacky.' Is this what you want for her?"

For an entire week the two of us could not settle on a name. Finally, my wife suggested Maracuja. We had been told by a safari guide, all the way back in 1974 during our visit to Virunga Park in Eastern Congo, that the maracuja was a passion fruit. Since drinking the delicious juice of that fruit in an even more delicious cocktail, Priscilla had thought that if God should bless us with a girl, she would be named "Mara," short for Maracuja.

Now, however, it was my turn to violently disagree. My daughter was never going to be called a fruit of passion! If Wa Katshinga was out of consideration, Maracuja would be an absolute nonstarter.

My wife is a very resourceful and creative woman, however, and she knew one way that was sure to win me over.

"Okay, honey," she proposed, once I had cooled off. "Let's look for the name Mara in the Bible."

This woman does not know when to give up and give in, I thought, but I agreed to open the Scriptures with her. I assumed that we would go through the motions and end up where we had started—with Wa Katshinga!

The first instance of something resembling Mara was found in Exodus 15:23. The name was spelled "Marah," and it referenced the bitter water the Israelites could not drink. Then, in Ruth 1:20, we read, "Don't call me Naomi…Call me Mara, because the Almighty has made my life very bitter" (NIV). Here was the bitterness again. Mara was definitely out!

Still, we kept searching until we reached the penultimate verse of the entire Bible. Revelation 22:20 said, "He who testifies to these things says, 'Yes, I am coming soon.' Amen. Come, Lord Jesus" (NIV). We learned from the Bible's study notes that in Aramaic, the expression *Come, O Lord* is "Maranatha." With that, we had our solution. I could live with Maranatha, from which my wife would get Mara for short.

We then quickly agreed on the rest of Mara's name: Mara (from Maranatha) Julienne (my mother's first name) Dinanga ("beloved" in my tribal language) Wa (of) Tshibaka. My wife would later describe our daughter's name as meaning, "Our Beautiful Beloved Is Coming Soon!"

When the four of us arrived in Nairobi, Citibank put us at the Intercontinental Hotel. There was a house waiting for us, but several repairs were still being finished.

The hotel was wonderful, but something in my spirit sensed that it was not a safe place for us to remain. That Friday evening, I was watching the news on the local TV channel. The president was shown interacting with members of the public. It did not feel right. Memories of similar scenes on TV in Liberia, pre-coup, resurfaced in my mind. Priscilla did not want to leave the hotel, rightly pointing out that we would be moving into a home that was not ready for us, but I insisted that we move on Saturday at the latest.

Sunday morning, we woke up to gunfire not far from our home in Karen, just on the outskirts of the city center. A coup attempt was in progress! It was unsuccessful, but we later learned that several people at the Intercontinental Hotel were accidentally killed.

Overnight, the bank's credit portfolio became problematic. Tough decisions were required. We needed to shore up the bank's liquidity, and write-offs of soured credits were required. Much of our focus would need to shift to collection and recovery of delinquent loans. The much-deteriorated macro environment also demanded a revisit of our organization and cost structures, right-sizing both in the light of the new market realities.

To make matters worse, Kenya's central bank introduced rules that would keep us underwater. It was impossible for the bank to make money in such conditions, so it was "crisis management" all over again. I was forced to consider new ways for the bank to make money. Turning around Citi's fortunes in Monrovia required every trick in my banker's playbook as well as a few tricks my team and I had to invent along the way. In fact, it took us an entire year to get our branch out of the red and into the black. This felt like a long time to me, but it exceeded the expectations of senior management in New York.

I simply hoped that when Citi considered our *next* move, they would manage to find us a location that was *actually* peaceful and relatively risk-free!

Not every banking issue during my time in Kenya was macro, however. One was far more personal.

My boss at the time was a gentleman by the name of Eric Lester. One day he and I were discussing a budget that I had proposed for the following year, and our discussion gradually became an argument. We spent an inordinate amount of time on a single item that did not seem particularly significant. Eric kept questioning it. I believed he was paying undue attention to something that was immaterial and he, perhaps, believed I was not taking his concerns about the item seriously.

Neither of us backed down, and the meeting entered a spiral. Our emotions were rising, our productivity was declining, and we were no closer to agreeing on what the final budget should look like. *We are wasting too much time,* I thought. *We need to move on!*

"Eric, I think we are sitting in the wrong chairs!" I said, half joking but also exasperated. "I think we should switch chairs!"

He immediately stopped moving, stopped talking. He stared at me. I could see that my offhand comment had not been received in an offhand manner! I had not been seriously suggesting that I should replace Eric. Rather, my ill-conceived comment had been directed at moving the meeting forward, past a minor disagreement.

The meeting did go forward after that, but things would change between us. Eric perceived, erroneously, that I was attempting to replace him. I understood what had happened, just as I understood there was nothing I could do to change his perception. Anything I said in my defense would be considered "damage control." The trust between us had been broken. In a way it had not been my fault, but I also knew that I had caused the rift with my ill-timed quip. Our working relationship was irreparably harmed.

Compounding the problem was another situation I remember when, at a reception to welcome me to Kenya, my operations manager (Rick Barlay, originally from Liberia) made a highly controversial statement. In a brief speech, this experienced and tough banking executive said, "To get to this position, A. T. had to work twice as hard as all of you here."

The "all of you" included Eric, my immediate boss, who was British, and James Johnson, an American to whom Eric reported. The statement had clearly not sat well with them.

As a result, the reviews I received from Eric soured. They ought to have been stellar since our team truly was able to turn the fortunes of the bank around. I was supported by top-notch bankers from Kenya, Liberia, and England: Martin Nzioka handled my liability management group, Rick Barlay was in charge of operations, Ellen Johnson Sirleaf helped me in opening doors with governments and banks in Central and East Africa, and Stuart Lawson was the head of corporate banking. They all moved on later, with Ellen eventually running for (and being elected twice) as president of Liberia.

Yet from that moment, it did not matter that I would meet and exceed all my goals for the year. Eric, although acknowledging the undeniable facts, would usually find something to say to downplay my achievements.

Citibank allowed employees to react in writing to such reviews. I made sure my bosses in both Athens and New York read my self-assessments, backed by facts, along with Eric's evaluation.

Facts don't lie. Results spoke louder than any concocted narrative by my boss.

CHAPTER 26

Compassionate Father

Kenya

PAINFULLY, OUR TIME IN KENYA WAS MARRED BY MEDICAL SCARES for each of our children.

When Niki was seven years old, one morning he woke up screaming in pain. "My head hurts, my head hurts!"

I suspected he was suffering from malaria, just as I suspected he might be exaggerating his pain. Nevertheless, we called our family doctor. Upon hearing Niki's symptoms, the doctor demanded that we bring him to the clinic as soon as possible. He suspected what I did not: that Niki might have spinal meningitis.

When a test confirmed this, we were told to rush to the pediatrician at the nearby children's hospital. The doctor laid out the probabilities for us, along with the appropriate treatment. We were to give Niki antibiotics and do everything in our power to bring his fever down. Even if we did that, the doctor told us, there was a strong chance he would go blind, or deaf, become paralyzed, or even all three.

"And you should prepare yourself for the possibility of his death," the doctor concluded. "There is also a chance he will survive, and be fine, but it is only a small chance."

Priscilla and I were in shock. We raced home with Niki, determined to do everything the doctor had asked us. But was that all that could be done?

"A. T.," Priscilla declared, gripping both of my hands with hers, "we need to pray, and we need to pray now!" To this day, my wife is the prayer warrior in our home.

Along with several members from our small international church, including our pastor, we decided to pray over Niki during the Sunday service. There was no change in his condition. Once back home, Priscilla and I continued praying for as long as it took for God to heal Niki. Our vigil began in the morning and lasted through the day. Niki's pain was coming in waves, which we interpreted as a hopeful sign. Constant pain would have meant the sickness was winning, whereas moments of painless rest seemed to mean our prayers were winning.

It was a long, long day. Niki's temperature spiked to 104 before receding somewhat. His pain came and went. We gave him fever reducers and kept damp towels on his forehead and neck and arms. Through it all, we declared our trust in God the Father. *You have given Niki to us,* we prayed, *and we know that You can heal him. We know that You can make him live!* We had moved Niki to our king-sized bed upstairs, and at one point, I picked him up, holding him in my arms as I cried and implored the Almighty.

With prayers such as these, and others that rebuked the devil, we prayed for hours and hours, until Niki opened his eyes and spoke.

"This part of my head doesn't hurt at all," he reported, rubbing the area above his left temple.

Halfway there! We kept on praying until Niki spoke again. "Now this side feels better too," he said, pointing at the right side of his head.

Almost there! For good measure, we prayed some more. We noticed that Niki's demeanor had drastically improved.

"Niki, Niki," I said, "how is your head?"

After blinking several times, and seeming to take inventory of his body, he sat up. "It's fine, Daddy. My head doesn't hurt at all!"

This news, of course, produced a great deal of weeping, laughing, and praising God. After which we went downstairs, prepared food for everyone, and then turned on a soccer match on the television. Niki fell asleep with his head in Priscilla's lap.

The next morning, after a visit to the doctor, we were told that Niki was fully cured. It was a diagnosis that did not surprise us.

Only one year later, young Mara faced her own health crisis.

Priscilla had been out and about in town, taking care of some errands, and she had left Mara in the able care of her nanny, Veronica. (Mara, by the way, called her Vionika.) While Priscilla was out, Mara began to suffer from diarrhea and vomiting. There was no way for Veronica to alert Priscilla to what was happening, so by the time my wife returned to our home, Mara was weak and dehydrated.

Priscilla had witnessed children in Congo die of dehydration, so she rushed to the hospital with Niki and Mara, who was quickly admitted. Before too many minutes had passed, Mara was in a bed and being attended to by nurses.

There was a problem, however. Because of all the fluids Mara had already lost, her veins had collapsed, and the nurses were unable to start an IV. That saline fluid was the one thing that would help her, and it seemed impossible to access the channels to her rehydration. Mara's skin grew waxen, and her stomach flaccid. The nurses began to mutter to each other in worried tones.

That was when Priscilla, holding Mara's head in her lap, began to sing "You Are My Hiding Place," over and over and over. Suddenly, Priscilla felt what she described as a water drop of peace dripping down into her soul. She understood in that moment that Mara was going to be fine. Mara was hidden in the protection of God the Father, and nothing would be able to change that.

All the tension and worry left Priscilla's body. She smiled at Mara, then looked up and smiled at the nurses. Seconds later, a nurse announced that she had found a vein in Mara's arm. Once a good vein was found, it was a simple matter for a nurse to pump bag after bag of intravenous fluids into Mara. In the meantime, Niki, who had not been allowed into the hospital because of his young age, managed to find the window where his mother and sister were. Upon learning that his sister was going to make a full recovery, he stood outside the window and happily read Dr. Seuss and Tintin, his favorite books!

•XOX•

Both medical issues reminded us how precious our children were and how precious every moment of time with them was.

Apart from our worries about our children's health, our living situation in Kenya was wonderful. We had a huge house for a young family of four. It was situated on twelve acres of land, far from the road. We invested nearly one year of our time in Kenya building an extension to it, with two more bedrooms and bathrooms. The water borehole also needed to be deepened for better and more reliable access to this indispensable commodity. We spent some six months enduring the noise from the equipment used to complete the task, but the outcome proved the effort worthwhile. We had staff to take care of the property as well as a driver, paid for by the bank. I paid for Priscilla's driver, a cook, and two nannies, who completed our domestic staffing needs.

Kenya was like a paradise for us. What else could a man ask for? Our house was so nice that when we moved out, the son of Kenya's vice president purchased it from the bank.

My banking hours were generally from eight in the morning until eight at night, not to mention extra meetings, dinners, and so on. If I could come home early, that meant extra family time with Priscilla and the kids, and I guarded my weekend time jealously. Most bankers belonged to a nearby country club, and much unofficial business was conducted on the links. Despite this, I chose not to take up golf. Instead, we joined the country club as a family, enjoying tennis and the swimming pool, activities we were able to do together. Niki and Mara loved running and fetching the balls for us, oblivious to the fact that I was destroying their mother at tennis, usually by six-love sets. When threatened with food (or other) deprivations, I would engineer six-one or six-two sets. She has her own side to this story, though! Still, the days we spent together were nearly always filled with affection and happy memories.

Throughout our time in Kenya, whether in good times or in bad, God continued to remind us that He loved us and that He was in control.

We could trust Him to lead us, just as sheep trust their shepherd. God had proved that He was not just *a* Shepherd but the Good Shepherd.

His loving-kindness extended to me personally as I faced my own crisis in Kenya.

The business culture in Kenya was soaked in alcohol. Perhaps owing to Britain's influence on the country, we all tended to be fond of beer, whiskey, and gin and tonic. Whether lunch with a client, a reception after work, or anything in between, a great deal of banking business was lubricated with a stiff drink.

I had always been a willing participant in the system, but at year's end 1984, I hit a low point. After yet again having too many drinks at an after-hours meeting, I arrived home, only to realize I was a bit inebriated. I did not like the drinking habit I had formed. Excessive alcohol, coffee, and tea had combined to cause intermittent burning in my stomach. After I was diagnosed with stomach ulcers, I understood my drinking habits had become unsustainable. I was unhappy with my inability to discipline myself, and seemingly unable to refuse a drink if the opportunity presented itself, in spite of what my body was telling me!

I determined that 1985 would, with God's help, be different. Before New Year's Eve, I fell to my knees and pleaded with God. I confessed that I could not control the amount I drank. "Take alcohol away from me," I cried out to God. "Take it away entirely. Help me God! Please!"

When I rose to my feet, I knew that God had indeed heard my desperate cry.

Beginning the following morning, January 1, 1985, I simply stopped drinking. I can testify that it was not my willpower that accomplished this, but the grace of God.

Even so, I was worried that my professional life would suffer. Would my coworkers and I have anything to talk about? Would business partners, actual and potential, steer clear of me? Or worse, misinterpret my abstinence as antisocial? Would they judge me or, inversely, fear I would judge them for their drinking habits? This was to say nothing of my personal life. What if I were no longer "good company" for people?

As I moved through my typical interactions at the bank and after work, I did not partake in a single sip of alcohol. If someone happened to ask me why I did not want to indulge in a drink, I had a ready answer. "I certainly would have wanted to in the past. But I asked God to take away my dependence on alcohol, and He answered me!"

Wonderfully, as the days and weeks and months went by, I was never judged by a single person. If anything, most were either surprised or impressed, and in both cases I was able to share about my faith.

Each time I interacted with someone about my newfound sobriety, the goodness of God was impressed on me. It reminded me of the Hebrews in the book of Daniel who, while captive in Babylon, partook of healthy food and drink rather than the wine and rich food of their captors.

My heart was filled with gratitude for God's grace.

AT's father, Alphonse Ngandu (middle third from the left) with friends. Picture taken before AT was born (likely early 1940s).

AT's sister, Godelieve Kayowa.

AT's brother, Kanyiki Robert Vianney, as territorial administrator during the Belgian rule.

Robert Kanyiki (AT's oldest brother) standing beside their grandmother, Kaku (Grandma) Wa Katshinga.

AT in high school (Bibanga) flying a kite.

AT and high school friends in Bibanga, DR Congo. AT is bottom right.

AT's (back row, far left) graduating class in high school, Bibanga, DR Congo, circa 1967.

AT at Dartmouth College, 1971, in front of his dormitory, Tuck Mall.

AT and PT wedding day (June 25, 1972) outside Columbia University's chapel.

AT and PT standing on either side of his mother, Julienne Ngalula, circa 1974.

Family portrait: AT and PT with Niki (L) and
Mara (R) taken in Liberia, circa 1982.

Family photo outside the house in Nairobi, Kenya circa '83 (in Karen, part of Karen Blixen's property).

Circa 1997 (with piles of cash during the 25th year anniversary of Citibank-Zaire). High inflation meant you needed a lot of devalued Zaires to buy goods.

AT surrounded by family in Kinshasa, including his late brother Antoine Tshiyombo sitting to his right (AT is wearing the dark jacket).

AT surrounded by family members in Kinshasa (AT in the center, wearing a yellow polo shirt).

AT and his eldest grandson, Josiah Athanase (19), visiting family in Kinshasa in July 2025. AT is third from the right and Josiah is standing beside him on the left.

Matthieu Nkongolo (AT's uncle and former chief of the Bena Kadiamba, succeeded by AT's brother Antoine Tshiyombo).

Chief Antoine Tshiyombo Muka,
succeeded by his son Muimbi Jean.

Chief Antoine Tshiyombo
with his Bible. Last days.

Jean Muimbi (current chief of the Bena Kadiamba) suceeded his father—AT's brother—Antoine Tshiyombo.

AT and PT enjoying a visit from their eldest grandchild, Denali.

AT and PT enjoying a Christmas outing with their family at the National Harbor in Maryland.

Tshibaka family in August 2025. Picture taken in front of AT & PT's home in Spotsylvania, VA. Not pictured is their oldest granddaughter, Denali.

AT and PT in front of their home.

AT and PT in Providenciales, Turks and Caicos Islands.

CHAPTER 27

A House Divided

Kenya

THERE REMAINS A CRITICAL EXPERIENCE FROM OUR TIME IN KENYA that I must mention, although the retelling fills me with pain, even to this day.

Our church in Kenya was intimate. I do not simply mean the relationships, though they were certainly intimate. The church was also so intimate that we met in a small school classroom. The congregation, such as it was, consisted of the Tshibakas, several Kenyan families, a few American families, various expats and businesspeople from the United Kingdom, and the pastor and his family. On Wednesday evenings, when we met for prayer and Bible study, all of us could cram together inside the pastor's living room.

Our pastor was a missionary from England, and he had come to Kenya with his wife, daughter, and son to lead our fledgling international congregation.

We had been introduced at church to a young Kenyan woman, Elsie, who was living with our pastor's daughter in an apartment near the university. Elsie was engaged to another Kenyan, Peter Maranga, who also attended the church. They both seemed to be upstanding young people.

One Wednesday, during our time together, our pastor shared that his daughter wanted Elsie out of the apartment they were sharing with only one day's notice. He did not share *why*, only that their whole family approved of the decision. After learning about this unfortunate development, Priscilla and I offered to take Elsie into our home, either until she could find a new place to live or until her marriage with her fiancé

Peter, a few months thence, when they would move into their own home together.

The reaction of our pastor surprised us. He was furious with our decision and told us we were undermining his authority and that he believed we were trying to take over the leadership of the church!

Priscilla and I were flabbergasted. What was going on in our pastor's mind? We tried and tried to understand his point of view, but the only conclusion we could reach was that his reaction was unhealthy. There must, we thought, be something going on behind the scenes to which we were not privy.

The following days and weeks seemed to confirm our suspicions. The next time all of us met together, our relationship with the pastor was clearly shattered, if not irreparably broken. To our faces he called us rebels, and at the conclusion of the service he instructed everyone else in attendance to avoid associating with us outside of church.

Soon came word that we were unwelcome at any church functions.

Even though Priscilla and I believed we had done the right and honorable thing, this rejection stung. We talked about what to do and concluded that we were no longer welcome at prayer meetings on Wednesday evenings, inside our pastor's home. We determined, however, that we would still go to Sunday morning services in the school classroom. We had done nothing wrong, and the school was neutral ground. We felt it was our church as much as the pastor's church. Not that we were trying to take over the church! We simply wanted to continue attending and worshipping together with everyone.

The first Sunday after this decision, we arrived at the school and discovered that the service was being conducted by a visiting pastor from Israel. It did not surprise me at all when the visiting pastor announced he would be preaching on Joshua 24:15. "Choose today whom you will serve," he read, and I nodded along. It seemed fitting, considering our pastor's incomprehensible decision. Except the visiting pastor's explanation of the verse made it very clear that he had been handed a brief by our pastor! "Are you going to follow your trusted pastor," he asked the congregation, "or are you going to follow the wayward Tshibaka rebels?"

I could not help myself. I stood immediately, despite Priscilla's attempt to keep me seated. "There are no issues with *us*," I responded. "In fact, we *are* following God and following the pastor. We have no ambition to take over the church. We are simply giving Elsie a temporary place to stay. And we are simply trying to worship with others in our church!"

That was not what the visiting pastor wanted to hear, although I did notice several supportive nods directed my way.

It wasn't long after we left the service that day that we heard the news: Our pastor was disbanding the church. Not officially, but practically. He would only be conducting "services" at his home, and only with the English members of the church. Meanwhile, the rest of us, most of whom were Kenyan or American, decided to meet at our home.

The following Sunday, this fledgling house church began with a great deal of introspection and humility.

It pains me to admit this, but not even a *month* of Sundays passed before our grand experiment foundered on the rocks of petty gossip and blame. It seemed we could not bear *not* talking about our former pastor's family. Rather than focusing on our own shortcomings, and more importantly on God, we were choosing to point fingers at others.

Weeks before, at one of our Wednesday meetings before the split, I had shared with the group from Matthew 7:1–2: "Do not judge others, and you will not be judged. For you will be treated as you treat others. The standard you use in judging is the standard by which you will be judged" (NLT).

We had all been convicted, opened our hearts to one another that day, shed tears, and hugged. It was a cleansing experience. How could we now, we the outcasts, turn around to criticize the pastor and our brothers and sisters in Christ? No, that was not right. We all agreed to self-examine, praying and leaving the ultimate judgment to God our Supreme Judge.

I should say that we did eventually discover the apparent facts of the matter. Our former pastor's daughter had been in a relationship with a Muslim professor at the University of Kenya. To continue inviting him to her apartment, she had to remove Elsie from the equation. She managed to convince her parents to take her side, despite the obvious conflict between their inhospitable actions toward Elsie and the professed beliefs of her parents as well as her own.

I share this story because to this day a part of my heart remains broken. Seeing division grow in the body of Christ marked me. Indeed, it felt as if the slander and splintering were a sort of cancer, spreading unchecked through previously cherished relationships. And to think it occurred over something so banal! If the pastor had denied the divinity of Christ, or if Priscilla and I had tried to destroy his leadership, perhaps then the accusations and ensuing division in our church would have been more understandable.

As it was, our church was broken over what amounted to a fight among roommates…and our hearts broke along with it.

After the church split, Elsie stayed for nearly half a year with us. When she married Peter and moved out, she soon became pregnant. The happy couple had asked us to have a prominent presence at their wedding. Soon Priscilla and I would be asked to be godparents, an honor that we joyfully accepted. (They are still married to this day, by the way, with many children! Peter is a retired captain with Kenya Airways.)

There are moments that mark your life indelibly. The splintering of our church was one such moment for me. Whenever I reflect on that difficult season of my life, I cannot help but feel pangs of guilt and regret. Scripture says that we are vessels of clay (2 Corinthians 4:7), and I have ample evidence that I am a cracked, broken vessel. To be blunt, I can leak like a sieve. I am all too aware that I might sow division, whether wittingly or unwittingly. What role did I play in the division and dissolution of our church? How much responsibility did I bear for the pain that followed?

I know that I can be direct and sometimes brutally honest. You will have to ask Priscilla how she might describe me! The lingering sense that I might have somehow caused the dissolution of our Kenyan church has, to this day, made me reluctant to serve in Christian ministries, especially in a lead role. It reminds me of the seventeenth chapter of John, in which Christ speaks about the unity His church should have. We in the church are called to be united in the same way that Jesus was united with His Father.

And we, in our church, failed.

A part of my heart remains shredded, nearly forty years later.

Why?

It was a question I could not stop asking as our church disintegrated, and it is a question I ask myself to this very day. Perhaps this is difficult for anyone to understand if they were not part of our small but burgeoning congregation. But as I write this from the perspective of an old man, able to look back on my entire life, I testify that not one issue in my banking career affected me as deeply as that church split.

Lord, have mercy on me.

CHAPTER 28

Persistent Prompting, Obedience Rewarded

Kenya

MY TEAM AND I HAD SUCCESSFULLY TURNED AROUND THE BANK in Kenya in my first year. Then the bank became increasingly profitable over the next several years. So perhaps it should not have been surprising to hear from Citibank about a new position. Although I was surprised when the call came from Kim Abbott, the man who had mentored me back in the Congo.

Kim informed me he was heading the international audit department for Citibank. He had positions open in Manila, Philippines, and Rio de Janeiro, Brazil. The Brazil responsibilities would cover six other countries in South America, but my office and team would be based in Brazil, traveling to those countries for business risk reviews or audits of Citibank entities.

Before I could process this offer, he complicated it. Kim was a gentleman. He wisely clarified that I still had the option of staying in Kenya, if that was something I chose to do.

"But A. T., it would be good for you to get exposure to another region of the globe. Think about your career five, ten years from now. The last thing you want is to be pigeonholed as a so-called Africa expert, right?"

He was right, but it would be difficult to leave Kenya. We loved our home. Priscilla and the kids were happy. I felt as if our life was in a good groove, and now Kim was asking us to leave and start something entirely new.

Priscilla and I decided to pray about it. Truth be told, we were not considering Brazil. We had visited Brazil the summer before as tourists. The TV programming in Rio de Janeiro had not seemed appropriate for children, at least during the few days we spent in that fun city. Nor did the overall lifestyle suit us. Thus, in our eyes, the choice was between Kenya and the Philippines.

Then we began to pray to God for direction. We were asking God to tell us whether to opt for the Philippines or for staying in Kenya, with the latter being our preferred option. The two of us agreed not to tell the other what we were hearing from Him. We prayed and listened, then prayed and waited, independent of each other. At the end of one week, we sat down over cups of tea to share what we might have heard. Which turned out to be nothing.

"So," I clarified, "you have not heard anything?"

My wife nodded. "And you haven't either?"

I nodded. We sipped our tea. "Perhaps we ought to fast?" she suggested.

So each of us prayed and listened, then prayed and waited, all the while fasting. And still nothing. No direction from God, despite what we thought were earnest and faithful prayers.

At last, it dawned on both of us almost instantaneously.

We had been asking God to choose between *two* places, but there were actually *three* doors opened to us. We had been asking God the wrong question! We were restricting His guidance to the choice we had already made. Brazil had to be put back on the proverbial table.

We continued to pray and listen and fast. Several days later, after dinner at our friends Rick and Princess Barlay's home, Priscilla and I decided to take a walk in their garden. After several minutes of silence, we turned to face each other and spoke simultaneously, asking, "It's Brazil, isn't it?"

In the days that followed, we gathered information on Brazil from the local embassy, and the Brazilian ambassador even invited us over for a meal at home with his family. He put on a real sales performance for the country, an introduction to life and culture in Brazil. For a couple we had only recently come to know, their hospitality was amazing, and at the embassy, the ambassador designated one of his consular officials to handle our entire immigration process.

Our paperwork sailed seamlessly through the bureaucracy. Priscilla and I knew we had made the right decision, with God's guidance.

Exactly one week before we were due to leave for Brazil, early in the morning I found a note waiting for me on the desk in my office. It had been hand delivered. Curious, I sat down, opened it, and began to read.

As I did so, I wept.

The letter was from our former pastor, and it was an apology for the way he and his family had treated me and my family. He asked if we could forgive him, and he asked if he and his wife could come to our house to ask for forgiveness in person. I collapsed forward onto my desk, head in hands, my shoulders inconsolably shaking as I cried. I felt a mixture of joy and relief, accompanied by a hint of the pain that the acrimonious split had caused. It seemed I had not healed fully from that experience, and the letter provided a type of salve for my soul that I had not known was needed.

My first phone call was to Priscilla. She too wept, joining me in tears of gratitude and thanksgiving.

My next phone call was to our former pastor. I thanked him profusely for the note and explained to him that he and his wife did not need to come to see us. We agreed to meet at his home that evening. As far as I was concerned, he was still God's anointed, deserving of our respect.

The reunion was incredible. We did not spend any time rehashing what had happened. Instead, the four of us prayed together. A sense of deep, cleansing peace came over all of us. Reconciliation was exactly what Priscilla and I needed before moving to another country. A huge weight had been lifted from our shoulders.

Yet God had even more restoration in store for us.

Several days later, Citibank organized a farewell reception for me and Priscilla. The venue was to be a large ballroom in the Hilton hotel. More than five hundred business leaders, government officials, and friends would attend. We had also made the decision to invite the members of our former church, who all attended.

As with our former pastor, nothing was said that evening about what had happened. We were reunited in happiness. Hugs and handshakes were given, and we returned to our home that night feeling as if we had been bathed in joy. No sense of fracture would accompany us to Brazil but rather the knowledge that our God was a God of healing and reconciliation. We were grateful, deeply grateful.

On the morning before we were due to leave for Brazil, I sat at my desk for the final time. In that quiet moment, I sensed a prompting from the Holy Spirit. *Tshibaka, you must apologize to your boss for your attitude toward him.*

What did I *do wrong?* I asked.

You must apologize, came back a persistent, gentle, firm, and unmistakable retort.

But it was Eric *who was in the wrong,* I continued my self-defense.

You must apologize!

I was not given a choice.

He was wrong in the budget meeting, I kept on arguing, *and he was wrong to treat me unfairly in my annual appraisals.* He *should apologize to* me*!*

The Spirit of Christ Jesus in me would not relent.

You must apologize!

Not a minute of the day passed during which my mind was not preoccupied with this issue. I could not focus on the many work-related tasks I had to complete.

I tried to organize my affairs, clean out my desk, and say my farewells to various staff members, but the entire time I was engaged in a spiritual battle. I knew what was required of me but steadfastly refused to yield. Pride and self-righteousness seemed to have the upper hand. My resistance—or better said, disobedience—was winning.

It was not until 6:00 p.m. that I finally decided to go to Eric's office, on the sixth floor of the building. I thought, *By now, Eric must have left for home or for drinks with friends or bank clients.* Still, I knew the only way to bring about a peaceful resolution to my inner struggle was to present myself to Eric and ask for his forgiveness.

I stood from my desk. "Okay," I said aloud, hoping to embolden myself, "I am going to his office now. It seems unfair. It is humiliating. But God is asking that it be done before my departure from Kenya. This is my last evening in Nairobi, my last opportunity to do right by Him. Yes, it must be done."

I took the elevator to the sixth floor and walked to Eric's office door, ready to knock. The thought returned to me that at this time of day, it was unlikely Eric would be in his office. If that was the case, I could simply leave. I would have thus obeyed God's call to right my relationship with someone I had offended. My conscience would be at peace, knowing that I had at least attempted to obey.

My plan fell apart the instant after I knocked.

"Come in," Eric said.

I entered the office and found myself face-to-face with my boss, who was standing in front of his desk. I knew I had to seize the moment without engaging in unnecessary niceties.

"Eric, I apologize for my attitude last year," I said in a rush of words, "and I am sorry I disrespected you."

There. I did it. But what would be the reaction?

Eric's eyes opened wider for the merest of moments, and then his gaze found a space somewhere over my left shoulder. He mumbled something inaudible. I extended my hand, which Eric shook firmly. Then I spun and exited. As I strode down the hallway, I listened carefully for the sound of Eric's office door closing behind me. When I heard the *click,* I allowed my shoulders to slump a few degrees.

Back in my empty office, a feeling of cleansing washed over me. In His grace and mercy, my loving Father had gently led me to repentance and reconciliation with Eric.

An image entered my mind. I saw myself walking across a barren land. My clothes were filthy, my hands and bare feet were caked with mud, and flies buzzed around my face. Suddenly, I came upon an oasis, and a voice invited me to bathe. When I emerged from the water, all traces of dirt and filth had been washed from my body. I understood immediately: It was only by forgiving my former pastor and asking for forgiveness from Eric that I had been forgiven, cleansed of the mud.

David's cry in Psalm 51 came alive to me: "Have mercy on me, O God, according to your unfailing love; according to your great compassion blot out my transgressions. Wash away all my iniquity and cleanse me from my sin.... Create in me a pure heart, O God, and renew a steadfast spirit within me. Do not cast me from your presence or take your Holy Spirit from me" (Psalm 51:1–2, 10–11 NIV).

God's faithfulness remained steadfast, unquestionable. I could now move to Brazil feeling liberated.

CHAPTER 29

Accused, Then Vindicated

Brazil

PRISCILLA AND I BOTH FELT AN INCREDIBLE SENSE OF PEACE ABOUT our move to Brazil. We knew God was leading our family across the Atlantic Ocean, and we knew He would continue to be our faithful Shepherd no matter what we encountered in South America. Unsurprisingly, given our track record of transitional challenges, our relocation did not pass without at least some difficulty. Fortunately, this time it was not something as dramatic as a coup d'état upon arrival! The issue was more banal: Our initial accommodations in Brazil were less than ideal because they were located in one of the most beautiful places on earth.

I was a senior banker, tasked with doing credit audits and business audits in seven countries: Argentina, Bolivia, Brazil, Chile, Peru, Paraguay, and Uruguay. Wherever my wife went, she was a respected community and church member, along with being a homemaker, piano tutor, and mother to our two young children. And yet Citi chose to house us, initially, in Le Meridien Copacabana Hotel, located directly on the famed, and infamous, Copacabana beach.

This was only until our permanent residence was ready, which was to be a beautiful apartment *also* located directly on the Copacabana beach.

If this sounds like paradise, it was not. What it meant, practically, was that I was forced to walk toward my office in the city center, wearing a banker's suit, while young people in speedos and bikinis were headed the opposite way, to the beach! It truly felt like torture.

Nevertheless, I soldiered on, telling myself not to ponder how delightful the weather was, nor how inviting the beach was. Business called, not pleasure.

Unfortunately, my business life was about to become a nightmare. Out of the blue I received a message from a former Citi colleague who was now the head of human resources in New York. "I wanted to give you a heads-up on something that could be a problem for you. Eric Lester is doing a comprehensive audit of the bank you used to run in Kenya, and he's building a case that you were knowingly paying yourself and certain expat staff too much money."

That seemed bad enough already, but the news got worse. A friend from the Kenya office, Omido, was the head of human resources there. He relayed that Eric Lester had asked him to help with the audit. In other words, Eric was out to get me, but he wanted to have an "independent" person bring the case so that he could keep his hands clean.

Clearly, Eric had chosen not to accept my apology.

I knew that an ally on the inside might be the only way I could prove my innocence. I begged Omido to fax me particular files from the Kenya office. They were copies of correspondence I had sent to our human resources headquarters in New York as well as to our regional head office, at the time based out of Athens, Greece. I recalled something about the files that I hoped would help me, and when my fax machine began printing out sheet after sheet, I began to read. It seemed Omido had been able to send everything I wanted—and there, clear as day on the correspondence, were my handwritten notes. Success!

At the time, Citi paid "hardship allowances" to expat employees working in crisis areas or areas with other hardships. The allowance in Liberia, for instance, was a 50 percent bonus, whereas in Kenya, the allowance was 15 percent. My handwritten notes had been addressed to my superiors, and they proved that I had actually pointed out the compensation amounts seemed too *high*. I had asked my HR team to follow up on the issue, which was hardly something a man trying to steal from the company would do!

Each time we questioned the hardship allowances, seniors in HR wrote back and told us not to worry. They assured me that the amounts were correct. And I had all of this in writing. I breathed a sigh of relief.

Eric discovered Omido had faxed the documents to me. He immediately fired Omido. My heart broke when I heard the news. It galled me that the loyalty of a trustworthy colleague had been rewarded with unjust treatment, and there was nothing I could do about it. I hoped Omido would find other employment quickly, but from Brazil there was nothing I could do to help him. Not to mention I was the subject of an active ethics investigation.

I soon learned that my case was being reviewed by Citi's highest-level ethics committee in New York. The documents Omido had faxed me *would* clear my name, I believed, but the investigation would need to take its proper course. I also learned Kim Abbott sat on the New York committee, along with several other people who had known me for years.

But none of those factors guaranteed the outcome of my case. Just as I had begun establishing myself in Brazil, it seemed as if I might be uprooted. Or, to choose a different metaphor, Eric's attack on my character felt like the sword of Damocles hung over my head. It was as if a single decision made by Eric could end my professional life.

Thank God I was continuing to read the Bible and pray in that season. The more I read God's Word, the more I could dare to hope. Each time I read a promise of protection, I would highlight the text, then sign and date the promise in the margin of my Bible.

One verse I read stood out to me in a particular way, and I committed it to my heart: "The Egyptians you see today you will never see again" (Exodus 14:13 NIV).

I understood that to mean that the trials I was facing would pass. How and when, I did not know, but I trusted God and God's timing.

It took three months for the ethics committee to reach a decision.

They let me know that any overpayment errors to expat staff were the fault of human resource supervisors at the time, the ones to whom I had written questions. Since I had "put the ball in their court," as it were, I was free and clear. Officially exonerated!

If only the phone call had stopped there.

However, the fact remained that I, along with expats under me, had been paid total compensation 35 percent higher than what we were entitled to during my tenure in Kenya. The difference was due to the bank continuing to pay us a hardship allowance at the Liberia rate of 50 percent rather than the lower hardship allowance at the Kenya rate of 15 percent. The ethics committee determined that the excess payments must be restituted to the bank. In breaking the news to me, the offer made was for me to take a $120,000 loan from the bank, with a reduced staff interest rate. In truth, it was a just and generous decision.

"It's the only way," they told me, "and it's out of our hands. Listen, you can take a loan from Citi and pay it back over time. That will let you keep your savings. Or..."

"Or what?" I asked.

"Or you can use your Citi savings account to cover the amount of overpayment."

I made the decision in an instant. Eric Lester's accusations had been polluting my life for months. I knew that if I were to take out a loan, each time I made a payment it would surface negative thoughts and feelings. Much better to be done with the matter once and for all! So, after consulting with Priscilla, I authorized the bank to debit my account and settle the HR snafu for good.

When Priscilla and I moved to Liberia in 1980, we had no penny saved to our name. Since then, we had put a little sum aside following my Liberia and Kenya assignments, only to see that safety net evaporate. We had nothing to show for fourteen years of a banking career. Even though my suffering at the time could not come even close to what Job of the Bible had endured, I drew my comfort from one of the profound statements he made: "Naked I came from my mother's womb, and naked I will depart. The LORD gave and the LORD has taken away; may the name of the LORD be praised" (Job 1:21 NIV).

And that is how, three months after arriving in Brazil, Priscilla and I found ourselves with an empty savings account and clear consciences. *The enemies you see today you will see no longer.* She and I prayed through the verse again, thanking God for His provision and protection. An end had been made, and Tshibaka had survived to bank another day!

I soon learned that Tony Mantsavinos, Citi's executive vice president (international), had visited Kenya. (Tony had replaced Jack Clark as EVP international). I do not know if that trip was planned before the ethics investigation began, but I do know that Eric Lester made a presentation to the EVP, they had dinner together, and then the EVP returned to New York.

The next day, Citi fired Eric Lester.

I felt relief at the news, yes, but also sadness. Eric's firing, and my exoneration, meant that I was in the clear, for good. Yet part of me mourned for my former boss. I could not know what had caused him to pursue his false claim about me. Ultimately, I knew that another of God's promises had been proven true. *The enemies you see today you will see no longer* took on a new level of meaning. I had nothing to do with Eric's firing. It had happened in the right way, through official oversight.

Everything that happened had come about because of the faithfulness and justice of God. The outcome reminded me of the story of Haman in the Bible, the hater of Mordecai, Queen Esther's uncle, and of the Jewish people. Haman was impaled on the pole he had set up to have Mordecai killed (Esther 7:10).

Eric had wanted me to be fired, or worse.

But God had other plans.

CHAPTER 30

Golden Covering

Brazil

ONE NIGHT AFTER DINNER IN OUR BEACHSIDE APARTMENT, I MADE a final decision I had been mulling over for some time. "This city is not a place for business!" I may have slapped the tabletop for emphasis.

"Tell me how you really feel," Priscilla responded, a twinkle in her eye.

"I will!" I answered. "I cannot continue to have Citi's regional business risk review office here. I cannot! And we cannot remain in this apartment and raise our children in this environment!"

After much discussion with my superiors at Citi, we agreed to move our regional headquarters to São Paulo.

At that time, Citi required expat staff in Brazil to reside in a secure location, which meant an apartment with 24-7 guards, a perimeter fence, visitation, entry policies, and so on. To be honest, after our experiences in previous countries, such a policy made a great deal of sense to me!

My wife had other ideas. "A. T., we are going to have a home in São Paulo," she informed me.

"Of course," I agreed. "An apartment can certainly feel like home."

Her stare let me know I was not comprehending her meaning.

"A *home*," she clarified. "Just us, in a house, with a garden out back."

Now I comprehended. But how would that be possible, given Citi's strict policies? Perhaps my wife would change her mind, with enough time.

She did not.

That night, I dreamed.

First, I dreamed of a small, neat house. It was an A-frame, but while the eaves touched the grass surrounding the house, the peak of the roof stretched impossibly high, all the way into the heavens. The roof of the house was made of gold.

Next, I dreamed of the same small, neat house, but this time the roof was covered in something much different. Instead of gold, the roof dripped with blood, which ran off the roof and soaked into the grass.

I woke up with a clear idea of what I needed to do. My wife would not be pleased, but I had no choice. I sat across from her at the breakfast table.

"Listen," I said, deciding to skip the preamble. "If we move into an isolated house of our own, there will be trouble."

She frowned at me.

"Definite trouble," I clarified. "I had a *dream*."

"Oh?" She took a sip of her tea, seemingly unconcerned for some reason.

I set out to explain the first dream, describing the golden-roofed home briefly before launching into a gory retelling of the second dream. When I reached the end of my description, I emphasized that the second home was a clear warning of danger for our family. Then I sat back.

Priscilla buttered a piece of toast and took a bite.

"Well?" I prompted.

"Let's think more about your dream," she said, "but later, because you need to get to work."

I did think more about my dream, and the truth came to me that same day as I worked. God was not warning us *away* from a home. Rather, God was promising us our home would be safe! The golden roof, which I had left conveniently unexplained, was a symbol of God's protective armor. And the blood was even better: It was the blood of Jesus, covering our home and our family, and even more precious than gold!

Accomplishing the goal of house rental required a significant amount of communication with Citi officials, but in the end the matter was settled. If we paid for our own guard protection, Citi would allow us to choose a house.

Priscilla found one with a garden out back, naturally. And in the coming years in São Paulo, while both of our neighbors' homes were broken into, ours was never touched.

"LORD, you alone are my portion and my cup; you make my lot secure" (Psalm 16:5 NIV).

CHAPTER 31

Divine Interruption

Brazil

AS THE REGIONAL HEAD OF BUSINESS RISK REVIEW, COVERING CITI'S businesses in Brazil, Argentina, Bolivia, Paraguay, Uruguay, Peru, and Chile, I had to travel almost constantly. My trips were not confined to South America but also included the United States, Australia, New Zealand, and Italy for various reviews.

Professionally, my banking years in Brazil were important. Because I made some tough audit rating decisions on major institutions, I enhanced my reputation for fact-based auditing, fairness, and objectivity. I was also forced to confront and fire a high-ranking employee in our São Paulo office. Some called me fearless, which was interesting. I was always eager to make the right decision. Perhaps some viewed me as fearless because others in the financial world were fear*ful* of doing what was right, especially if what was right was also difficult or unpopular.

In any case, my banking accomplishments in São Paulo meant that my career with Citi was advancing suitably.

But that also meant that for the two or three weeks I traveled each month, I felt torn from my family. Sometimes, when saying goodbye, it was as if my skin was being ripped from my body.

There were so many common activities I wished to share with them each week, yet more often than not our relationship took place across a long-distance phone line. Niki and I enjoyed kicking the soccer ball in the street and rooting for the Brazilian teams on television. I had chosen São Paulo to support, while Niki favored Corinthians. On several occasions I was forced to leave for the airport in the middle of a match, precipitating many hugs and kisses and professions of love.

Mara was (and continues to be even now, to her chagrin) my baby girl. She preferred to sit by her daddy on Sundays when, after church, we would all go to a restaurant together for lunch before rushing home in time for a soccer game on TV. She could do no wrong, at least in my eyes. When occasionally she would be caught wrongfooted, a mere stare from me would provoke tears to gather in her eyes, causing my heart to melt. It was a very effective way for my darling girl to avoid punishment.

One particular memory from that season always makes me smile. The nation of Mexico was hosting the 1986 World Cup, the biggest sporting event in the world. As it happened, Brazil's team reached the quarterfinals of the tournament, and their opponent was France. Brazil was, and is, mad for its football, and it seemed the entire country was gathered around television sets to watch the historic showdown between two world powers.

We had carefully built relationships with our Brazilian neighbors, but all our hard work nearly came crumbling down because of nine-year-old Niki. While Priscilla, Mara, and I watched the game inside, Niki decided to wander into the street and watch in a more fun and social environment. The game was full of scintillating attacking and stout defending, but when the final whistle blew, sending the game to penalty kicks, we learned that Niki was vocally rooting for France, even though he was outnumbered one hundred to one!

This was a huge faux pas, and it would have no doubt had relational consequences. We were only spared, I think, by Niki's charming personality and young age. He certainly angered our neighbors...but when the beloved Brazilian team lost 4–3 in the penalty shootout, Niki's pro-France rhetoric was soon forgotten—and replaced by neighborhood-wide weeping and gnashing of teeth!

Of course, my absences were difficult for Priscilla and the children as well, although they adapted to life in São Paulo. Both Niki and Mara attended an excellent American school, and each child grew up with a proficiency in languages. Niki knew some French and some Lingala from the Congo, and both children picked up Portuguese during our time in Brazil. (As they continued to move around the globe, their language capacity would grow even further. Today, both speak Spanish and read French, and Mara speaks German as well!)

We joined a Foursquare house church and continued to deepen our prayer lives and our relationships with the Lord. In fact, one occurrence confirmed to us beyond any shadow of a doubt the goodness and provision of our God.

It was an otherwise unremarkable afternoon in my São Paulo office when the still, small voice spoke to me again.

Stop. Pray. Now.

I sensed someone had suffered a grave accident and was in imminent danger of death. I could not explain this as anything other than a divine prompting.

Immediately, I called Priscilla, fearing the worst, but she and the kids were safe. "You need to pray," she affirmed, "but not for us."

God, I don't know what You are asking, I said, *but I will pray.*

I locked the door to my office and knelt on the carpet. How should I pray, knowing no facts about the situation?

It seemed that trusting God's guidance was my only option, apart from disobeying and refusing to pray. I closed my eyes.

God, would You touch this person, would You spare this person's life?

One week later, Kim Abbott called.

He related that his wife, Alice, had been in a serious car accident. A large truck had struck her sedan on the driver's door. Alice had suffered forty-four broken bones, a punctured lung, and a host of other injuries. She was stable but still fighting for her life.

I inquired about the time of the accident. As Kim relayed the timeline of events, I realized God had prompted me to pray at the exact time Alice had reached the operating table.

"The doctors were able to save her life, thank God," Kim said, his voice shaking. "But…"

I sensed I should wait. I heard him draw a long breath.

"But they are saying Alice will never walk again."

My heart sank. Kim and I prayed together for several minutes, and then we said goodbye. Priscilla and I were determined to continue praying for Alice's recovery, and we thanked God for the healing He had already accomplished in her life. We could not know what Alice's future held, but we knew that God had answered our prayers for the preservation of her life.

CHAPTER 32

Our Dream Home

Brazil

OUR TIME IN BRAZIL WAS NEARING ITS END. THREE YEARS HAD passed in what seemed the blink of an eye. Back then, a three-year assignment was quite normal, so in a professional sense it was time to move on.

At a personal level, as well, Priscilla and I felt it was time to make a change. We had made friends with our neighbors and learned the best places to shop for produce, meat, and bread. Jean and Ana Rozwadowski, Dermot and Janet Shean, and so many other families had become dear friends, and remain so to this day. Our children had enjoyed their schooling and we had discovered the beauties of a new country. Despite the difficulties of being away from each other for so many days each month, we persevered with the same Tshibaka family attitude that had carried us through before. But we were certainly not going to live in Brazil forever.

So what was next?

I was in New York when Citi provided half a dozen countries from which Priscilla and I could choose our next posting. New Zealand, Nigeria, Ecuador, Saudi Arabia…it was quite a globe-spanning list! The positions were varied as well, with offers such as risk manager, chief credit policy officer, managing director, and chief risk officer.

To make the decision even more challenging, two different Citi executive vice presidents were fighting hard to secure my services in their respective regions. A certain Mr. Baily wanted me to remain in Latin America, and he insisted that Caracas, Venezuela, was the best site for my next posting *and* for my family to live. Priscilla agreed and aggressively pushed for Caracas, by the way. Our short time in Rio de Janeiro had not sated her appetite for tropical beaches!

On the other hand, Mr. Gunther Greiner, a German who oversaw Citi's operations in Europe, pressed me to move to Spain. As we chatted in the New York office, Gunther saw an opportunity to personally convince me. He began to lay it on thick.

"Listen, you are the guy for this. You are perfect. Some of my guys are here in New York, ja? Right now, you can meet with them. HR, my chief of finance, and other guys. Let's get the meetings set up!"

"Thank you," I responded, "but I need to talk to my wife back in São Paulo first."

"No, no, no," he insisted. "Listen to me. This is what you will do. After the meetings here, you will fly to Madrid, ja? And once you are there, you will look at our operations. If you still cannot decide, we will understand. But first fly to Madrid. This is how you will decide."

Clearly, he wanted to seal the deal before my wife could offer any input about Venezuela, or before I could field a better offer from a different Citi post.

There was a certain logic to his plan. Going to Spain would be clarifying, one way or another. How could I say no to the trip?

The man had done his homework. Before our meeting in his office, it seemed to me he had read everything he could about me. Normally, in an interview of this nature, I would have expected him to put all kinds of questions to me, to assess my suitability for such an important position on his team in Europe. Instead, Gunther spent the hour talking to me about my background and why I was a perfect fit for the chief risk manager job, Iberian division (Spain and Portugal). He argued, convincingly, that going to another emerging market would tag me with the "emerging markets expert" label. This was like the reasoning Kim Abbott had offered in convincing me to pursue my banking career out of Africa after fourteen years on the continent.

"Rather, A. T.," he counseled, "I strongly urge you to enter the *developed* markets of Citibank through Spain and Portugal, a good transition region for you."

Unable to convince me to decide without Priscilla weighing in, Gunther had me meet with five of his direct reports in different functional areas, including his chief of staff. My response to each of them was, "Thank you, but I still need to return to São Paulo and discuss with my wife."

It was then that Gunther played his last card. He was no longer asking. I sensed a veiled you-can't-turn-me-down order when he said, "A. T., you will return to São Paulo, but through Madrid, Spain. I want you to see the city and meet Amador Huertas, the managing director and division head, and some of his senior staff. They are your potential future colleagues."

The following day, I found myself gazing out an airplane window at the sprawl of Madrid. A Mercedes-Benz luxury car picked me up at the airport and took me to the Villa Magna, arguably the best hotel in Madrid at the time. Amador provided me with a condensed tourist experience: tapas, plazas, cathedrals, and delectable desserts.

"So..." he said slowly, hopefully, "have you made up your mind?" I thought the word *finally* was implied in his tone of voice.

I thanked him for the tour and told him I had learned a great deal about Madrid. "Thank you for all the time you have spent on me. But I *still* need to talk to my wife about this decision!"

Amador shook his head and chuckled. "Still?" he clarified.

"Still!" I laughed.

"Well, in the meantime, we have some properties to show you. These are places you would be staying with your family," he half-jokingly offered, "when you move here?"

Again, how could I say no?

The bank driver took me to a sprawling mansion in a prestigious neighborhood called Somosaguas. It had seven bedrooms, a swimming pool, and a lush garden. "Fulgencio Batista, the former president of Cuba, had lived there," I was informed. "And, next door, lived arguably the richest man in Spain at the time, José María Ruiz-Mateos."

Our tour continued, and the driver showed me a newer neighborhood, La Moraleja. He helpfully pointed out how close both neighborhoods were to good schools: one an American private school and the other an international private school.

Frankly, I was impressed…by everything! I knew Amador ran a top-notch business operation. He was a personable, smart man, one whom I would be happy to work for. Professionally it would be an excellent move. And of course I was flattered by the attention he heaped on me.

Still, Priscilla and I were a team. So even as my whirlwind visit to Spain came to an end, I confessed to Amador that I had not made up my mind about his offer. I thanked him wholeheartedly but reiterated that I wanted to spend time talking with my wife before deciding. We needed to have a 100 percent agreement. The implicit message I was conveying to Gunther and Amador, along with their teams, was that my wife was going to be the final decision-maker.

Amador grabbed the opening with both hands. "Of course, of course!" he agreed. "This is why you will have Priscilla come to visit Spain as well? She must be 100 percent on board, as you say!"

While Amador was doing his utmost to woo me into Spain, Gunther was, from New York, making phone calls to several of his division executives in Europe who knew me well, directly or by reputation. James Johnson had been the division executive based out of Athens to whom Eric Lester was reporting during part of my time in Kenya. He had now moved to assume responsibility for Citibank's operations for Northern Europe, based out of Frankfurt, Germany.

Rafael Buenaventura was the division executive for Southern Europe, based out of Milan, Italy. He was Amador's direct boss. (When he left Citibank several years later, Rafael returned to his native Philippines, where he was appointed governor of the central bank. I was very sad when I learned of his passing away due to health complications. A great man and a dear friend!)

James and Rafael called me separately while I was still in Madrid. Each urged me to consider Gunther's offer and expressed their delight at the prospect of me joining Citibank's European team. Gunther was resolute in his determination. He was not going to accept no as an answer.

I wondered if perhaps Priscilla would be persuaded by these additional appeals…not to mention my excitement to move to Europe for the sake of my professional growth.

When I arrived back in São Paulo, Priscilla could sense my excitement about Spain, even as I tried to recount a factual list of the pros and cons of the move. I informed her as well about Amador's offer to bring her to Madrid for a visit.

"You know I would still like to move to Venezuela," my wife reminded me. "Think of how the kids and I could relax on the warm, tropical beaches while you are jet-setting around the globe to bank!"

"Does this mean you will not visit Spain?" I asked.

"Who said anything about that?" she countered. "Why would I turn down a free trip to Spain?"

On her flight to Madrid, Priscilla had prayed. *Lord, if this is the right place for our family, and if the right home exists for us, would You show me a sign I can't mistake?*

When she arrived at the first house, its garden was in full bloom. The delicious scent struck her the moment she opened the car door. Wisteria. Roses. And best of all, the rarely blooming jasmine. I will note here two major preferences of my wife. First, she loves to smell the flowers and will spend long hours in her garden planting and nurturing them. Second, she would happily live anywhere she could enjoy a fresh ocean breeze.

Thank You, Lord, Priscilla prayed, breathing in the scent again and again. *I know this is where You want us. Thank You for answering my prayer.*

As it turned out, the smaller house with the elaborate garden was taken off the market. The owner, Spain's ambassador to Morocco, had passed away, and his wife canceled her plans to rent the house. But the seven-bedroom mansion became my wife's preferred fallback. The smells of wisteria around the veranda, the swimming pool on the back of the house, and proximity to the American School of Madrid combined to make it an ideal choice for us.

So it was that Gunther Greiner had his wish; the Tshibakas decided to move to Spain after all.

I knew Madrid, Spain, was our next destination. Yet I could not help pondering the route that had taken us to that point.

To this very day, I cannot fully explain why Gunther Greiner pursued me in such a manner. He was a German business executive whose portfolio was Western Europe. I was a Congolese who had never lived in Europe. Why did he pursue me, specifically?

More puzzlingly, why did Gunther Greiner not give up when I was reluctant to accept his proposal? Most other people in my position would have jumped at his offer. Gunther was feared within the bank as a tough, no-nonsense leader. Why would he commission Amador to personally invest time with me, and go as far as asking several division heads in Europe to call me?

Looking back, I have only one explanation: God's grace.

If it had only been up to my wife, we would have moved to Caracas in the blink of an eye. And, left to me, we would have ended up in Nigeria, the largest Citibank franchise in Africa with the greatest promise for growth back then. The offer was made to me during lunch in a restaurant near Citibank's 399 Park Avenue headquarters. I had turned that offer down, gratefully, as I knew Nigeria was out of consideration for Priscilla.

In the end, it did not matter that I would have been the country corporate officer, or CEO, of Citibank Nigeria. Neither did it matter that we missed out on the beaches of Venezuela. God had a better plan for the Tshibakas: Madrid, Spain.

CHAPTER 33

Laughter and Light

Spain

OUR NEIGHBORHOOD IN MADRID, CALLED SOMOSAGUAS, WAS utterly delightful. It was the best place we ever lived as a family. Tree-lined streets curved back and forth across the hillsides. White and brightly painted houses stood here and there, surrounded by fields and trees, all perched on the edge of the massive city park known as Casa de Campo. Somosaguas itself was crisscrossed by sandy paths and dotted with ponderosa pine trees, serving as a buffer between us and the urban hustle of metropolitan Madrid. Priscilla made friends quickly, both with neighbors and through our involvement with Centro Cristiano Vida Nueva, part of the International Church of the Foursquare Gospel, one of the Protestant denominations in Spain. Soon it was common for her to walk those sandy paths in deep conversation or prayer.

You will recall we had originally chosen a house that belonged to the Spanish ambassador to Morocco, but it was taken off the market and we were forced to "settle" for a seven-bedroom mansion. I joked with my wife that we would have to buy a great deal of new furniture, only to regret my joke when her eyes lit up. Originally she had not been keen on the mansion, owing to the size of both its garden and its interior. But it soon came to feel like home.

Nearly every home in the vicinity was surrounded by tall hedges. The entrance to our home passed through green metal gates that opened inward automatically. Our driveway then circled a large fir tree in front of the house before returning to the street. Surrounding our home were wild plum trees that, late in the winter, put forth beautiful pink blossoms. There were also laurel bushes and poplar trees, whose silvery leaves shimmered in the breeze. A lovely lawn wrapped around two sides of our home, providing ample space for Niki and Mara—eleven and eight years old, respectively—to play games with their friends.

In the rear of our home, Priscilla's beloved wisteria vines produced a delightful fragrance in March and April each year, while petunias, impatiens, and other flowers contributed a rainbow of colors. An in-ground pool was the centerpiece of the backyard, but the space held other attractions as well. Closer to the stone patio was a barbecue grill and a basketball hoop, while beyond the pool was a volleyball and badminton court, along with a relaxing hammock.

Inside, the floors were a mix of parquet wood and tile, all illuminated during the days by many large windows. On summer evenings, which could be quite warm, we enjoyed swimming in the illuminated pool, then padding around barefoot on the patio, or even inside the house, feeling the coolness of the floors on the soles of our feet.

If this sounds like paradise, in many ways, it was. Not that every person in the neighborhood shared our delight. We did have a certain obstreperous neighbor who would yell at me in the summers, demanding that Niki and Mara make less noise during the traditional afternoon siesta time. However, that was when my children were waking up for the day, at which point I told them to go outside and play!

Niki and Mara's school, the American School of Madrid (ASM), was less than a ten-minute drive from our home, and certain friends lived so close to us that they could ride bikes to visit them. Niki loved the freedom of planning his own social schedule, and Priscilla and I loved that he was making friends and exercising. Around that time, we decided Niki and Mara would not be allowed to watch television during the school week. They would focus on their homework, and if they had extra time, they could play a sport, read a book, or hang out with friends. Niki made a habit of returning from school, doing his homework, and then riding his bike to a friend's home to play basketball. We were thrilled.

Several months later, we decided to join a video club as a family. This would allow us to see the latest movies on VHS from the comfort of our couch, in English no less, rather than traveling to the Spanish-language cinema in the city. During the first movie we watched, Niki proclaimed that a good scene was coming up. During the second and third movies, he spoke some of the key lines along with the characters on screen. During the fourth movie, he suggested he might skip the end because he already knew what was going to happen. After some light interrogation, we learned that his "basketball" friend was also a "movie" friend, and he had seen some movies we had yet to watch!

Mara, for her part, preferred to hang out with the boys. She would rather be shoved into a mud puddle than be subjected to the circles of gossip and backbiting that seemed to be prevalent in the social circles of girls her age. I recall one mixed-gender pool party Mara attended. She reported to us that the boys had decided to work together to throw her in the pool, but she had turned the tables, pushing every single boy into the water and then laughing from the edge. She could always handle herself.

Both Niki and Mara were stars in the various shows that were produced at the ASM, including *Cats* and *Guys and Dolls*, in which they played two of the main characters. They also shined performing together one of the songs from *The Phantom of the Opera*, delighting parents, teachers, and students, and bringing tears to our eyes. Priscilla and I could not help but be reminded of Mara's first large gathering rendition of "You Lift Me Up." She made us burst with pride, and in the process, she acquired even more friends, including the daughters of the ambassador of New Zealand to Spain and a high-ranking official from the US embassy. Her friendship with the daughters led us parents to develop closer relationships as well.

Priscilla and I were fortunate to enjoy our children at home most weekends, due in great measure to the fact that my wife made delicious meals and strategically determined to have treats of all kinds available for our children and their friends. Our home was the go-to place! We got to know and love their company, especially on weekends.

Moving to Madrid was the best thing that had happened to our family. Our home was filled with laughter and light.

CHAPTER 34

Shielded by My Redeemer

Spain

OUTSIDE THE HOME, MY BUSINESS AS CHIEF RISK OFFICER FOR Spain and Portugal continued to flourish.

Several years into our time in Madrid, I could have moved on to another position. Opportunities were always available within Citi's global network, and I had spent a relatively normal amount of time with that set of responsibilities. A senior credit officer, a member of Citicorp's credit policy committee, visited twice in one year and strongly urged me to consider moving to Japan as chief risk officer for Citibank in that country. I met with him secretly at the Madrid Ritz-Carlton Hotel, on his second visit and attempt at persuasion.

"A. T., Chairman John Reed has asked *me* to ask *you* to reconsider your position on Citibank Japan," he said. "This is a critically important career move, considering the significance of Japan for the bank." There was no way for me to tell whether John Reed had made the request or whether this was a tactic to get me to a yes response.

I was torn between a career move and the reality of life in Madrid. Priscilla and I had visited Tokyo previously as tourists, reconnecting with a Japanese colleague who used to work with me in Kinshasa as representative of Mitsubishi Bank. Takashi Suzuki had taken us around Tokyo, exposing us to the beauty of the city as well as its tight living accommodations. On a day with good visibility, we could admire the magnificence of Mount Fuji from the upper floor of our hotel. Nonetheless, I knew Priscilla was not keen at that time to entertain any thoughts of leaving Madrid. Additionally, my boss, the Iberia division head, had strongly urged me to remain in my position for the foreseeable future. We had been delivering great results: strong, growing, and sustainable profitability along with sound internal risk management and controls. We enjoyed an excellent working relationship, and we were finding favor with both coworkers and clients.

That is how I decided to turn down the offer of the position in Japan.

"I am truly flattered and grateful for the offer," I told the senior credit officer. "I had broached the idea of moving after our last encounter. Amador, my Spanish boss, feels we still have a lot of unfinished business in the Iberia division. And to be totally frank with you, a move now is a nonstarter for Priscilla and my teenagers. But please convey my heartfelt gratitude to the chairman."

As I further considered the issue, I understood remaining longer in one job was, for the first time in my career, a legitimate option. Previously in my career, moving posts relatively often had made sense. As a younger banker, I needed to do the bidding of my supervisors, which included relocating my family numerous times and averaging three years in any one country prior to my Madrid assignment. I had learned so many things during my career and served Citibank on three continents. No longer was there a risk of being pigeonholed professionally if I stayed in one place, and the kids were thriving at home, in school, and beyond.

So it was that our family chose to remain in Madrid, a decision that made all four of us quite happy. As the saying goes, "Happy wife, happy life." The decision assured peace in the Tshibaka household.

That is not to say my business life was entirely without difficulty. By God's grace, I had not tasted alcohol since January 1, 1985, in Kenya. My determination to refrain from alcohol faced a sterner test in Spain, owing to the wine culture.

For example, one of my duties with Citi was to lead some of our relationship managers on client calls.

These officers were responsible for developing and deepening the breadth and profitability of our business relationships with corporate, bank, institutional, and government entities. Our relationship managers were expected to deliver exceptional service to our target clients, anticipating and addressing their needs punctually. While their regular calls on clients had a primarily business focus, one of my roles as chief risk manager was to ensure they *also* watched for any emerging risks or problems with the client's business. Surfacing problems early would allow the bank to take preemptive steps, both to help the client manage those problems and to minimize their impact on the bank's portfolio and profitability.

My role went beyond watching for problems during the calls. Firsthand understanding of the clients' plans and needs allowed for speedier decision-making when I was subsequently presented with credit proposals. Our relationship management philosophy thus emphasized a balanced approach that aimed to maximize relationship-level returns while ensuring downsides were responsibly and proactively managed. That's what we called a well-rounded banker.

Among our portfolio of clients was Sogrape Vinhos de Portugal, a major winemaker located in northern Portugal. Because of the significance of their business portfolio with Citi, I took with me a larger-than-usual delegation of managers. We planned to visit the vineyards and production facilities, discern the current and future needs of the business, and do it all with a deft personal touch. In return, Sogrape Vinhos graciously welcomed us with their entire management team.

Of course, this plan entailed touring a winery in a country (and an industry) known for its hospitality. Naturally, our hosts wished us to sample every type of wine they were producing. Each time a waiter offered me a glass, I would take it, swirl it around, exclaim about the bouquet…and then subtly set it aside on a nearby table. The trouble was, by the time we had been presented with all their products, I was standing next to a table absolutely covered in unsampled wine glasses.

Fortunately, no one seemed to notice my subterfuge. Lunch, however, was another matter. I was seated at a banquet table next to the Sogrape Vinhos chairman, and I understood instantly there would be no place for me to hide my wine. To make matters worse, port wine was added to the table. Every person present seemed to be drinking glass after glass after glass, while I alone had a single, untouched glass in front of me.

Surely our hosts will notice I am not drinking, I worried to myself. *Will this insult them? Will it harm Citi's business?*

Yet despite the increasingly obvious fact that I was the only nondrinker present, not a single negative comment was made. Quite the opposite: As our visit ended, several on the Sogrape Vinhos team mentioned their respect for me.

Later, I reflected on the client call. I understood that when *God* is the one at work in our lives, we need not fear any outcome. I knew in my soul that the cessation of my drinking and smoking had both come from God, not from any special willpower or strength on my part. Therefore, I trusted God would be equally present in whatever happened because I no longer drank or smoked. Abstaining from alcohol did not impact even a penny of my business relationships, and for that happy outcome, I was doubly grateful to my Creator.

Although my alcohol abstinence did not have an adverse effect on my life or business, years later, I did resume drinking again, but only red wine. I felt I had the Lord's permission in this, and I remain grateful for everything He taught me during my dry spell.

Priscilla experienced a deep gratitude to God during that time as well.

Recall that we had been praying for Kim Abbott's wife, Alice, ever since her life-threatening car accident in Brazil. After we moved to Madrid, Priscilla and I were invited to a Citi conference outside of Lisbon. We had not been updated recently about the Abbotts, other than to know they would be at the same conference. We were anxious to see them.

The first night of the conference, Priscilla and I arrived fashionably late. We entered the reception, and both of us stopped in our tracks. There, in the center of the room, was Alice, *standing* beside Kim. She was laughing at something that had just been said. They looked entirely ordinary, which was so out of the ordinary that we could scarcely process what we were witnessing. Priscilla was so overcome with joy that she ran to the bathroom, hoping to find a place to cry and praise God in relative privacy.

The following morning, we met the Abbotts on one of the tennis courts. Kim was able to hit balls to Alice, and as long as they were within her reach, she was able to return them. This from a woman who, according to doctors, would never be able to walk again.

One outcome of God's goodness filling Priscilla and me with gratitude was a new ministry. With the blessing of Centro Cristiano Vida Nueva, we began to develop our relationships with missionaries. The value of the American dollar had dropped by a third against the value of the Spanish peseta, and it became increasingly common for missionaries to "crash out" of their ministry in Spain, simply because of the underlying economics. This was often accompanied by a sense of introspection and even personal failure.

Some of these missionaries truly needed to take time off, while others needed to be encouraged to keep up the good fight. Priscilla and I made it *our* mission to encourage and support them as best we could.

This took the form of praying and talking at our home, sometimes for hours at a time. Certain missionaries who needed a bit of refreshment were invited to stay in one of our spare bedrooms. At worst, they would return to their home countries with a feeling that they had been heard and loved. At best, they would be reenergized to return to their missionary endeavors.

They were a tremendous blessing to us as well, a source of encouragement and sustaining prayer whenever we had difficult situations requiring their prayer support. Many became some of our closest friends up to the time of this writing.

CHAPTER 35

We'll Take It!

Germany and Spain

IN 1995, AFTER I HAD BEEN IN MADRID FOR SEVEN YEARS, CITI launched a new initiative to support more than one thousand of the largest global businesses.

Out of the blue, I was approached to join the effort by Truett Tate in Citi's Frankfurt office. If I accepted the position of emerging markets region head for the global relationship bank, my territory would cover Eastern Europe, Central Europe, and Central Asia, and I would work out of Frankfurt, Germany. From Citi's perspective, I was the preferred candidate. The HR head in New York had also reached out, telling me there were six other candidates under consideration, but my skillset and history with the bank meant I would be able to smoothly transition into the position. It was mine to take or forgo. The idea was attractive to me as well.

But my perspective, and the perspective of the bank, were not the only ones that mattered!

I raised the issue that evening at dinner. Niki was away at university, and the three remaining Tshibakas were gathered at the table. I spoke around the edges of the issue, and I could tell Priscilla was listening, whereas Mara had largely tuned out my "work talk."

The instant I spoke the phrase "potential new position," I could tell I had crossed a line.

Priscilla's fork froze in midair, above her plate. Mara looked at her mother, then me, then back at her mother. Her mouth was agape.

"A. T. . . ." began my wife.

I knew there was no going back. I quickly divulged every detail of the job, including the location.

Priscilla set down her fork with a bit more force than was strictly necessary. "Frankfurt? *Germany?*"

"No way, Dad," added Mara. "Just *no way*. I still have two years before I graduate from high school! What about all my friends?"

"And what about Madrid?" asked Priscilla. "We *love* Madrid. We have our house, all our friends, and our church. We're comfortable and happy here. We are not moving!"

The following day, when I related this news to my prospective boss in Frankfurt, Truett Tate, he was undeterred. "At least bring your family up for the weekend, A. T.," Truett insisted. "Your wife and daughter will love the culture of the city!"

The truth was that Priscilla and Mara would love the free trip, as would I. Even so, I did not expect it to make any difference in our decision. That night at dinner, I told my wife and daughter, "Listen, Mr. Tate would like us to visit Frankfurt, and he will show us around the city. We cannot refuse a free trip like this, can we?"

"You're right," Priscilla grinned. "We can't. Not that it's going to change my mind, but why not get a free vacation out of the deal?"

"And shopping too!" added Mara.

"Welcome to Frankfurt, A. T.!"

Truett was waiting at the airport stairs for us, holding wide his arms and smiling.

He lifted our luggage into the trunk of his immaculate Mercedes E-Class and invited us to ride with him. "Notice, no company driver," he said as we took our seats. "I will be your driver today. Even better, I will provide you with a personal tour of Frankfurt!"

The city was a mix of medieval stone and ultramodern glass and steel, all bisected by the Main River. Truett pointed out the Citibank building and informed me my office would be on the fifth floor, just across from his. After the city tour was completed, it was time for dinner. Truett's wife, Dorthe, met us at a fancy sushi restaurant downtown, and everyone delighted in sampling akami, spring rolls, and spicy tuna. Everyone, that is, except me. I ordered a steak, well done!

We shared a wonderful conversation, and once Truett graciously covered the bill, Dorthe made a suggestion: "So…who wants to go clubbing?"

Mara immediately and vocally approved of the idea, and soon the five of us made our way to a nearby discotheque, where we danced the night away. (Our daughter shared later that she had not been impressed with our dance moves. We had apparently embarrassed her.) When at last we left the club, Truett informed us we would not be staying at a hotel. Rather, he and Dorthe would host us in their home.

As we walked to his car, Mara tapped me. "Dad, your boss…" she began, before stopping to search for the right word, "…is *cool!*"

At Tate's home, Truett stopped me and said, "Listen, A. T., tomorrow morning, Citi will send a driver for you and Priscilla and Mara. We have selected a few houses for you to look at…"

I interrupted, saying, "This will not make a difference…"

He patted down my objection with his hands, and continued, saying, "A few houses for you to *look* at with an agent, nothing more. This is just in case you change your mind, you see. In that case, it will be good to know which house you prefer?"

This was becoming a pattern: my seniors trying to entice a family relocation by showing us fancy houses. I should note this technique was not entirely without merit! Yet I had not made up my mind about the move, and as far as Priscilla and Mara were concerned, we were enjoying a wonderful, free trip to Germany.

The following morning, the first home we were shown by the Citi-approved agent was a twelve-bedroom manor that had once been owned by the Rothschild family. Inside, it consisted of dark, paneled wood, chandeliers, and hunting trophies, while outside it was surrounded by an acre of manicured grounds. I pretended to admire the home as we strolled through, but on the inside, I was mortified. I imagined hosting a senior from New York in such a mansion. *What kind of impression would they have?* Worse yet, our bedroom would be a five-minute walk from the kitchen!

The second house we were shown had belonged to some sort of high-ranking military officer in the United States Army. It was a modern four-story townhome that was clean and nice, but my wife and daughter had been spoiled by our home in Somosaguas, so "nice" was not going to move the needle for them.

The last house the agent showed us was much larger than the town-home and far less ostentatious than the Rothschild mansion. The floor-plan was well conceived, and the home had been recently renovated. Several walls had been replaced with floor-to-ceiling windows, and the main ground floor room was massive. It had been an outdoor swimming pool that had been paved over with granite tiles and enclosed with glass, creating picture windows opening on the lawn, a bubbling brook, and a nearby Japanese garden ringed with red maple trees. I watched from a distance as my wife and daughter took in the view, then moved together into the modern kitchen. They put their heads close and spoke quietly.

Then I heard my wife ask Mara, by way of confirmation, "Yeah?"

"Yeah!" answered Mara.

Yeah what? I wondered, walking toward them. I noticed Priscilla was grinning. "We'll take it!" she announced, unprompted.

"Yeah!" laughed Mara, "We'll take it!"

Before I could formulate a sentence, the agent pounced.

"Did I hear…"

"You did," answered Priscilla, pulling Mara into a hug, "we'll take it. It's perfect!"

Slow down, I thought. *I have not even decided to accept this position!*

•XOXOX•

The process was relatively straightforward from that point. Now that I had conditional permission from the Tshibaka women to move to Frankfurt, I needed to consider if I truly wanted the position.

I did!

So I moved to Frankfurt right away, with my personal computer and a single suitcase full of business attire.

Meanwhile, Priscilla and Mara remained in Madrid. The three of us decided it would be wise for Mara to finish her sophomore year of high school before moving to a new city. When her school year was completed, I returned to help them pack the personal belongings we would take with us on our flight to Frankfurt. For the rest, we enlisted a shipping company to pack and ship separately.

At last, after eight blissful years in Spain, it was time to say goodbye to Somosaguas.

Now that Germany was in front of us and Spain would soon be behind us, I felt an overwhelming sense of peace and gratitude about our time in Madrid. I knew Priscilla did as well. It was the sort of realization that made the transition to Germany easier, despite having to leave so many good things behind. In short, it was "mission well done," on all fronts.

As we rolled around the circular drive for the final time, and our house grew smaller behind us, tears were certainly shed.

"We're leaving our home," Mara said from the backseat.

Then the automatic gates closed behind us, and that chapter of our lives came to a close as well.

CHAPTER 36

Flourishing in Frankfurt

Germany

FRANKFURT WAS A LOVELY PLACE TO WORK. THE CITIBANK building was a short walk from the opera house, Alte Oper, which made it possible for Priscilla and me to rendezvous there for an occasional date whenever my work and travel schedules allowed. Both my office and Truett's office were walled top to bottom with glass, making them simultaneously transparent and private. Having offices adjacent to each other meant closer interactions whenever we found ourselves overlapping in Frankfurt. Our territory included Russia and the whole of Eastern Europe and Central Asia. That demanded a great deal of travel for meetings with our local management teams and joint calls with them regarding subsidiaries of global companies that fell within our target market.

I had moved from risk management to the business side of the bank. I was thrilled to be part of the senior management team charged with opening new markets and tapping into the business potential they presented. The Soviet Union had crumbled a few years earlier. Consequently, the emerging markets presented both great opportunities and significant difficulties. There were the typical pains inherent with any new business venture but also macro-level economic, political, cultural, legal, and regulatory challenges.

We kept busy. Many decisions had to be made on staffing as well as target client and product selections. Policies and procedures manuals had to be written and translated into the local languages. Time had to be invested in training the staff to ensure a seamless and flawless delivery of the bank's products and services to our chosen target market customers.

But we were successful. Business performance for the region rapidly improved, with profitable and growing operations across our assigned territory. Risks were tightly managed, and we were pleased with our progress.

During our time in Frankfurt, and the nearby town we lived in, Königstein im Taunus, we came to appreciate the direct nature of the German people. Upon meeting our neighbors for the first time, Priscilla prepared a cake for them, which the three of us took to their door, aiming to introduce ourselves as we had done in other countries. We handed the cake to them and let them know we were their new neighbors. As we said our goodbyes, the husband said clearly and very slowly for emphasis, "Thank you for the cake and the visit. Please don't expect us to become your friends."

We kept smiles on our faces, but we felt hurt. Later, however, we came to appreciate our neighbors' forthrightness. Because they knew we would be in Germany for only a few years, they did not want to waste time investing in a friendship with us. Even though we would not have dreamed of saying such a thing, we understood, and respected, their logic.

Another time, I needed to refresh my stock of passport photos. I found a local shop, and the photographer, a young woman, refused to sell me the twenty-four photos I was asking for.

"No, sir, I will *not* give you twenty-four," she insisted. "I will only give you four."

We argued back and forth. Frustrated, I inquired what kind of business she was running. I was a customer, prepared to pay for her services, and yet she refused to help me!

"Sir, if I develop twenty-four photos, and they turn out to be not what you want, you would be wasting your money on a poor product," she explained. "That is why I will develop four. If they turn out badly, the cost will be bearable for both of us."

I understood and felt immediately grateful to her. Later, the thought occurred to me: In America, the photographer would have encouraged me to buy forty-eight instead of twenty-four and enticed me with a bulk discount!

On the home front, Priscilla and Mara were adapting quite well. Each made friends within Königstein and surrounding towns, both among the expat community and German people.

Mara enrolled in Frankfurt International School, located in the next town over. She quickly blossomed in her new school, whose mascot was the Frankfurt Warrior. Besides her academic success, she threw her heart and soul into competitive soccer and basketball. Priscilla and I, when my work allowed, accompanied her on some of her road trips around Europe for matches and tournaments. On the pitch and the court, she earned the nickname "Predator," after the famous movie series from that time. To opposing team members, she was awesomely frightening, both in her dribbling moves and the way she would stop to shake her braided hair. She never held anything back.

Mara continued to be involved in theater and music as well. It was the latter talent that attracted the attention of a German music agent. He believed Mara could become a professional pop star and consequently presented us with a contract that would have allowed Mara to embrace a music career at age seventeen. We met to negotiate terms and conditions, and eventually we arrived at a draft contract. Importantly, it gave Mara's parents final approval on the lyrics of any song she would be asked to record. After much discussion as a family, we concluded that a move into the music industry was not the best plan for a high schooler. It seemed Mara had a choice between pursuing a college education and forgoing college to focus on music. We said no to the music agent, and possible fame, but Mara accepted the decision.

CHAPTER 37

A Steinway Incentive

Germany

YEARS EARLIER, NEAR THE END OF MY TIME IN BRAZIL, I HAD MET a Citibank Executive named Dipak Rastogi during a trip to the bank's headquarters in New York. Dipak was a once-in-a-generation banking genius. Of Indian origin, his short stature belied what would be his outsize impact on global banking. He had graduated top of his class in business school, after which Citi immediately hired him and put him to work as a trader. He excelled and was promoted at an incredibly rapid clip. In fact, he was among the elite cadre of bankers who invented derivatives. When we were introduced in 1988, I was performing an audit of his derivatives business in New York, and I noticed Citi executives were already eyeing him for a senior leadership position.

In 1998, I was working in Frankfurt when Dipak called me out of the blue. Truett was moving on to greater things elsewhere, and Citibank wanted Dipak to be exposed to managing a geography and customer relationships. He had clearly proven himself on the product side of banking. His new responsibilities would round out his banking experience, thus positioning him for even more senior executive positions in the bank.

"A. T., I have been hearing a lot about you from my colleagues. You remember we met years ago in New York when you audited my business?"

We exchanged pleasantries for several minutes, and then he got to the point.

"A. T., I have been appointed to replace Truett as executive VP responsible for Central and Eastern Europe as well as Central Asia. I want you to join me. You will be my right-hand man for that region. In addition to your global relationship banking responsibilities, you will be the chief risk officer for Central and Eastern Europe and Central Asia."

I was intently listening, registering the surprising development.

"I will share more face-to-face. I am right now in Moscow and will travel through Frankfurt on my way back to New York. Can we meet at Frankfurt International Airport?" he asked.

I considered his words. Something seemed a bit too good to be true. I was curious and excited, true, but at the same time apprehensive and concerned. I decided to hold off the many questions popping through my head. They could wait for the meeting in person, so I confirmed my intention to meet him at the airport.

My apprehension and concern shared two main causes. The first was that I was comfortably settled in my work in Frankfurt. I enjoyed the collegial atmosphere in the office, and my business trips to CEECA (Central and Eastern Europe and Central Asia) countries provided a welcome change of scenery, both professional and cultural. And now I was being asked to leave my stable and comfortable life in Germany to resettle in Warsaw, Poland? Dipak had made it clear during our phone conversation that he was seriously considering moving our regional headquarters to Warsaw. He wanted us to base our leadership team inside an emerging market, and Poland seemed an ideal location for that move.

The second concern revolved around breaking the news about this potential move to my wife. Thankfully, Mara had already moved and joined her brother at Amherst College.

I did not have to confront and try to convince two women with their own agendas—agendas that did not always seem to align with the opportunities coming my way on the professional front. Assuming I accepted Dipak's offer, which was not yet a done deal, how would I get my wife to bless the move and, if possible, do so enthusiastically?

When we finally met that evening, Dipak and I talked nonstop for some three hours, which at the time seemed like an eternity. Dipak tackled all my questions regarding his expectations for how the position would combine global relationship banking and risk management. We also covered at length his game plan and objectives for the region. As we talked about how we would work together, he further sweetened his offer by piling on more roles to my new position. I would also head Citicorp venture capital business for CEECA. At the time, the latter business was headquartered in Prague, Czech Republic.

Our conversation went on and on, and I felt increasingly unable to dissuade him. The reasons he wanted me to join him were myriad, but most important, at least from his point of view, I was the perfect candidate to head the multifaceted portfolio of businesses and functions he would be delegating to me. At one point, he paused and looked at me with unflinching, self-confident eyes,

"A. T., I don't give up easily. We will work together," he said with finality, as one who already had his fish hooked and was patiently weighing options for pulling it into the boat. He was tenacious, yes, but he also seemed sincere and trustworthy.

"Why don't you process all that we covered during our conversation this evening?" he suggested. "I will call you from New York and we can start mapping out our next steps."

Nonetheless, I was still assessing him, quietly. Would we have good chemistry in our relationship? Would we develop and nurture collaborative interactions, or would we have to navigate many collisions, even as we pursued mutually agreed-on goals? *If he is so stubborn in his pursuit of me*, I wondered, *will he listen to sound advice when offered?*

Still, I was mentally prepared to say yes at our airport meeting, but I held back. There were yet other conversations to be had—namely, with my permanent *boss* at home. The face-to-face with my wife was going to be more complicated, demanding a great deal of tact.

"Dipak, you have been so kind to think of me. Thank you for stopping in Frankfurt and for the time you have taken to share your vision for CEECA and the work ahead. I will give serious consideration to your offer, but I must first discuss all of this with my wife."

I would be remiss if I did not, at this point, drop *another* name who I know was proactively rooting for me behind the scenes. Usama Mikdashi was a member of Citicorp's credit policy committee. Like Kim Abbott, he was well respected and a great influence within the bank. Sam, as we called him, was the same man who had shown up earlier in Madrid, twice, to attempt to persuade me to take the chief risk management position for Japan. Originally from Lebanon, he likely was aware of my performance at the Beirut Training Center decades earlier and must have been following my career very closely since then. He was one of the people Dipak had gone to for input on me. I am grateful to him and so many others the good Lord placed along my life's path. Scripture comes to mind: "Even to your old age I am He, and even to your advanced old age I will carry you! I have made you, and I will carry you; Be assured I will carry you and I will save you" (Isaiah 46:4 AMP).

How would I broach the subject with Priscilla? Another move would not be welcomed. She had a happy life in Königstein. She enjoyed her women's group through our church, had regular tennis dates with me, and loved teaching piano lessons to kids from the area. Not to mention, Warsaw had only recently emerged from the darkness of communism. Even though it would only be Priscilla and myself moving, *any* move entailed the effort and stress of packing, unpacking, and then adapting to a new culture. Worse, we would have to leave church and friends behind, yet again. My wife had truly sacrificed to leave Spain for Germany. As it turned out, she enjoyed Germany…and I would be asking her to leave for Warsaw?

I decided to take a direct approach. "Look, I am thinking of accepting Dipak's offer to move to Warsaw."

Talk about direct! The effect, however, was negligible. Priscilla, for some reason, did not react to my statement.

I cast around for another way to approach the subject. Priscilla and I had always wanted children. We had even used the term many to describe my vision in the past. She came from a family with two other siblings, while I came from a family with five other siblings, though only five of us had survived childhood. I had made it very clear while dating Priscilla that my goal was a minimum of five children. To achieve that, we would first *work* on producing three boys, to be followed by two girls.

God, however, determined that we would have a boy and a girl first. Priscilla felt she had achieved her goal with a boy and a girl. And going from two to five children no longer seemed possible. She had rebuffed any attempt from me or my family to bless us with at least one more child. I was now in my early forties, and Priscilla was approaching forty. It was too late to keep pushing the impossible. As Priscilla kept reminding me, just because Sarah gave Abraham a child in her old age did not mean the same would happen for us!

In the past, I had attempted to use the promise of a grand piano to attempt to sway my wife toward having more children. However, she had categorically stated it would not happen, and I had irrevocably taken the grand piano off the table as a bargaining chip.

A thought occurred to me. *Perhaps I could get Priscilla to accept moving to Warsaw in exchange for a grand piano?*

For a pianist of her caliber, owning a grand piano would be akin to an art collector owning a famous painting. Whenever in the past I had mentioned a third child and a piano in the same breath, Priscilla's response would be, "If I have another kid, I won't have time to play the piano! The offer is not realistic."

I therefore decided on a different approach. "How about a move to Warsaw in exchange for a grand piano?"

That caught my wife off guard.

I continued, saying, "Warsaw will be wonderful. Do not ask me how I know. I just think we will have a lot of opportunities and exciting things to do there. The grand piano is back on the table...if *you* agree to move there with me."

Now I had my wife's attention. Her raised eyebrows asked for confirmation.

"You will have a grand piano," I affirmed, "*and* you will have time to play it!"

Her eyes took on a faraway look as a beautiful smile graced her face. She breathed a single word, and with it I knew we would be moving to Warsaw.

"Chopin!"

CHAPTER 38

London Calling

Poland, Austria, and Germany

SOON, THE TWO OF US WERE ABLE TO MOVE FROM FRANKFURT TO Warsaw, and Priscilla was able to take delivery of her grand piano. Finding the right grand piano proved difficult. While Poland was the birthplace of Chopin, Priscilla and I had decided to travel to Austria, the country of Mozart, in search of the perfect model. Unfortunately, Priscilla decided she did not favor any of the pianos on offer in Vienna, but that did not stop us from attending a performance of the Vienna Boys' Choir.

Our next step was to make an appointment at the Steinway factory in Hamburg, Germany. To my wife's trained ear, Steinways were too "brilliant" sounding, at least as represented by the models available in the United States during her upbringing. Fortunately, the story was different at the factory in Hamburg. Priscilla was granted two hours to try out various models, and when Claude Debussy's *Clair de Lune*, played in the upper register on a seven-and-a-half foot Steinway, brought her to tears, she knew she had found her grand piano.

If the piano was hard to choose, so was a home in Warsaw. Unlike previous moves, we did not enjoy the luxury of looking at as many houses. Thinking creatively, Priscilla identified a home still under construction. A deal was struck: If we could pay six months of rent up front, the builder would allow us to customize the lighting, flooring, appliances, and so on. Dipak approved the six-month rental advance, and the amount was sufficient to complete the house.

In Warsaw, Priscilla and I enjoyed the low cost of living, a welcome break after Germany and Spain. We practically survived on filet mignon and French cheese. At that time, an entire filet was ten dollars, as was a massage for Priscilla. What we missed in the variety of food choices was more than compensated for by the freshness and quality of our groceries.

We grew fond of Poland. It was cold and dark in the winter, yes, but we found the people to be warm and welcoming, and the landscape held a spare beauty whenever we ventured outside of Warsaw. Across the street from the Citi offices was one of the largest opera houses in the world, the Teatr Wielki, where we were treated to shows regularly. All that was needed was for Priscilla to call and tell me a particular show was running at the opera house. Then she would join me at the office, and we would walk together to the show.

The same was not true of movie theaters. I once took her out to see a film, and we were told to return at the same time the following day. We learned movie theaters were usually packed, so we resolved we would stick to shows at the opera house.

Unfortunately, less than a year into our time in Poland, Citibank decided to move the Warsaw office to London. Although this decision was spearheaded by Dipak, I saw the logic in it. Warsaw made better sense on paper than in reality. International travel to and from Warsaw was not adequate, and communications were unreliable. That made it difficult for the efficient functioning of a regional office. I agreed with the decision to move, but I still had to break the news to my wife.

I began with a trial balloon at dinner one night. "Out of curiosity, what would you say if we had to move to London?" I asked. I prayed, for my own safety, that my light tone and small smile would convince her I was joking.

"Ha!" she responded. "Don't even mention the word *move* again! That's a bad joke, Tshibaka!" (When she forgot about A. T. and transitioned to *Tshibaka*, I knew she was upset with me or had determined a scolding was warranted.)

I looked around the room at several boxes from Frankfurt, belongings we had yet to unpack. I quickly changed the subject.

Several weeks later, I brought up the subject again. By then, enough time had passed that I was relatively sure my bride would not kill me…

and I was right. Priscilla sighed, but in truth she agreed with the decision. She knew that London would be a better place to live and a better location for our office in the long run. The UK had far more to offer in cultural and culinary attractions than Warsaw, and shopping would be a delight for Priscilla. We would join a new church and make new friends. The transaction closed without me having to resort to begging… or bribing…or both.

London was calling, and the time had come to answer.

CHAPTER 39

Microfinance and Poverty Alleviation

London

THE THREE YEARS I SPENT WORKING FOR DIPAK RASTOGI WERE among the most challenging, but also the most fulfilling, of my career to that point. He had become a close friend, and as it turned out, we would support and encourage each other through our careers and beyond.

You will recall he had fought hard for me to join him as chief risk head for Central and Eastern Europe, Central Asia, and ultimately the Indian subcontinent, Middle East, and Africa. To further entice me, he had asked me to continue as regional head for global relationship banking in the same geographic region.

This was a heavy load to carry, but I thrived on it. We were able to open full banking operations for Citibank in new markets such as Ukraine, Kazakhstan, and Slovakia. The Russian crisis of 1998 added to the demands of my position, as much extra travel and time were needed for difficult and sustained negotiations with our Russian obligors, particularly our counterparts in the banking sector.

Priscilla and I found a place to live in Cobham, roughly forty minutes from London. I worked extremely long hours in that season of my career, often taking the last train out of London and arriving home around midnight!

Work commitments did not prevent us from joining a local church. The International Protestant Church in the nearby town of Esher became a place of spiritual nurture and deep friendships for us.

It was at this church we met Adrian Merryman and his family. During our friendship, he shared with us about an international organization that focused on poverty alleviation. Opportunity International, he informed us, strove to provide individuals with a hand-up rather than a hand-out, using targeted microloans and other products tailored to the needs of the poor such as savings accounts, microinsurance policies, and financial literacy training. As a banker and advocate for poverty alleviation, this was a cause that greatly appealed to me.

Priscilla and I sought to learn as much as we could about Opportunity International, which at that time was assisting more than a third of a million people worldwide.

Many stories were shared with us by Adrian and others, but one in particular made a lasting impression.

There had been a woman in the Philippines who, along with her children, lived inside a literal garbage dump. Upon waking each morning, she and her children scavenged the dump for scraps of food and nearly worthless items that perhaps held some fraction of worth for them. This all-day activity was undertaken separately by each family member, including the smallest children, so that more ground could be covered. As a father, my heart broke for that family.

Providentially, the woman heard about Opportunity International from another scavenger. After applying to the program, she was granted an initial loan of only sixty dollars. With that modest sum, she purchased the necessary cooking supplies and ingredients to make traditional Filipino donuts, which she had learned how to make in her youth. She then sold the donuts on the street outside the garbage dump. Each day she divided her profits between donut ingredients, loan payments, and savings. And rather than relying on the moldy scraps of food discarded by locals, the mother was able to buy fruit and fresh bread for her children.

As word spread of the mother's baking talents, her clientele grew by leaps and bounds. She sold dozens of sweet treats per week, then a hundred, then several hundred.

Eventually, the family was able to move out of the dump and into stable housing. All the while she was acquiring business skills and squirreling away small amounts of money. It all added up and, several years after her initial loan, she opened the doors to her own restaurant in the city. Later, she was to launch a transport business, having purchased a few *jeepneys* or small buses with the profits from her restaurant.

By the time her story was told to us, that hardworking, resourceful woman had sent her daughter for studies at a university in Canada and, instead of waking up in the dump, she was employing dozens of locals with good jobs. She had achieved all that...not with a hand-out, but with a hand-up from Opportunity International.

Her story stunned Priscilla and me. It set my mind and heart racing. I found myself pondering Opportunity International as I went about my duties at work. I became convinced that the organization was the perfect place for me to use my banking experience to help others living in abject poverty, as I once had.

With that in mind, Priscilla and I joined Opportunity International as volunteer supporters. We became immersed in the nuts and bolts of how it functioned. Opportunity International emphasized financial training wherever they operated, which at the time was in around thirty countries. Potential clients were placed into groupings of perhaps twenty to thirty people. Each class was taught by someone from the organization and covered financial literacy: budgeting and bookkeeping, cash flow management, entrepreneurial and stewardship principles, and so on. The participants were taught how to handle themselves as borrowers, taking responsibility to repay their loans within the agreed contractual time frames and conducting their businesses ethically.

While these classes were ongoing, Opportunity International staff would observe which participants seemed to have leadership and entrepreneurial potential, demonstrated by their grasp of the concepts and the way they related to their fellow participants. When the training concluded, "trust groups" would be formed with around a dozen members each. The groups would agree to their own governance structure, usually choosing a president, a treasurer, and a secretary from among the members. Group members met weekly to review and share experiences from the preceding week, pay loan installments due, distribute new funding from Opportunity International, and discuss any new business initiatives members were contemplating. This could range from growing, roasting, and selling peanuts to producing leather sandals. At that point, the group could approach Opportunity International for a loan with which to launch the business. With each cycle of loan repayment, the group could ask for a larger loan, using it to grow the business, with the goal of becoming self-sustaining.

I was most impressed with the effectiveness of the trust groups. Each member supported and cross-guaranteed the others. Because of this mutually supportive setup, one "bad apple" would be unable to ruin the bunch. Whether for excellent reasons, such as a shared sense of purpose, or weaker reasons, such as not wanting to appear unfit compared to one's peers, the loan guarantee was almost ironclad.

Over time, participants could graduate into smaller trust groups. A woman who sold sandals, for example, might leave a dozen-member trust group and join a group with five or fewer members. And it was these groups which went on to produce individual borrowers, along with small- and medium-sized enterprise owners, who became sources of employment within their communities. Thus could the virtuous cycle from poverty to self-empowered job creation be completed.

Opportunity International arrived in our lives at the perfect time. Priscilla and I had begun pondering what it would look like for me to retire. When would the best time be, and where would we live? More importantly, how would we give back our time, talents, and finances to the work of God's kingdom?

I was relatively certain I would not work until I passed away. And I was *certain* I wanted to make a much greater positive impact outside of professional banking before I was too old to be effective.

These considerations occupied our hearts. We did not yet know the next chapters in the story of our lives, but we suspected Opportunity International would be part of our post-banking life together.

CHAPTER 40

From Refugee to Risk Titan

New York and London

I MOVED TO NEW YORK CITY IN JULY 2002 AS CHIEF RISK OFFICER for the newly created Citigroup International. Following the merger of Citicorp and Traveler's Group in 1998, a new banking giant was born: Citigroup. With that development came the renaming of the international part of the bank as Citigroup International. Citigroup wanted to harmonize risk management policies across the merged entities.

More specifically, the new senior executive team in New York had heard about our disciplined approach to risk management in Central and Eastern Europe, Middle East and Africa Group (CEEMEA). In early 2002, I organized a risk management conference in Prague, Czech Republic. Attendees included seniors from New York: Chuck Prince, then Citigroup's chief operating officer; Petros Sabatacakis, Citigroup's chief risk officer; and Ann Goodbody, the senior-most credit officer for Citicorp. Ann was due to retire, and the three of them surprised me with the news that the bank had chosen me to replace Ann after her retirement mid that year.

As it turned out, crafting the necessary policies with my counterpart from Traveler's Group was far easier than instilling them at cultural and practical levels, especially in a transaction- or deal-driven organization, one that differed from the relationship-focused approach that had characterized Citicorp. More and more, bankers around me seemed to be motivated by bonuses and self-advancement. As I led, trained, or mentored them, I sometimes felt I was beating my head against the proverbial wall.

My banking culture was not their banking culture. It was as if we were attempting to marry radically different cultures, and while I knew something about that at a personal level, I was frustrated at a professional level.

Even as the culture drifted in what felt to me like the wrong direction, the leadership situation for my part of Citigroup stabilized with the appointment of Stan Fisher, who joined as vice chairman and president of Citigroup International. He had previously been deputy managing director of the International Monetary Fund. Upon his arrival, I had a dual reporting line to both him and Petros Sabatacakis, a fine man of unquestioned ethics and integrity, who was appointed chief risk officer of Citigroup. Stan and Petros were both excellent leaders. Warm and friendly, but no-nonsense when it came to risk-related decisions, they supported me unequivocally on some of the tough calls I had to make from time to time with respect to significant credit transactions.

As always, I endeavored to do my work with integrity, seeking to accomplish what I knew was in the best interest of the bank.

Priscilla and I lived in Ardsley, New York, a forty-minute train ride from my office in New York City. I was grateful that the commute gave me time to think about and pray for my wife, Niki and Mara, my extended family, and the challenges facing me at work.

At the time, Niki was completing his doctorate in law at Harvard Law School and dating a beautiful and bright young woman, Kelly Hartline, who would become his wife. Mara was finishing her BA at Amherst College, working on a double major in Spanish and German.

If everything went according to what Priscilla and I were planning, I would retire from banking at the end of 2004 and then deepen my involvement with Opportunity International.

Just after moving from London to New York City, Ken Vander Weele, president of Opportunity International Network, visited me in my office to offer me the position of chief operating officer of Opportunity International Network. I declined. I had just begun a new position with Citigroup, where a gargantuan task of joining cultures awaited me. Still, the meeting confirmed in my heart that Opportunity International held a place in my future.

It was during my time working for Citigroup in New York that my former boss in Frankfurt, Truett Tate, called me. He was working for Lloyds TSB Bank in London.

"A. T., let me ask you something. Are you happy?"

"Yes!" I replied, without hesitation. I was doing what I loved, after all, and not quite ready for retirement. Perhaps he had not been expecting such a definitive response.

"Oh, well," he responded, sounding casual, "I simply wanted to know if you are happy, and you are. Good, let's stay in touch."

I thought nothing of his question until, several months later, he called again. After we exchanged pleasantries, he asked, "How are you really doing these days? Are you sure you are happy?"

That certainly sounded like a loaded question. I reiterated that I was happy, but he was, it seemed, after something else. "I *am* planning to retire, even though I am happy. I cannot bank forever, after all. Why do you ask?"

"The grapevine has it that you are coming to London on a business trip," he told me. "If I were to arrange several meetings, would you mind talking to some of my colleagues? No commitment, A. T., I just want you to hear a little bit about Lloyds TSB Bank."

I agreed. It was August 2004 when I went to London on a business trip. With retirement from Citi looming, I saw no reason *not* to speak with the various bank officers. What was the worst that could happen?

Truett had arranged meetings with what amounted to a hiring committee for me! I spoke with the head of human resources, senior bankers, and even the CEO, all as part of an effort to convince me to leave Citi and join LTB as risk director for their wholesale and international division.

My plan *had* been to retire at the end of 2004, not merely from Citi but from professional banking. At that point, I wanted to focus on supporting the work of Opportunity International as a pro bono volunteer.

Additionally, Priscilla and I had chosen the plot of land in Virginia on which we would build our dream home for our retirement years.

Yet, as I pondered Truett's offer, I realized the timing of my retirement from Citibank could change slightly. Why not continue to be productive while our home was under construction? Why not work with a trusted friend and embark on a new banking adventure for a short time?

So it was that I decided the best way to retire was to continue working full-time at another bank, at least for the time being.

CHAPTER 41

To Everything There Is a Season

New York

On December 14, 2004, I sent an email to Citi employees in the seventy-seven countries I was overseeing. I would like to quote from it at length because it captured an important moment of transition in my life.

> Dear One and All,
>
> "There is a time for everything, and a season for every activity under heaven…" (Ecclesiastes 3:1).
>
> After a little over thirty-three years with Citibank, I have decided to retire. My retirement is effective January 1, 2005. As most of you know, this has been a fruitful and varied career. Looking back, I am truly thankful for the many great professionals and good human beings I have had the privilege to work with and for the many contributions made toward creating the great institution that we all came to love, and our competitors came to fear, if not emulate:
>
> We opened new franchises in new emerging countries and built the business from scratch.
>
> We managed difficult country crises, from bloody coups d'état to economic/financial crises and natural disasters.
>
> We put people first and made sure they were safe since they were to be instrumental in helping us reposition the business for growth.

We were tough and yet objective and fair in the way we assumed our auditing responsibilities for Latin South during the turbulent mid to late 1980s.

We built a vibrant business in the Iberia Division, with quality credit process and portfolio.

As part of the geographic business leadership of the Global Relationship Bank in the mid-1990s, we organized, galvanized, and motivated the relationship management teams who, through a consistent strategy and focused execution, have made a positive and lasting impact, building a peerless customer organization.

In CEEMEA and in EM Credit Risk Management, notwithstanding the periodic crises characteristic of emerging markets, we built sound credit disciplines and contributed to the building of a robust and yet paced, predictable, and sustainable business growth.

We have held on to the strong belief and have been guided by the unshakable principle that, of all the responsibilities we shoulder as a financial services company, developing people and helping them to advance as far as their abilities permit must rank at the very top of our goals.

I go with the unique honor and joy of having served with colleagues who have had such a tremendously positive effect on my growth as a professional and as a human being. I am equally pleased to see a number, those whose lives I may have wittingly or unwittingly touched, in positions of responsibility and continuing to make a real difference for our shareholders, for our customers, for the communities we have the privilege to serve, and for our colleagues.

Keep up the good work and choose to do the right thing, and to do it right always, including when this may entail some personal cost! I wish you and your loved ones a blessed and joyous holiday season!

In closing, I shared a favorite inspirational quote, taken from Bob Buford's *Half Time: Changing Your Game Plan from Success to Significance.*

> "Then there is the reality of the game itself: The clock is running. What once looked like an eternity ahead of you is now within reach. And while you do not fear the end of the game, you do want to make sure that you finish well, that you leave something behind no one can take away from you. If the first half was a quest for success, the second half is a journey to significance."

From success to significance and with gratitude,

A.T.

Less than one month later, five days from my sixty-first birthday, I would no longer be working for Citi, after serving the company for thirty-three years.

Despite my colleagues' insistence, I did not want an elaborate farewell. Nor did I need one. My years at Citi had defined a large portion of my life, yes, but that did not mean I wanted to stand up in front of colleagues at our head office to be celebrated, or worse, to be waved off! I simply wanted to leave remembering the long-lasting relationships I had made and the problems my teams and I had been able to tackle without fear or trembling. A corporate farewell seemed akin to displaying myself like a museum exhibit.

Unfortunately, my wishes did not prevail. My colleagues would not relent in their campaign to lure me back for a proper farewell. Even after I had left, I was pestered to return. Whether in emails or phone calls, the sentiments I heard were the same. *Please, A. T., come back for a goodbye. We need to have a proper goodbye.* You *need a proper goodbye.*

Suspecting the pressure would never relent, I relented! Soon after agreeing to a farewell party, during a business visit to New York in the summer of 2005, I stepped out of the company car at 399 Park Avenue at the foot of the forty-one-story Citibank building. I knew it would be my last visit to a building in which I had spent countless hours. Indeed, as I craned my neck to look upward, I recalled a certain youthful Dartmouth graduate who had entered another Citibank building with trepidation more than three decades before. While it seemed like a moment ripe for self-reflection, in my mind and heart, I had already moved on to the next season of my life, anticipating all that was in store. I was eager to attend the party, say my piece, then depart as quickly as possible, with minimal fanfare.

There was one condition about the party in which my desire had prevailed: The number of attendees was to be kept to a minimum. Rather than inviting all the bank's senior staff, as would have been typical for someone in my position, we had invited people only from my department and the department of my counterpart, Dave Bushnell, who was hosting the event.

When it came time for me to give a speech in response to the very generous words Dave had directed my way, I knew exactly the message I wished to convey. I wanted my last words to my colleagues to cut through all the rush and bluster of banking and reveal the heart of the matter.

"My friends, thank you for all of this." I gestured at the food, drinks, and decorations. "If you will allow me, I would like to say a few words."

Cheers and clapping answered in the affirmative. I looked down, took a breath, and began the speech I had been composing for several weeks.

"Every day you are called on to make difficult decisions, as professionals with responsibilities in the bank. But every day you must strive to make those decisions as *people*, with intellect and conscience, not merely as bank employees. All of us are confronted with choices in life. No matter the job, no matter the position, we will be required to make choices. Some are simple choices all of us would make. Others, however, are more difficult, requiring courage. I believe it is in those moments that we will discover who we really are, what we are made of, our real character.

"I have no doubt each of you will reach a fork in the road. You will have to make a difficult choice that only you can make. Perhaps it will be tomorrow, or perhaps it will not be for weeks, months, or even years, but you *will* reach a fork. When you do, I believe you will *know* in your heart which way is right and which way is not. At that moment, avoid shortcuts. Avoid short-term thinking. Do not focus on plaudits, or bonuses, or attempts to earn the approval of your coworkers or supervisors."

I paused and scanned the faces. I had the full attention of all present.

"Rather, at each fork, do what is *right*. Do what is right for this bank in the short *and* long term. Do what is right for the bank's stakeholders, including its customers, shareholders, staff, regulatory authorities, and communities it serves. Doing the right thing has consequences, and those consequences will not always be positive. Sometimes doing what is right can be costly, but do it anyway. Allow a 'Well done!' from your conscience!"

Without saying it, I was thinking of several verses of the Bible I had come to appreciate as applicable to my approach to professional work. "Whatever you do, whether in word or deed, do it all in the name of the Lord Jesus, giving thanks to God the Father through him.... Whatever you do, work at it with all your heart, as working for the Lord, not for human masters, since you know that you will receive an inheritance from the Lord as a reward. It is the Lord Christ you are serving" (Colossians 3:17, 23–24 NIV).

With that, I held up my glass for a final toast, and the room, which had been completely silent, erupted in applause.

Lloyds TSB Bank informed me that the paperwork needed for me to live and work in London was still being finalized. However, they had an American office in New York, located on the Avenue of the Americas. I could work out of that office for several months until it was time to move to London.

So, bright and early on a Monday morning, two days after retiring from Citi, I boarded the train for New York to begin my new job with Lloyds TSB. I allowed myself to reflect on my career to that point.

Thirty-three years and eleven country moves and related promotions. Through it all, I had shown myself to be what people often termed "old school," very disciplined and serious about adhering to bank policies and procedures.

Old *guard* might have been a more accurate term. I valued operating by the book as trained by Citicorp, but not *only* by the book. I also understood the importance of sound business management and the worth of developing and nurturing solid relationships. With each passing year, I met more and more bankers who thought nothing of ignoring essential social and business requirements, to say nothing of the temptation and growing willingness to skirt sound banking disciplines.

I could understand and work with a staff member who made an honest mistake or an unintentional error of judgment. Spending time mentoring such a staff member was always satisfying to me. Intentional violations of sound banking disciplines, whatever the reasons or motivations, were something I found hard to tolerate.

I knew some of my fellow executives, especially the newer ones in the merged conglomerate, viewed my values negatively. This was to be expected, and it was compounded by the fact that I had the final say on credit proposals they had spent a great deal of time on. I often asked them to address issues in their proposals, which could result in changes to the deal structures and more negotiations with clients. Still, I tried to understand and respect where my fellow bankers were coming from, and I hoped they could understand and respect that I was doing my job.

As I surveyed the banking landscape, it seemed many had lost their way. I was coming to suspect the path forward was actually a return to the past. I had wanted to change the culture of Citigroup. That had been the mandate given to me by Petros Sabatacakis in 2002 during a conversation at that risk management conference in Prague. A tall task to be sure! There was so much left for me to do. So much, in fact, that my spirit understood I would never accomplish it in my lifetime.

My lofty goal had been to instill integrity and discipline at every level of the bank. Perhaps labeling that aspiration as "lofty" was an error.

Rather, it was merely what was to be expected from excellent, well-balanced bankers!

I wondered if the situation would be different at Lloyds TSB Bank.

CHAPTER 42

Transitioning to Retirement

London

BACK TO LONDON FOR ROUND TWO!

Priscilla and I located temporary accommodations in Walton-on-Thames and resumed our attendance at the International Protestant Church, where we reconnected with old friends.

The contract I had signed with Lloyds TSB was for two years, though at the end of that contractual arrangement, I was asked to extend my stay at the bank indefinitely. While I recognized the offer as a testament to my banking skills, experience, and reputation, the offer conflicted with my vision for the future.

Over the previous half decade, my heart had steadily put down roots outside of my professional life, specifically in the field of poverty alleviation. That did not mean I lessened my effort as a banker, of course. It simply meant I was actively praying about what God was calling me to do and when He was calling me to do it. My motto, as always, was to serve where I could be used for a worthy cause.

My plan to work only briefly with Lloyds TSB Bank soon crashed on the rocky shore of reality. We negotiated and agreed to a six-month contract extension, during which efforts would be made to hire my replacement.

I was responsible for risk management for the wholesale and international division of the bank. This division encompassed all corporate and investment banking as well as commercial businesses (small and medium-sized enterprises, or SMEs). The role and consequent responsibilities demanded a compromise on my part. The request to extend the contract itself was not unreasonable, but the indefinite timing of it was. I was already investing time and finances into Opportunity International's work. Serving a few more months with the bank seemed the right thing to do.

As the six months approached without a replacement in sight, I became apprehensive.

Rightly so, as it turned out.

"A. T., would you reconsider our permanent employment offer to you?" That was the unexpected query I received from the division's HR head.

My heart was already outside formal banking, and I was growing excited about the prospect of banking for the poor through microfinance. Thus, I reiterated my decision to retire, emphasizing the pull to engage in helping the needy more fully, as a volunteer. And the sooner the better.

Yet the bank would not take no for an answer. Truett Tate, being the genius salesman he was, tried another strategy. He knew that focusing on the poor was not the only thing driving my urgency to move on.

"A. T., I know you would like to be close to the family, particularly your grandchildren," he said. "Would you consider moving to New York to assume the managing director's responsibility for Lloyds TSB North America? It's an important business for us. In this role, you would be responsible for our corporate activities, headquartered in New York City, and our private banking business, based out of Miami, Florida. You will, of course, continue to head risk management for the wholesale and international division until a replacement for that component of your responsibilities is found."

At that time, our son, Niki, and his amazing spouse, Kelly, had blessed us with two children: Denali, born in 2004, and Josiah Athanase, born in 2006. Niki and Kelly would add Joseph in 2009, Justice in 2012, and Elora in 2014. I will share another detail about a motivating factor in my decision to retire when I did: my daughter-in-law. We were going for lunch in Washington, DC, during one of my visits in early 2007, when Kelly pulled me back for a one-on-one chat.

"Dad, when are you thinking of retiring? You know, the longer you stay working abroad, the less exposure you will have to your grandchildren. They will not recognize you," she said with the logic and persuasion of the trained lawyer she was.

What could I say in response? She made complete sense and gave me good food for thought.

Our daughter, Mara, added two boys to our quiver of grandchildren: Xander Athanase, born in 2016, and Xavier Kadita, born in 2019.

Knowing my fondness for both my children and grandchildren, Truett knew which buttons to push to get my attention. I was not a stranger to accumulating job responsibilities, even without commensurate adjustments in my compensation. I was intrigued.

More negotiations led to an agreement that I would remain another six months with the bank, wearing two hats: risk management for the division and temporary managing director of Lloyds TSB Bank for North America. Effectively, that meant I would be the CEO, so of course I agreed and signed on for what I earnestly prayed would be my final period of service.

Despite my hectic banking schedule, I enjoyed moments of wonderful human connection. For example, I was asked to share at a wholesale and international division "marketplace" conference while still in London. The various parts of the division had booths where they presented innovative ideas and new products. The theme was about achieving success in one's professional career. Essentially, I was asked to share a bit about how I had achieved success in my banking career. Truett promoted such gatherings, both for the cohesion of the team and to encourage creativity and cross-fertilization.

By that time, I had attended enough meetings to understand the expectation was to present something like a plan with bullet points, or a year-by-year outline, or a theme such as "Seven Steps to Success." At best, such presentations credited beloved mentors for their sage advice, while at worst, they merely puffed up the intelligence, hard work, or creativity of the speaker.

I chose a different route. I was old enough, and secure enough in my career, that I believed I could "do my own thing" without suffering any consequences.

At the meeting, I stood and faced the group of my peers, determined not to be remembered as a "self-made man."

"I got to where I am today," I began, "by the grace of God."

That captured the room's attention!

Then, over the course of my talk, I summarized my background and shared some of my life story. Beginning as a young, penniless refugee who feuded with his teachers, I had ended up at the uppermost levels of global banking. That was unlikely enough, but because I knew my audience believed deeply in hard work and meritocracy, I decided to sharpen my point by sharing additional details. What if I had never thrown down my hoe in the middle of a baking hot field? What if my high school principal had not held a pilot's license and volunteered to fly me back and forth to Kananga for tests and interviews? What if I had never met Priscilla? What if I had not heard Citi was hiring? (What I did not add to the list of unlikely events was the question "What if I had never become a follower of Jesus?")

By the end of my brief talk, I knew I had not impressed all my listeners. At the same time, I had at least demonstrated the possibility that my career depended on the grace of God. My speech had broken the mold, all too common in my industry, that shaped young bankers to "take what was theirs" and "earn what they deserved." If merit was *truly* the only criterion for success, I would never have been there to deliver that talk. In fact, in my presentation, I shared that I had never asked for a promotion in my career, a revelation that produced many raised eyebrows and at least one audible sound of disbelief.

Clearly, I had worked quite hard throughout my banking career. Perhaps much harder than my peers! However, I did not want that to obscure the message that the grace of God had abounded beyond measure in my life, moving me to want to excel at whatever responsibilities were given to me.

The following evening, after most of the employees had already left the building, I walked from my office to the nearest water cooler to get a drink. On my way back, I crossed paths with a young woman in the hall. She stopped me with a question. "Mr. Tshibaka?"

I smiled and nodded.

"I heard your talk yesterday about God's grace. I became a Christian only three months ago. I was wondering, could we start a prayer group here?"

Perhaps we could! I told her I would like to talk to her more the following day.

When we met in the staff lunchroom, I inquired if she knew any other Christians from the bank she could invite. She did, as did I, and so it was decided that we would launch a prayer group.

The dozen or so attendees began to meet before work on a weekly basis. We gathered to share our concerns and joys with each other, sometimes about work, and other times simply what was on our hearts as people. We would read a verse or two out loud and then spend time together in prayer. The group was one of a countless number of confirmations that God was faithful and working in the hearts of His people, mine included.

CHAPTER 43

Unexpected Response

London

EVEN AS I WORKED FOR LLOYDS TSB, MY HEART CONTINUED TO BE drawn to the call to love and serve the poor, and Opportunity International was my chosen vehicle for achieving that mission. If the cause was so important, how could I justify keeping it to myself? Wherever and whenever I had an opening, this was something worth sharing with others.

Naturally, I discussed exciting opportunities such as this with Truett Tate, and soon Truett and his wife became supporters of the poverty alleviation mission of Opportunity International. Several others from our division began proactively contributing to the organization. That, along with my unending enthusiasm, had a spillover effect in our London office. Additional colleagues asked me how they could participate. It wasn't simply that they believed in the goals of Opportunity International, although they most certainly did. Poverty alleviation was a worthy cause. There was also the appeal of *how* Opportunity International went about its mission. The organization was practicing cutting-edge banking in areas normally overlooked by the mainstream banking community, and thus it generated a great deal of positive interest. Several of my office-mates even attended an Opportunity International conference with me in the United States.

It is true that I had assumed several of my colleagues would be attracted to the ethos of Opportunity International. At the same time, I was aware that the overt Christian nature of the organization would put some of them off. It was a solid institution with an enviable track record, yes, but over the years I had experienced firsthand the reluctance of certain secular friends and institutions to participate in anything that was Christian or even remotely religious. In a way, I could not fault such a position. If it came from a place of conviction, well, I too lived by my convictions.

Just before our annual budget and strategy meeting at a retreat, several LTB coworkers approached me to ask if I would be willing to share information about Opportunity International with the wholesale and international division executive team.

I kept a straight face as I agreed, but my mind was racing. After securing permission from Truett Tate, I allowed myself to feel a sliver of excitement. The more people who wanted to hear about Opportunity International, the better!

My enthusiasm was somewhat diminished, however, when the head of our HR department approached me with some details. "The team can't wait to hear from you at the meeting. We have a fifteen-minute break if that works for you?"

I forced a smile. *Beggars can't be choosers,* I reminded myself, *but a quarter hour is barely enough time to scratch the surface.*

I could speak at great length about Opportunity International, but fifteen minutes? I wondered how I could best communicate the essence of the organization in such a short time. Not that I cared about how my presentation would be received from a personal standpoint, but whenever I was given a platform to speak about Opportunity International, I always considered the impact my words might have. What if even one person invested in a microloan? What if ten or twenty did?

Now the calculations were even more difficult. What if my presentation was so abbreviated that my words had a *negative* impact? If there was a chance I could turn people away from Opportunity International, perhaps I should make excuses and choose not to speak at the budget and strategy meeting.

However, after Priscilla and I prayed about the situation, God provided an answer. The fifteen-minute window *was* too short for a speech, so I would not speak at all!

Instead, I would present a fourteen-minute video that my daughter, Mara Julienne, had recently produced as a tool we planned to use in our own advocacy for the poor.

Six months earlier, I had traveled to Ghana with Priscilla and Mara, along with representatives of the Dikembe Mutombo Foundation. With the help of a young filmmaker, a family friend from our time in Madrid, Mara had conducted many hours of on-the-ground interviews, which had been edited down to a fourteen-minute video, accompanied by a wonderful soundtrack provided by Mara, sharing her singing gift via some of the popular Christian music of that period.

The video clearly presented both the reach and the impact of Opportunity International as witnessed in Ghana at Opportunity Savings and Loans. I knew in my heart it would be the best possible representation of our work.

As it happened, the Lloyds TSB bankers were the inaugural audience to view the video. I had funded the production of cartons of the video and CD for my own fundraising efforts with individuals, family foundations, churches, corporate and multilateral entities.

When the video ended, the lights were turned on and I looked around the room. I did not know the faith background of all my colleagues on the executive team, but I knew not all of them were Christian. We were nonetheless friendly with one another and mutually respectful. From what I could tell, among our staff there were a handful of cultural Catholics. Several Jews. One or two Protestant believers and more than a few atheists. This was the group to which I had just shown a film about a Christian nonprofit.

"A. T.?"

I turned my attention to one of my colleagues.

"I have only one question," he said. "How do we get involved?"

"Yes," agreed another colleague. "What are the next steps?"

"How exactly can we help?" asked a third colleague.

Everyone was nodding in agreement. My heart began to beat faster as I said a silent prayer of thanksgiving. Rather than creating a negative impact, sharing Opportunity International's work with my colleagues was unexpectedly fruitful. I was caught completely unaware by the unified positivity of my colleagues' reactions.

As I began to answer each question, the fifteen-minute presentation became an hour-long brainstorming session. Together, we set specific goals relating to participation and fundraising.

Truett's executive assistant, Paul Szumilewicz, a wonderful young man with undeniable compassion for the poor, offered to coordinate following up with all my colleagues, as the consensus pointed to each of them desiring to share about the organization in their own departments. I left them and went back to my room at the resort where the meeting took place.

Then I cried. I allowed tears to flow, tears of joy and gratitude for God's amazing grace and provision.

Soon thereafter, I was able to invite the CEO of Opportunity International UK to come speak to the employee leadership group responsible for philanthropic activities. He fielded some tough questions, including about the level of Christian proselytizing. We kept the focus firmly on poverty alleviation, a cause that resonated with the group. We emphasized that microfinance was a way to give a hand-up to someone in need. Opportunity International staff weren't there to convert people but simply to love and serve.

That is how my colleagues became involved with Opportunity International, not only as a funding source but also as a pool of motivated volunteers. They organized and drove the effort on their own time, ultimately deciding to deliver on a concrete goal: funding one Opportunity Savings and Loans branch for the poor in Ghana. To that end, we determined that raising at least 350,000 British pounds would do the job.

What happened in the following months astounded Priscilla and me. To reach their lofty goal, my colleagues undertook a staggering array of volunteer activities. I heard of people who gathered sponsors for marathons, including one man who raised more than 14,000 pounds, traveling for a race in Paris, France. Others passed hats and pamphlets around London's underground transport system, asking for change on behalf of Opportunity International. Some chose to have monthly deductions taken directly from their salaries. Truett later decided to encourage people by introducing a company matching gift program. He led by example with his own giving, inspiring even more of our staff members to be involved.

Months after my retirement from banking, I learned that Truett and Dorthe, his wife, had decided to provide a six-figure donation, through Opportunity International UK, to support the education of orphaned children of one of the clients of Opportunity Bank Malawi. The mother, a widow, had passed away after a long illness. What generosity! What a blessing!

At the end of this volunteer whirlwind, the employees had raised and invested more than one *million* pounds for the Ghanaian branch and other activities of Opportunity International globally. Lloyds TSB Bank became a strong part of the Opportunity International family. HRH Princess Anne became a "matron" of the organization, and visited Opportunity clients in Ghana, Mozambique, Peru, and the Philippines. She joined various Opportunity events in London, with her very presence attracting many in the business community to the cause.

In a moment of reflection, I thought back to the afternoon when, despite my trepidation, I had shared the fourteen-minute video with my colleagues. When the meeting ended, and I was alone, I had wept, thanking God for His faithfulness. It had been all God's doing…all of it! I would be forever grateful for my colleagues' enthusiastic and fruitful investment of time, effort, and money. I knew, beyond any doubt, that God was doing a great work, both through Opportunity International and in the hearts of my colleagues. I also knew, deep in my soul, that my commitment to Opportunity International was God's calling for a season of my life. It was a calling I embraced with humility and joy, grateful that He would judge me worthy to partake in His mission, which was a ministry of eternal consequence.

As it turned out, in my role as temporary managing director of Lloyds TSB Bank for North America, I had been provided an apartment on Times Square in New York, mere blocks from the bank's North American headquarters. The location allowed me to walk to and from work each day. It was the best arrangement I had ever enjoyed in my career.

Still, I was ready to retire—again!

The retirement house Priscilla and I were building in Virginia had recently been completed, and we had already moved our personal effects from London into it. Additionally, I was primed to begin serving Opportunity International, as I sat on their US board of directors as well as their global board.

December 2007 arrived. Six months after my second six-month extra stint with Lloyds TSB Bank, I retired from formal banking, and this time it stuck. On January 10, 2008, Priscilla and I moved into the house that would anchor our retirement. And on January 15, 2008, I stepped onto my first flight to Houston, with Priscilla by my side, to fundraise on behalf of Opportunity International.

CHAPTER 44

Too Generous for the Tax Man

New York City

BEFORE I TELL THE STORY OF MY FULL-TIME WORK WITH Opportunity International in more detail, I want to relate the story of two government audits I was forced to endure.

Each year, we continued our involvement in charities with worthwhile causes. In addition to Opportunity International, we supported NGOs such as Africa New Day, the Eleazar Wheelock Society, Children in Christ, and Samaritan's Purse. We wanted to have an impact wherever possible, contributing to credible organizations with value-aligned missions and a good track record.

Because of the priority we placed on generosity, our giving ended up being "too high" a percentage of my annual pension payments and director's fees, at least according to the New York State Department of Taxation and Finance, which chose to audit my tax returns. In addition to suspecting I was giving too much of my income to charitable causes, the department also believed I was traveling too much, both domestically and overseas, with fewer days shown for my presence and work in the state. In short, my giving and traveling set off alarm bells for them.

To provide greater detail on what transpired, let me add that my taxes had been professionally filed by Price Waterhouse, and I knew for a fact that everything was in order. The taxation department did not know before it chose to audit me, but I am quite fastidious when it comes to documentation. In the early stages of the audit, the agent had accidentally confirmed to me that "everything seemed to be in order." They simply could not believe that "a Congolese," a permanent resident in the United States, could travel as much as I did or spend as much as I did on charitable causes.

To put it bluntly, they suspected I was showing high giving and travel rates to reduce my tax burden, and not for any other reasons.

Recall that in my work with Citi, I headed up risk management for emerging markets, stretching from the southern tip of South America to Southeast Asia. Certainly, I did not visit every office, but I traveled to key locations as necessary. Reasons for traveling varied, from dealing with emerging crises, to visiting one of Citi's subsidiaries for preemptive quality checks, to leading sessions at one of the bank's training centers in America or Europe. All these required me to travel, none of which counted well deserved family vacations during the year. Travel was a key element of my job description.

To fulfill their mandate, the taxation department asked me to provide receipts for every plane ticket and car rental, copies of bank and credit card statements, acknowledgments or receipts from recipient charities, and any document that would be relevant in supporting the information provided in my tax filings for the previous two years.

As can be appreciated, this process was less enjoyable than frequent trips to the dentist, but after many months of sweat, tears, and anxieties, the agents assigned to my case informed me I was in the clear. They had determined that I did, in fact, travel constantly for legitimate reasons, even as I resided in the United States for legitimate reasons—twin facts that ought to have been apparent from the outset. They also concluded that my giving was legitimate. Priscilla and I were simply generous.

The following year I was audited again, this time by the Internal Revenue Service. Once again, the agents expressed high levels of skepticism about what seemed to them extravagant philanthropic giving.

Our charitable giving had always been consistent, set as a high percentage of what I earned. When I retired, we gave even more as a *percentage*, because I was no longer earning a regular salary, even as our giving remained unchanged. Whatever I earned from for-profit board appointments went to the various philanthropic causes Priscilla and I were supporting. Such tax-deductible donations did not include the aid given to numerous members of my extended family, primarily for health needs and for the education of my many nieces and nephews, aunts and uncles, distant cousins, and childhood buddies. We often had to draw from whatever we had in our retirement savings to support such charitable and family giving.

This drew the attention of my friends at the Internal Revenue Service. "How in the world," they must have asked themselves, "could a retired guy be giving this much out of a reduced income? He must be hiding money in some kind of tax haven!"

Rather than providing innumerable travel receipts, as I had been required to do the previous year, I was asked to present evidence of charitable contributions across multiple years. Whereas Price Waterhouse played a role in my New York State audit, this time around I was on my own with the IRS. To make this audit even more *enjoyable* than the last, the agents required me to present the evidence in person, in Washington, DC. This meant driving many cartons of painstakingly gathered documents to IRS headquarters.

Once I arrived, a young Black American man went through each of the cartons in my presence, looking at every single document. He was about the age of my own children. Politely, professionally, methodically, he examined each piece of documentation in a process that seemed to take forever.

"Sir," he said eventually, "it appears everything here is justified, but I don't have the final say. I'll have to report to my boss, and then get back to you with the final ruling."

On my drive back home to Virginia, I reflected that I never again wanted to be in the crosshairs of a federal agency.

Several months thereafter, I received a letter in the mail from the IRS informing me I had nothing more to worry about. The news was a relief but also a temptation. Certainly, I did not want to interact with

IRS agents again…so perhaps we ought to give less generously? After all, we could cut our giving drastically while still contributing far more than the average taxpayer.

I believe this temptation came from the devil. Perhaps Satan had not reckoned with how stubborn Priscilla and I are. Righteously stubborn, we hope! Jesus Christ has been, and always will be, our indescribable gift. When He sacrificially gave Himself on the cross for our sakes, He set the example for us to be extravagant givers, in honor of Him.

Should this draw the attention of my friends at the Internal Revenue Service again, I now have all the pertinent documentation organized by year and ready to deploy. It is meticulously organized, so if federal agents suggest in the future that I have not learned my lesson, I will politely and quietly opine that *they* have not learned their lesson! Perhaps I will also respectfully suggest that they leave this old man alone to peacefully spend the rest of the years allotted to him by God.

It is all too easy for us to make assumptions about our fellow humans. In some ways I cannot blame New York state and the IRS for casting a skeptical eye on me. Yet, whatever God has blessed me with, I strive to give back to God, without grumbling. I look at generosity not as a duty but rather as a way to demonstrate gratitude toward God, who owns it all, including me. Giving away what I have been given demonstrates obedience to Christ, who calls me to be His hands and feet to those in need. After all, His grace has abounded in my own life. He has guided and blessed and provided beyond what I could ever have dreamed or imagined. There is nothing I can do to out-give Him!

PART FOUR

AFTER SUCCESS, SIGNIFICANCE

FRUIT OF A LIFETIME OF PREPARATION AND PASSION 2008–2011

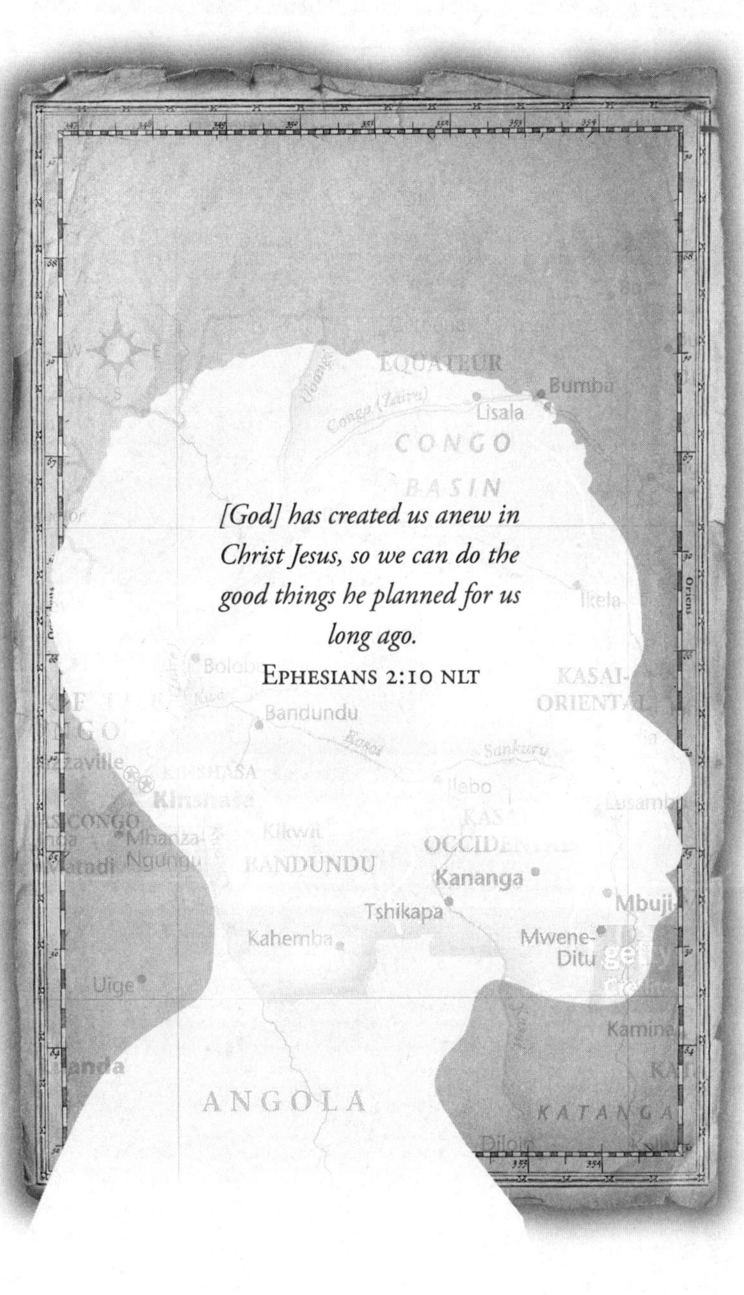

[God] has created us anew in Christ Jesus, so we can do the good things he planned for us long ago.

Ephesians 2:10 NLT

CHAPTER 45

All They Really Need Is an Opportunity

By the start of 2008, I had, at last, officially retired from my professional banking career. I had not, however, retired from working.

Since January 15, 2008, I had been traveling almost constantly on behalf of Opportunity International. Initially I paid for the trips with my own funds. I reasoned that every dollar the organization saved was a dollar it could use on behalf of its clients, the poor we were serving. Eventually, I discovered I was burning through my savings account at an unsustainable pace, and Opportunity International began to pay for my trips. This motivated me to work even harder. I wanted every trip to be a net positive for the organization's finances.

In June of that year, I was invited to give the keynote speech at Opportunity International's "Opportunity Summit" in Chicago.

My speech traced the contours of my unlikely life path, paying particular attention to the elements I had in common with many of the clients of Opportunity International. I shared that I had lost my father when I was quite young, and grown up in poverty, nurtured by a mother and family members who did their best to invest in me and who made countless sacrifices on my behalf. More importantly, I shared my certainty that my mother would have been an ideal client for Opportunity International, had it existed back then. She was resourceful, diligent, and creative. A microloan would undoubtedly have changed her life for the better, and through her the lives of so many others.

I shared with the audience that this was the heart of my motivation to serve Opportunity International.

Jesus Christ calls us to love and serve the poor. I was born one of those poor people, and countless others loved me and helped me, setting my life on an entirely new trajectory. What I now wanted was to give everything I had to make a difference in the life of someone else.

My speech went quite well and garnered a hearty round of applause. Choosing to retire from professional banking and using my talent and passion on behalf of Opportunity International felt like the best decision I had ever made. While the applause died down, I looked to the front row and found the face of my daughter, Mara. Unbeknownst to most of the attendees, Mara had composed a song about Opportunity International. As I sat, she took her place on the stage, and the opening chords of her song filled the room. When her clear voice sang the first lines, I knew everyone present was utterly captivated by her message.

It's a look of desperation in a hungry child's eyes
Can there be any salvation for the many bound and tied?

Her song continued powerfully, reminding her listeners that prayers are necessary but not sufficient. We know how we can make a difference, and so we must. Christ calls us to set captives free, and it is our human duty to respond. We are God's instruments here on earth. She asked, *Can you imagine what it feels like to make a family whole?*

Finally, she brought the song home, asking her listeners to imagine a better future, for everyone.

All they really need is an opportunity
Someone to stand up and give them one more chance
People need to have an opportunity
Someone who can bring the people hope

How could anyone resist a message so beautifully and artistically delivered? Every eye was locked on Mara as she sang, and when the final note faded, there was a single moment of complete, captivated silence. Then the applause arrived like a thunderclap. The audience leaped to its feet, and the ovation went on and on and on. I could not have been prouder of my daughter.

During the rest of the conference, it was quite amusing to be introduced to someone, only to have the person respond, "Oh, you are *Mara's* father!"

My role as keynote speaker had been justifiably forgotten! She increased, while I decreased...delightedly.

CHAPTER 46

For Such a Time as This

THE FINANCIAL CRASH OF 2008 AND 2009 HAD DIRE CONSEquences for the global economy. Opportunity International was not spared from the upheaval. It was clear our operations would be affected, though unclear in what ways or for how long.

I recall a board meeting that took place in Kampala, Uganda, in March 2009. Our president and CEO had recently resigned. The board chair and two other members of the board invited me to join them in a room at the hotel where we were staying. With two bottles of white wine on the table, they went straight to what was on their minds after having allowed me a sip from my glass.

"You must take the CEO role for Opportunity International, A. T.," I was told. "You *must*, for the sake of the organization!"

Initially I refused to consider it, even on an interim basis. Surely there were other qualified applicants available. I thought back to the way our church in Kenya had suffered such an acrimonious split. Since that heart-rending experience, I had said to myself I would not take on a leadership position in a Christian organization. I did not want ever again to be the reason for division in the body of Christ.

I thought, *If I consented to lead Opportunity International, would something similar happen because of me, or despite me? Would I, whether wittingly or unwittingly, be the cause of division in the body of Christ?* When I shared my concerns with the board, they were entirely unmoved. Rather, they insisted I accept the position, with the stipulation that it would be for only three months, until a permanent replacement was identified.

They contended that my banking background made me the right man for the job, and I knew, logically, they were right.

Therefore, despite some fear and trembling in my heart, I agreed to become interim CEO…just in time to greet the news that we would run out of cash in several months.

That would mean no new loan disbursements to existing clients. We could not take on new clients or open new field offices. We would be unable to pay either in-country staff or staff at our American head office. In other words, Opportunity International would close its doors.

I thought back to my first encounter with the work of Opportunity International on behalf of the Filipino mother and her children living inside a city dump. I recalled how a single $60 loan had empowered her to make a living *outside* that dump rather than *on* it, and about how she had created jobs for dozens of others.

To my very core I identified with the goal of all Opportunity International clients: to become self-sustaining business owners who would positively impact their communities. I was absolutely unwilling to allow this organization to close.

A realization came to me. *I think we can save Opportunity International. By God's grace, my thirty-year career has built me for this moment!* I knew we needed to both cut costs and continue to raise money. Cutting costs, in the near term, would mean reconsidering the structure of the organization. It would be a way to survive. And raising money would provide the ongoing cash we needed to return to a state of health as well as invest every possible dollar in our various countries of operation.

It was time to get to work.

Our first staff meeting after I became interim CEO took place in Oakbrook, Illinois. I needed to rally the troops.

"What we are doing is God's work," I shared with the team. "His work, not ours. God *is* demanding something of us, which is that we give this our very best. What happens after that is up to God." I did not want us to be broken by a spirit of worry but rather to leave the matter in God's hands, even as we went to current and potential donors, offering our very best.

The team was passionate and began the hard work of saving Opportunity International, for the sake of our clients.

To that end, we agreed on certain individual fundraising goals. We were extremely motivated, sometimes to a fault. I recall a time I was in California with another team member. She was sobbing, head in hands, because she did not believe she would meet her target for that trip. I encouraged her to continue doing her best and reminded her God was in control.

In truth, however, all of us shared her worries.

Even as we knocked on countless doors, we were working behind the scenes to secure Opportunity International's corporate support. We received annual grants from organizations such as Mastercard, Bloomberg, Citigroup, and the Gates Foundation. We desperately needed to preserve and then expand that funding stream if we were to survive. Such organizations were willing to partner with Opportunity International despite our identity as a Christian organization because of our innovative solutions for poverty alleviation. Essentially, Opportunity International pioneered the creation of several new banking mechanisms, tailored exclusively for the poor.

The calculation was relatively simple. A poor woman might need a loan to open a business, yes, but where would she *keep* her savings? There were no banks in most of these underserved communities. Most poor people targeted for assistance by Opportunity International had never been inside a bank. And keeping cash at home was extremely unsafe. Not only could it be stolen but there would be an ever-present temptation to use it unwisely. That was how we came to create microbanking institutions for the poor. This creation included the infrastructure as well. For example, in Malawi, we used modified steel shipping containers in villages to serve as banking facilities.

Our vision continued on to microinsurance: credit, health, life, and, for farmers, weather-indexed insurance, all tailored to the needs of the poor.

As more and more clients moved through Opportunity International's trust groups, we noticed a new chance to innovate. Suppose a client was successfully climbing out of poverty, only to fall victim to a tragedy, such as a cancer diagnosis or a truck accident. Microinsurance would allow people overlooked by traditional banks to protect their futures, and the futures of their families, no matter what unfortunate event befell them. We pioneered weather-indexed agricultural insurance policies, so even with a catastrophic harvest, the farmers could receive funding to survive.

To me, such products and innovations were exciting, life-giving, and confirmed God had led me to the right place at the right moment.

CHAPTER 47

Bringing Opportunity to the Congo

Half a year later, Opportunity International was still afloat, but struggling. I was beginning to regret taking the role of CEO.

Hard choices lay ahead. I decided to communicate honestly with Opportunity International staff. There was a continuing need to cut costs, which meant we would need to reduce staff levels. It was a chicken-and-egg problem in some ways. We needed staff to raise money for the future, but at the present we no longer had the cash to pay all those staff members. Yet firing staff now could lead to a reduction in future financial health.

There was no way around our present reality. Until we could increase our budget, we needed to continue funding existing and future loans. That was, after all, our entire mission. Through a painstaking process of reviews, interviews, and agonized prayers, we made the decision to part ways with a few employees.

I cannot overstate the difficulty of that choice. Letting go of colleagues who were excellent at their jobs tore at my heart. All of us were at Opportunity International because we believed in its mission. Many of the employees had worked closely together for years. I was overwhelmed by deep sorrow and heartache each time I called a person into my office to deliver the bad news.

It was more difficult to motivate people after that. Nerves were on edge. I did my best to help the staff focus, but the situation was grim. I used every bit of my time, energy, and management skills to explain our predicament and encourage all of us to think about the mission. This was easier said for me, of course. I had voluntarily decided not to draw a salary from Opportunity International when I accepted the CEO position, an additional way for me to give back. The staff members, however, needed their salaries to feed themselves and their families.

Beyond that, the only thing that remained was to walk my talk, as they say. I traveled as if my very life depended on it, which perhaps it did! With staff from Opportunity International, I visited current and potential donors, as well as philanthropic organizations, across the country. San Diego. Chicago. Atlanta. Portland. New York. Minneapolis. Houston. Phoenix...the list went on and on.

At the same time, we were looking at potential countries into which to expand, assuming funding sources materialized.

One memorable decision was about whether to open Opportunity International operations in the Democratic Republic of Congo. Several of my colleagues had it in their hearts that a country of more than eighty million people, most of whom were living on less than two dollars a day, simply could not be neglected. The obstacles were indeed great, but the needs were much greater.

Naturally I paid extremely close attention to the discussion, which was frank and open. The negative aspects of opening an office there were all too clear. In the preceding two decades, Rwanda and a half dozen nations around the Congo had been involved in fomenting instability on its eastern borders: rebellions, wars, and genocides, resulting in the deaths of more than five million Congolese in the space of five years (1998 to 2003). And this was to say nothing of the day-to-day difficulties of operating a developmental organization in the country, which ranged from food insecurity to the fact that Congo ranked near the bottom of the world in terms of corruption and governance. How would we convince staff to move there, and how would we guarantee their safety?

On the other hand, we believed God was calling those of us at Opportunity International to the places of greatest need in the world, not merely to areas that were stable and safe.

Ultimately, we decided that if we could raise six million dollars specifically toward work in the Congo, we would begin to fund and staff projects there. This, in addition to the other needs of the organization, became one of our revised objectives: raising funds for Opportunity International as a whole and covering the potential expansion into the Congo.

But that was not the end of the story. Opportunity International senior management and several board representatives convened a special meeting to answer a single question: Assuming we raised six million dollars, and we could enter Congo, *should* we go there? Was this an appropriate move for the organization, considering the many negatives attached to the country?

We were all convinced about the need. But the move? Opportunity International management in charge of Africa were vocally opposed to the idea. They highlighted the need to continue building our existing work in African countries. Expanding into Congo, they suggested, would be a risk in itself, in addition to taking focus and resources away from current operations. This opinion was respectfully questioned by others, who asked if adding an additional country might help Opportunity International's presence and reputation on the continent.

The discussion went on and on. I have been at tables for many lengthy meetings over the years, but this was one of the longest. The list of pros and cons filled the whiteboards and extended onto large sheets of paper taped to the wall.

Almost an entire day later, we were at an impasse. Blessedly, Ken Vander Weele, at the time president of Opportunity International Network, suggested a secret vote, with only two options: yes or no. This suggestion was enthusiastically accepted, if for no other reason than that it would insert a break into our marathon meeting. Folded pieces of paper were passed out, and each of us considered what to write.

I knew I would vote yes. The difficulties and risks were undeniable, but in my heart the decision was clear. But what of the others present? It seemed likely that the vote would reflect the back-and-forth nature of our meeting, with something close to an even split.

Soon our votes were collected, and the result was tallied and announced.

"It's unanimous. We're going into Congo."

The joy hit me in the chest and quickly spread to every limb. I grinned. Then I stood and left the room, lest I start weeping, laughing, or both at once! I knew in my soul that God had moved in that room, shaping the decision to accomplish His will in Congo.

I must add a cautionary note to this joyful reminiscence. Our Enemy, the devil, grows upset when God's people understand and experience God's guidance. As I left the meeting and entered the hallway, my knee literally ceased to work. It buckled, and I fell against the wall, scarcely able to stand. The pain was horrific. I had injured that knee severely in 1975 while playing soccer, and it had caused a bit of trouble since then, but nothing like this. I gasped, forced myself back to both feet, and took a tentative step. I gritted my teeth, then took another. It felt as if my knee had been replaced by a ball of fire. *This is the Enemy*, I told myself, *unhappy we are doing the work of God. He is attacking me physically because he knows he has already lost spiritually*.

I allowed the idea to fill my mind and heart. Was it true? Yes, it was! It was no mere coincidence that my knee had flared up, and because it was no coincidence, I knew we had made the right decision. That healing realization helped me continue down the hallway, each step less painful than the last.

I knew the money had not yet been raised, but I also knew God had opened a door and was inviting us through it.

CHAPTER 48

A Generous Man, Moved by God

MEANWHILE, FUNDRAISING WAS CONSTANT. I HAD NEVER TRAVeled more frequently, or worked more diligently, in my entire life.

Every time we prepared to enter a meeting, we would pray outside. We desperately needed God's blessing! This meant we could have no agenda of our own, no matter how tempting it might be. Our budget numbers strongly suggested we *should* have an agenda, such as raising a certain minimum amount from the donor we were calling on. But we understood that our job was to be faithful in sharing how lives were being transformed through Opportunity International's work. We left the outcome of our meetings in the hands of God.

Let me relate a story that illustrates this.

In 2009, a colleague and I visited the offices of Bob Perry in Houston, Texas. A kind and generous man, Bob owned a construction company. He had been a faithful donor to Opportunity International in the past but had never contributed more than fifty thousand dollars in a year. Having just shaken hands, and before we could sit down at a circular mahogany table, Bob thought it wise to manage expectations for our visit. "We want to let you know up front that things are very tough for us because of the financial crisis. We won't be able to give anything to Opportunity International this year, but we do appreciate you taking the time to visit."

That sort of message was becoming disturbingly common. Still, we needed to continue sitting down with people. No one knew how long the financial crisis might last, and in any case, we wanted to honor long-standing relationships with donors, through good times and hard times.

"Thank you so much for receiving us," I began, once we were seated in his office, along with his CFO. "We wanted to update you on how Opportunity International is doing and how we've used your past contributions."

The construction magnate was eager to hear how his money had been used. He asked many specific questions, which I answered as fully and honestly as I was able. At the end of an hour, I ventured, "Is there any additional information I can provide for you?"

The man shook his head no. His CFO shuffled a few papers, looked at his boss, and then back to me. "I'm sorry," he said, "and thank you for your time, but we can't donate this year. The crisis has impacted our business. I'm sure you can understand."

I wondered if he was trying to endear himself to his boss. The introductory message from Bob had been very clear, and clearly understood.

I nodded my agreement, although it would be a lie to say I was not disappointed. Yes, they had told me not to expect a contribution. On the other hand, I had been hoping for a change of heart, and his engaged manner had led me to suspect one might be forthcoming. But I knew that I had done my duty. It was time for me to give the situation to God.

We all stood and shook hands. I inquired if I could use the restroom before leaving, and I was directed to a door at the back of the office. When I returned to the office, the construction executive was gone, but his CFO remained. "Mr. Tshibaka," he said, "the CEO wanted me to let you know he has decided to donate five hundred thousand dollars to Opportunity International this year."

I managed to reach the rental car before I began to weep. I had answered all the donor's questions clearly and accurately, but the donation had not been secured by my persuasiveness. I knew with certainty that God had been at work in Bob's heart. There was no other plausible explanation. Incredulous, my colleague and I decided to take a few minutes to express our gratitude to God our Provider, God of the impossible, before proceeding to our next visit.

We experienced many such providential stories that year. God's faithfulness was so fully on display during this difficult time that I must relate one more story.

Opportunity International had been the beneficiary of a wealthy mother and her wealthy daughter. The daughter was in her twenties and believed in the mission of Opportunity International. She had committed to giving millions of dollars to the cause of poverty alleviation.

But tensions arose between the mother, the daughter, and our organization. The mother and daughter wanted to see things (meaning their projects) done in a certain way, and they felt Opportunity International was not listening to their concerns and that we had not been sufficiently supportive. The relationship was clearly in danger and in need of repair.

Thus, it fell to my team and I to meet with them in their offices in Chicago. The prayer we said in the rental car that day was among the most fervent of my life! The weight of what was at stake almost overwhelmed us. We knew we needed God to guide our hearts and words and grant us favor.

The hand of God was once again on our meeting. By the end, our teams were able to draft a memorandum of understanding, and immediately following the meeting, the mother called me aside and placed a check in my hand for $150,000. By the end of that year, the mother had given Opportunity International over half a million dollars, and the daughter had donated over five million dollars!

All told, we were able to raise more than forty-four million dollars that year, enough to ensure the mission of Opportunity International would extend into the following year and beyond.

Everything we achieved was due to the faithfulness of God. At every meeting, God's grace and favor went ahead of us. We were well received, at times extravagantly, even when we felt inadequate in some of the encounters.

I recall expressing to Priscilla that God was working so far beyond my expectations that I could scarcely believe it.

My beloved smiled at me.

"A. T.," she chided gently, "maybe you need new expectations."

CHAPTER 49

Remembering Another Giant in Philanthropy

It was January 2010, and Priscilla and I were enjoying some vacation time on the white sand beaches of the Turks and Caicos Islands. In 2002, while living in London, we had discovered the island of Providenciales as a warm and sunny escape from the damp monotone of the English winter, and we had been returning each year.

My phone notified me that a friend was calling. "Hello, Dikembe!" I answered. "How are you?"

My caller was Dikembe Mutombo, the famous NBA player who, like me, was a native of the Congo. He had launched a thirty-million-dollar hospital in Kinshasa.

"I am well," he answered in his distinctively grave voice, "but I will be even better if you come join me in Toronto."

Flying from a tropical island to Canada in January was not something I was initially inclined to do. As Dikembe filled me in on the details, however, his call began to make sense. He had a meeting scheduled with a couple who wanted to donate money to worthy Congolese needs. Apparently, the husband had given the wife five million dollars to contribute where she saw fit, as a way of "giving back" to the source of their fortune. The husband had made his money in the mining industry in the Congo, and the wife had heard me speak previously at an Opportunity International event.

"Listen, A. T.," Dikembe told me, "I just want to make sure she makes the *right* decision!" He would be fundraising for the Dikembe Mutombo

Foundation, but the bonus was that the family wanted me to share about Opportunity International and its microfinance work as well.

When I hung up, Priscilla agreed I should make the trip.

She also agreed—heroically, I might add—to "keep the sand warm" in my absence!

After arriving in Canada, I was soon introduced to the couple. They hosted a nice reception with their wealthy friends. Following that, we had a conversation about their potential investment in Congo. Of course, I had a particular opinion about that, but to begin with, I kept it to myself. Investment in several sectors was discussed, such as palm oil and coffee in agriculture, but for various reasons none of the schemes fit what the couple was looking for.

Once this became clear, I decided to push for Opportunity International, beginning with our new operations in Kinshasa and finishing with what could happen throughout the rest of the country.

Unfortunately, the husband had read some negative news reports about microfinance in Mexico and India. It was true that some organizations had placed profits above the poor, but I knew Opportunity International was truly different. Alongside me, Dikembe spoke passionately about the hospital in Kinshasa. I wholeheartedly supported Dikembe's pitch for his foundation, and from that time on, I would visit the hospital whenever in Kinshasa.

In the end, the Dikembe Mutombo Foundation received a quarter of a million dollars from the couple. I learned, a few months later, that the couple also had donated fifty thousand dollars toward poverty alleviation through Opportunity International Canada. They were pleased to be giving back to Congo, and Dikembe and I were pleased that our mission had been a success. He was offered to join the couple in their private jet for the return trip to the United States, whereas I headed to the airport so I could rejoin my wife on the beach in Providenciales. No doubt she was having a difficult time enjoying her seaside spot without me!

My return trip to Turks and Caicos was eventful. I had to transit through the United States, and therefore needed to present my Congolese passport to United States immigration officers at the airport in Canada. The officer took my Congolese passport. He studied it, taking note of the fact I had been in Canada for only a single day.

"Sir," he asked politely, "why did you come to Canada, and where are you headed?"

I explained that a former NBA star had asked me to leave Turks and Caicos to come raise money for our native Congo.

"No," he said, studying my face, "why did you *really* come?"

I explained again, adding a bit more detail about the Dikembe Mutombo Foundation and Opportunity International.

"You interrupted your vacation in the Caribbean," he asked incredulously, "to come to Canada for a fundraising mission?"

I answered in the affirmative, which did not satisfy him! "Sir, you must go to the back office to see my superior," he ordered me. "I don't buy your story and can't justify letting you in the US."

"But I have a permanent residency in the United States," I responded, "and my papers are in order…"

This did not help. My unwieldy passport was stuffed into an orange folder, and I was escorted into a back room. *Here we go again,* I thought. *This gentleman must think I am here on some fishy business.* The stubborn part of me nearly asked him to confirm my suspicions, but the wiser part of me kept my mouth closed.

After I told my story to the second officer, he was similarly skeptical. "*No* one would leave a vacation like that to come here. No one!" he half-shouted.

I suggested the officer could call my wife, still in Providenciales, to verify I was being truthful.

At last, I was able to bury them with an avalanche of corroborating details, and I was allowed to continue my journey. I wish they had been more receptive to the situation. Rather than saying I could not be telling the truth, what if they had pondered the possibility that what Dikembe and I were doing was an excellent use of time and energy? In the end, it was hard for me to blame them. Bureaucrats often think in well-established patterns.

When at last my passport was stamped, and I was grudgingly wished a pleasant trip, I could not help wondering if the officers needed a tropical vacation themselves.

Upon my return to Turks and Caicos, I discovered Priscilla had indeed saved a spot on the beach for me, and we finished a pleasant vacation.

In the six years I served with Opportunity International in an official capacity, we witnessed God's goodness and provision far too many times to recount. Never in my career had I invested as much effort into a single organization. I had averaged sixty- and seventy-hour weeks at Citibank, but Opportunity International was even more intense. When my time to leave arrived, I felt I had given my all. And when I was approached a few months later to rejoin the Opportunity International board, I gratefully declined.

I was physically and emotionally exhausted. I had run the good race, and fought the good fight, and now it was time to cheer from the sidelines.

Today, I am thankful that Opportunity International continues to thrive, reaching and impacting more and more beneficiaries, and hitting more and more milestones. I am thankful for the team God has assembled to continue serving His little ones.

PART FIVE

REMINISCENCE AND GRATITUDE

INVESTMENTS OF ETERNAL CONSEQUENCE 2011–PRESENT

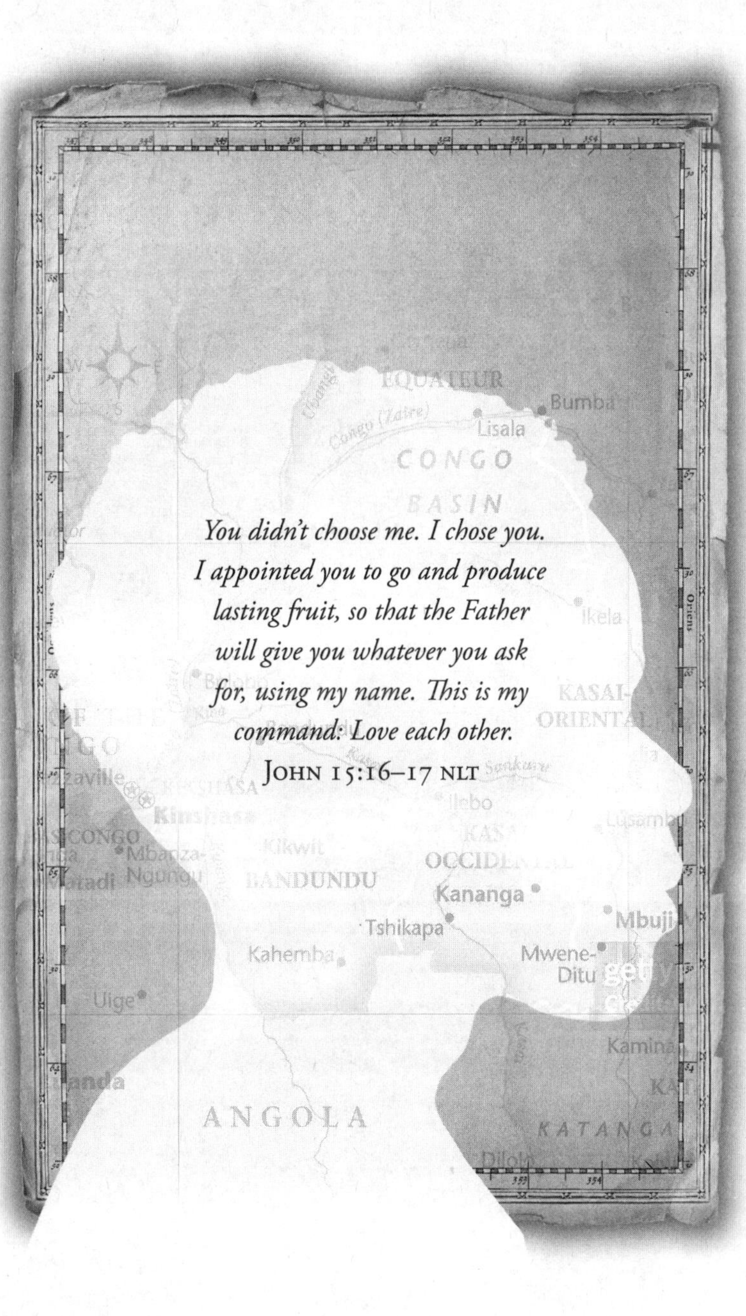

You didn't choose me. I chose you.
I appointed you to go and produce
lasting fruit, so that the Father
will give you whatever you ask
for, using my name. This is my
command: Love each other.

John 15:16–17 NLT

CHAPTER 50

Becoming an American

I DOUBT IT HAS ESCAPED NOTICE, BUT I CAN BE A STUBBORN MAN. When I was detained unjustly in Mobutu's jail in 1973, something hardened in me. The Congo was as much *my* country as it was Mobutu's. More so, in fact! I determined I would be a citizen of the Congo for my entire life, even if I no longer lived in the country. Nothing would budge me.

That noble decision, however, caused issues throughout my career. International banking required me to travel a great deal. Many jobs require international travel, but it is not an exaggeration to say that during my career, I was in the top one-tenth of 1 percent of international travelers.

Even that staggering amount of travel fails to capture some of the difficulties inherent in my case. Although I lived all over the world, returning to Congo to visit my family and feel the soil of my homeland was a regular part of my life. Whenever I visited Congo, to leave I was required to obtain a report from the security services, affirming I was in good legal standing and was authorized to leave the country. Then, to reside in whichever country Citi currently employed me, I had to obtain and continually renew a variety of visas. All this necessitated many conversations with various officers and officials, during which I was forced to explain, cajole, and sometimes nearly beg.

Before too long in my career, I had filled my passport entirely with entry and exit stamps. Normally, this would have been an opportunity to obtain a new passport and rid myself of the old, full one. However, I still had visas in multiple full passports and was forced to staple new passports to the old ones.

In a case that would be unthinkable in today's travel environment, I went to the Congolese embassy in Brazil for a new passport. None had been sent to the embassy by authorities in Kinshasa. I had important business trips that could not be delayed, yet the embassy hatched a clever plan. The decision was made to cut blank pages out of someone else's passport and staple them into mine, a simple solution that worked perfectly. At that time, the different countries I visited, including Russia, were lax about such things.

Eventually, I collected a grand total of *five* passports used for travel, attached to one another in a most unusual and unwieldy bundle. The poor immigration officers!

Then, in 2013, something odd occurred. As I had done so many times before, I applied to the Congolese embassy in the United States for a new passport. I traveled to Washington, DC; filled out the required documentation; and waited, only to be told months later, in December 2013, that they did not have enough applications to justify contacting Kinshasa. Instead, I would have to wait…or I could travel to Kinshasa personally if I wanted the process expedited.

Without a new passport, I would be unable to travel at all, so this was a matter needing urgent attention. It so happened that I had a business trip to Kinshasa in early 2014. I seized that opportunity to share my passport issues with a friend in the Congo, a distant relative from my clan. He held a high-level post as an ambassador and adviser to the president. Over dinner in his home, he asked for the batch of used passports in my possession, and he promised he would see what he could do to help.

Sadly, he became mired in the quicksand of corruption. When he checked into my situation, he was told by officials at the foreign ministry that, no matter how diligently they searched, they simply could *not* find my original passport application and required documentation. My friend understood how important this case was to me, so he slid a $100 note to the official in charge. Miraculously, the official "discovered" my file and issued a new passport for me on the spot.

My blood boiled when I heard what had happened during a follow-up dinner with him and his wife. Perhaps I should have expected such a situation. I knew such shady dealings were common. But here was an extremely powerful and well-connected government official, part of the very Ministry of Foreign Affairs, which was responsible for passport issuance, having to resort to bribery to resolve my passport problem. Totally unacceptable!

For me, it was the proverbial straw that broke the camel's back. I had a sense that life was too short to continue dealing with such petty unscrupulousness. Upon returning to the United States with my new Congolese passport, I determined that it was time to reconsider my citizenship commitment and, later in 2014, I applied to become an American citizen.

Reality had sunk in. How could I possibly justify continuing to put myself in such frustrating situations?

My case was an easy one. I had an American wife, American children, American bank accounts, and a principal home in Virginia, and I had given thirty-three years of my life to an American bank. As if this were not enough, I had dutifully paid my fair share in taxes and made other contributions to federal programs such as Medicare and Social Security. I had entered the United States legitimately, with a work permit and a senior position at a major global banking institution.

Predictably, I passed the citizenship test and interview with the Immigration Department in November 2014. On March 18, 2015, I was sworn in as an American citizen at a government office in Richmond, Virginia.

Procuring my United States passport was trivially easy after that, and so were my interactions with immigration officers from that point forward!

CHAPTER 51

Africa, a New Day

ONE OF THE GREATEST JOYS OF MY LIFE HAS BEEN CHEERING FROM the front-row seats and supporting the amazing, inspiring works of faithfulness others are accomplishing.

For example, a Congolese couple I know. Camille Ntoto is from the Bakongo tribe, and his wife, Esther, is from my tribe, the Baluba. In the early days of their dating relationship, both worked for a Christian radio station in Kinshasa, Radio Sango Malamu (Radio Good News). Providentially, they were able to obtain scholarships to study in the United States. Camille obtained a BA in intercultural ministries, pastoral ministries, and biblical studies, after which he earned a master's degree in leadership. Esther achieved a BA in intercultural ministries, with a minor in communications.

In the final days before graduation, Camille and Esther received an email from a friend describing the terrible suffering people were enduring at the hands of genocidal rebels in Eastern Congo. In anguish, they shared the communication with a trusted professor. He was sympathetic but asked them pointedly, "Now that you know this, what are you going to *do*?"

His words sparked a flame in the hearts of both Esther and Camille. They had recently become citizens of the United States, but they chose to leave the relative safety of America and return to the Congo in 2005 as missionaries. Up to that point in time, Eastern Congo had suffered an estimated 5.4 million deaths within a five-year time frame (1998–2003), according to data by the International Rescue Committee. It was still relatively common to read about men emerging from the bush and murdering scores of innocent people. Pockets of rebellion and fighting still roiled the countryside. It was in that toxic mix of deadly violence and insecurity that Camille and Esther chose to place themselves.

Initially they moved to Goma, on the shore of Lake Kivu. There Esther worked for an organization called Light of Africa. It ran a hospital for the women of Congo who had been abused or suffered atrocities. Most of them had been victims of severe physical and emotional trauma. Even when their bodies healed, they were often subjected to rejection by both their families and society at large, and they carried emotional wounds as well. Esther worked hard to rehabilitate and reintegrate the women into society. Her daily encounters were heart-wrenching and emotionally draining for her as well.

Her husband could not remain indifferent to what he was observing, day in and day out.

One night, after another difficult day in the hospital, Camille said to Esther, "*Cherie* [darling], we can't just continue dealing with the consequences of the evil carried out! Men are the perpetrators of these atrocities. We will not solve the challenges facing our sisters without addressing the root cause, our brothers. What can we do to change this situation?"

Thus was born a new ministry, the Sons of Congo. Esther and Camille created a Bible-based, modular training program that could be broadcast via radio. The lessons taught men about their responsibilities as husbands, brothers, fathers, sons, leaders, providers, and protectors. Soon it was picked up by more than fifty radio stations across the country. Men could listen anywhere. Even a rebel in the bush, sharpening his machete or cleaning his rifle, could hear the teaching and choose to put down his weapons. He could choose life for himself and for others.

As the program gained in popularity, listeners began to call the radio station with testimonies. Sometimes these were tearful confessions, but other times the testimonies were positive, sharing decisions made by men to reintegrate into society and to become life savers, in lieu of being life takers. Husbands who used to drink and visit prostitutes (and worse) were holding down jobs and coming home from work sober. They were depositing their paychecks at the bank and caring for their spouses and their children. The Sons of Congo program began to gain traction, building momentum and attracting the attention of government officials and local and multilateral organizations operating in the region.

It was then that Esther and Camille were again prompted by God. It was as if their Creator was telling them, *You have done a good job here. You have a program to train, educate, and transform men into responsible leaders. Now I want you to do something about the youth of the Congo.*

Thus the Leadership Academy was conceived and launched. It was a six-month program for those in their teens and twenties. The program was designed to help participants learn from their elders' mistakes and to adopt a solution-driven leadership approach to challenges they saw in their communities. Each participant was required to take a hard look at his or her community and report back with problems needing to be addressed. Thereafter, they were required to identify one problem and describe how they would go about addressing it. Then, with feedback from the trainers and other participants, they were sent out to execute and report back.

A case study was provided by a young man, Dieudonne, who graduated from another youth-centered program launched around that time but for needier families, Generation Hope. Dieudonne decided to focus on illiteracy. He knew most women in his village could not read and write.

As he asked around, he discovered untapped resources in his community. There were teachers who, outside of school hours, could volunteer their time. Similarly, pastors might be willing to help during the week when they did not have sermons to prepare or congregants to visit. He thought, *If I could just convince a few of these people to begin giving lessons...* And then he got to work organizing.

One year later, more than three hundred formerly illiterate women from his village could read and write.

Neighboring villages heard about the transformation and decided to launch their own literacy programs. Before long, the program attracted the attention of a Swiss NGO with grant funding applicable for the sort of program launched by Dieudonne. The young man who began this had no resources, at least in the eyes of the world. But he used his heart to see a need, his brain to solve the problem, and his relationships to gather the necessary resources together.

Money helps, but it is not a panacea for all life's problems. One's motivation for work—any work—must go beyond material gains. The Swiss NGO began paying salaries and providing other incentives to the teachers and pastors in Dieudonne's village. Soon a mindset of entitlement set in. Rather than taking pride in improving their community, the teachers began to expect payment for overtime and bonuses for sacrifices beyond the call of duty, at least in their self-assessment. Then, when the grant funds were exhausted, and no replacement funding sources materialized, teachers and pastors abandoned their participation in the literacy program.

Fortunately, Camille and Esther decided to add literacy training to the Women of Congo Program. During one of my annual visits to Goma, I was delighted to see one of the ladies go to the blackboard and write her name and a few phrases. We shared in the pride she exhibited for having achieved such a life-transforming milestone.

It was then that Esther and Camille were *again* prompted by God. They had reached the youth, but what about the children? A school was needed to marry excellence in academics with depth and growth in a Christian worldview. "If God is going to transform this nation and its leaders," reasoned Camille and Esther, "we must start at the earliest age possible."

They knew if they could shape the minds and hearts of the youngest members of the community, over time more and more residents would grow up with sound character and a healthy outlook on life. Congolese citizens would not be guided and ensnared by a culture of violence and corruption but rather by a new generation of men and women working hard toward the betterment of their own lives and the lives of others in their families, their communities, and their country.

The following year, their elementary school began with a single grade and fewer than forty students. Each year they added a grade, along with the necessary staff and physical space. The results from statewide exams have so far been spectacular, and well above the average for the country.

The *Un Jour Nouveau Leader-In-Me School* had nine grades and over 2,300 students prior to the most recent massacres and conquests of Goma and Bukavu by M23 rebels. We are praying it will become self-sustaining and start contributing toward its own expansion and the ministry's other programs. (In America, *Un Jour Nouveau* is known as Africa New Day: www.africanewday.org.)

To complete the strategic vision God had put on their hearts, the couple added two more programs: Generation Hope (previously mentioned), to offer leadership training to orphans and youth from poorer families, and an Entrepreneurial Hub, to train and assist people with vision and initiative to launch their own small businesses, monitored and supported by qualified team members and external experts.

For three years, beginning in 2017, I made the conscious decision to visit one of the Sons of Congo groups whenever in Goma. Each ten-member unit was well organized, with a president, a secretary, and a treasurer. On my first visit, we met in the modest living room of the group president's home. After explaining how they came together and some of their objectives, they shared a story that caught my attention.

Years earlier, they had each contributed small sums to a self-managed fund that allowed the group to buy two pigs, one sow, and one barrow. By the time of our meeting, they had forty pigs. The group showed me a single piece of paper containing their business plan. It was enough for me to see that they wanted to acquire equipment from China to be able to produce sausage with meat from their herd. The cost of the equipment was estimated at a little over twenty thousand US dollars. We brainstormed together on how such a large sum could be sourced, including the option of asking for a bank loan. Camille and I had called on the leadership of several local banks during my visit to gauge their appetite for supporting business initiatives of *Un Jour Nouveau*'s aspiring entrepreneurs.

I was very pleased by the story the Sons of Congo group had shared with me, and I encouraged them to persevere, forsaking some of the urgent short-term needs and patiently investing in the future to further grow their business.

When I returned to the group the following year, my first question concerned the evolution of the pig business. The group president was visibly embarrassed and profusely offered his apologies. "Mr. Tshibaka, I don't know what to say. The herd headcount was dramatically reduced as consumption and cash needs dictated satisfying the group's short-term emergencies."

While understanding the rationale, it was my turn to be visibly disappointed.

On my *next* visit, the group president welcomed me with a wide grin. Other members displayed faces that seemed to mean they were proud and happy with where they were. I learned that while they had not yet launched the production of sausages for the Goma market, the herd headcount had surpassed forty. Additionally, they had launched a poultry business, and they took me to visit the four hundred or so chicks they had purchased. Then, to crown a very pleasing visit, they took me to the furniture-making business they had also launched that year.

Returning to the story of Esther and Camille, it was around the time their school had four grades that, yes, God prompted them again!

They had reached older men and women, through Sons of Congo and Women of Congo. They had reached boys and girls through Leadership Academy and Generation Hope as well as children through *Un Jour Nouveau* School. They had built a media ministry in collaboration with (by now) some sixty-five radio stations, with an estimated audience of six million, and they had launched an entrepreneurship hub as another opportunity for beneficiaries of their programs to put into practice the leadership principles they were taught.

But then, they heard this question from the Lord: *You have been effective at delivering services with transformative impact for My people, but where is My church?*

Thus was born the *Un Jour Nouveau* Chapel. The church has grown and today is a congregation of about one thousand regular attendants.

I am amazed when I reflect on the incredible impact of *Un Jour Nouveau* (Africa New Day), delivering so much despite limited resources. I sat on the board of the organization for a few years, two of them as its chairman. I admire Camille and Esther and love the work they do, sacrificially and with great passion. Our daughter, Mara, who was instrumental in opening our eyes to the reach and impact of this ministry, was asked by the board to be chairwoman. Until her resignation in late 2024 to focus on her boys, the word through the grapevine was that she was doing a terrific job—a far better and more tactful leader when compared to her predecessor, her father!

But I do not view myself as an integral part of their operations any longer. Rather, I wish to illustrate the grace and goodness of God. God, who desires all to be saved (1 Timothy 2:4), is at work across the world through the actions of those who follow Him. Like a fruit tree growing in a desert, God's Word bears fruit even in the unlikeliest places.

It brings to mind a conference hosted by Esther and Camille that gathered young people and adults from across the Congo. At one session, a woman who had suffered horrific atrocities shared her story with the gathering. She had been raped, tortured, and sexually mutilated. Her mother and her daughter had suffered similarly.

Esther stood up and faced the young men in attendance. "Among you, there are people who have done things this woman is describing," she declared. The already silent room became absolutely so. "Now, which one of you is going to stand, come here, and ask forgiveness on behalf of the men who did this?"

Every pair of eyes drilled into the floor. No one dared to stand. Esther refused to back down, until at last one young man tentatively raised his hand.

"Come up here," Esther insisted.

He did.

"What have you done?" Esther prompted.

Haltingly, the young man described things he had done. He had killed and tortured. He had raped.

Tears soaked his face, as they did Esther's.

"Now it is time," Esther instructed the young man. He knelt at the feet of the woman.

"On behalf of the men who hurt you," he began. He stopped, then found the humility to continue, saying, "I beg for your forgiveness."

There was complete silence, apart from the weeping. Before the woman could speak, a second man stood, clasping his hands over his heart. A third man stood, then fell to his knees, crying. Two more men stood and took tentative steps toward the front of the room. The Holy Spirit was at work, healing and bringing about forgiveness and reconciliation.

No matter how rich one is or how poor, each of us has been blessed. Each of us is blessed to be a blessing.

When we see a need, do we remain indifferent? Or do we help?

I believe help can take limitless forms. It may be as simple as placing a hand on someone's shoulder and praying for their life. It may be as complicated as founding a radio ministry, a youth leadership program, a school, and a church in conflict-torn Eastern Congo. In either case, the fruit depends on the faithfulness of God. And we know beyond a doubt that He will be faithful.

CHAPTER 52

Conduit of God's Goodness

My beloved daughter, Mara, and a Polish American young man were married at our home in Virginia, on the boat dock.

The day of the wedding, the weather was as perfect as it could possibly be. It had been raining for days previously, but midmorning the sun came out in full. By evening, halos of light danced through the branches of the tall trees surrounding our dock and reflected off the waters of the lake. The groom arrived at the dock on a boat to meet his bride, who was radiant in a dress adorned with shimmering Swarovski crystals. Hydrangeas, green and white, matched the colors of the wedding party. Priscilla and I strove to take in the scene, but in truth our hearts were filled far past the point of overflowing. Joy seemed to seep from our pores.

During the reception at the Fawn Lake Community House, Mara leaned close to speak with me… and I accidentally spilled my glass of red wine down the front of her dress! She was escorted to the bathroom by two of her bridesmaids, while her husband hovered outside the door. (Do not ask about the first words that *my* beloved, Priscilla, said to me!) When Mara emerged at last, he approached, only to discover he had ripped Mara's train with his foot. Mara looked around the room. There remained a twinkle in her eyes and a smile on her face, as if she was assessing how such a comedy of errors had befallen her.

Our daughter-in-law, Kelly Tshibaka, approached Mara with a matching but authoritative "I got this" smile. Seconds later, she had cut Mara's train completely free and pointed her toward the dance floor.

Mara needed no encouragement. She and her husband led the celebration, and the gathered friends and family danced and danced and danced. My daughter's spirit and happiness are truly irrepressible.

Late that night, after Mara and her husband had left for their honeymoon and our guests had gone home, Priscilla and I stood together on the boat dock, our arms around each other. There was no need for words. We were blessed beyond measure. So, so far beyond measure.

As I put the final touches to my story, our daughter is going through a difficult season in her life, causing Priscilla and me deep emotional hurt and pain. Nevertheless, Mara is using her life's story to minister to others who are faced with complex challenges. For that reason, I rejoice and thank God as He alone is the holder of her today and her tomorrow. We trust that, as I have seen repeatedly in my own life, the Lord will use her trials for good.

I believe with all my heart in the reality God describes in the book of Genesis, chapter 12. God does not bless us in order that we should hoard His blessings. Rather, we are to be a conduit of God's goodness and provision. We are blessed in order that we might bless others.

All of Scripture testifies to this truth. Jesus summarizes *all* the law and prophets by commanding me to "love the Lord [my] God with all [my] heart and with all [my] soul and with all [my] mind" and to "love [my] neighbor as [myself]" (Matthew 22:37–39 NIV). The book of James observes that any so-called faith *not* accompanied by good works is dead. To this end, we give as generously as we possibly can, as a way of testifying to our love for God and demonstrating our love for our neighbors, no matter where on the globe they live. At last count, Priscilla and I have more than 320 relatives from my father's side of the family, who are scattered across the world. We support the family with prayers, words of encouragement, and financial and material assistance to the extent of our ability. The needs are as varied as they are overwhelming, for education, health, bereavement, and small entrepreneurial initiatives.

I am reminded of the support I received growing up and the exhortation in the Bible to provide for our relatives and immediate family members (1 Timothy 5:8). Truly generous giving can never be compulsory. We do not give out of obligation or to earn favor with others. Rather, we give because Christ is working *in* and *through* us to bless others. After all, as we read in Ephesians 2:8–10, "It is by grace you have been saved, through faith—and this is not from yourselves, it is the gift of God—not by works, so that no one can boast. *For we are God's handiwork, created in Christ Jesus to do good works, which God prepared in advance for us to do.*" (NIV emphasis added). It is out of love and gratitude that we strive to do good in the world.

In the end, we never give *things*. Not really.

We give our money, yes. Our skills and expertise. Our fervent prayers and faithful friendships. Sometimes we give pallets of food or provide college tuition.

But in life there is only one thing we can truly give, and that is ourselves. We do this in the name of Jesus because Jesus gave Himself for all of us. Our whole lives ought to be a response to that.

My humble prayer is that my life has been, and will continue to be, one of service and loving-kindness, to the best of my abilities as a broken vessel, until my Lord and Savior calls me home.

EPILOGUE

Until He Calls Me Home

Let the redeemed of the LORD tell their story—those he redeemed from the hand of the foe.
PSALM 107:2 NIV

AND SO WE'VE ARRIVED AT THE END OF MY STORY, A TALE UNIQUE TO me. We all have our own stories, and I have told mine to the best of my recollection, sharing events that have shaped my character.

I am now sitting on our deck, under the awning that no longer protects me against the sun. Fawn Lake looks unusually calm, and the birds' chirping produces unrehearsed melodies pleasing to my ears. The sun's rays reflect on the trees, giving them a bright and rich green. It is a beautiful springtime evening in Virginia. I have always loved this time of the year, especially with winter in the rearview mirror.

I look back on my life with gratitude for the opportunities given to me to share God's marvelous works. I hold that where we start is not where we end in life. God gives to all of us, His created beings, grace abundant and undeserved. Whether we thankfully receive it and put it to work in our lives is on us, not on Him. In Job 8:7 we read, "Though your beginning was small, yet your latter end would increase abundantly" (NKJV).

I don't claim to be rich by any stretch of the imagination. Still, as I reflect on the trials and challenges I have overcome during my earthly journey, I can truthfully say that I consider myself richly blessed.

How can I explain that move from the Catholic school to a Presbyterian one in Tshibombo? Why Dartmouth? And how and why Citibank? Against all odds, how did this son of the Congo have the tremendous blessing of a uniquely precious pearl, the woman who would become my trusted and faithful companion for over five decades?

Life has brought us our fair share of struggles, but we were not alone through it all. If Priscilla and I sing, "We are blessed, we are blessed, we are blessed," it is because that is the predominant sentiment we choose to focus on.

We have wonderful children in Niki and Mara, endowed by their Creator with great intellect and life-guiding wisdom. They both attended Amherst College and graduated with top honors.

Niki went on to obtain a juris doctor from Harvard Law School, and Mara obtained a masters of science in global affairs from NYU.

Our grandchildren—Denali, Josiah Athanase, Joseph, Justice, Elora, Xander Athanase, and Xavier Kadita—are all growing well, nurtured in God's Word by their parents.

We are also grateful for the gracious hand of God on our extended family, most of whom have decided to accept Jesus Christ as Lord and Savior. Priscilla and I are aware that they live, for the most part, in extreme poverty. We find it our call to help, especially in cases of medical emergencies and university education for promising kids. We help support the educational needs of twenty to thirty kids (possible because university in Congo is "cheap" relative to Western standards), with a dozen or so graduating each year with degrees in disparate fields such as medicine and cosmetology. It gives us extreme joy when we receive the annual scorecards through my eldest nephew, Etienne Ngandu, who's seventy-one years old.

And then there is the greater circle of influence out there, the younger people the Lord sends my way to mentor, those still in college, and young entrepreneurs who may seek my counsel. I always find it a privilege to make myself available as much as possible. Their success is my success, encouraging me to give even more of myself. Scripture says, "When someone has been given much, much will be required in return; and when someone has been entrusted with much, even more will be required" (Luke 12:48 NLT).

In June 2024, I decided to relinquish all my board positions, for-profit and nonprofit, to concentrate on finalizing my story. Two months later, in August 2024, I received a call from Dr. James Mwangi, managing director and chief executive officer of Equity Group Holdings, a fifteen-billion-dollar total asset footing financial institution with operations in seven Central African countries.

"You have been highly recommended by Mr. Wolfgang Bertelsmeier, chairman of our DRC subsidiary, *Equity Banque Commerciale du Congo*. We have problems and ambitious strategic objectives in the country. Your professional profile tells me you can greatly help us," he said to me, his demeanor projecting sincerity and trustworthiness.

Intrigued, I thanked Dr. Mwangi and told him I would seriously consider his offer and follow up once I'd made my decision. I told Priscilla what had just happened, adding, "Sweetheart, as attractive as this new development sounds, I am reluctant to return to serving on a board again. I want to focus on my memoir." She agreed to pray for guidance with me. I further read all that I could about Equity Group Holdings and Equity BCDC on the Internet. The mission of the group stipulated offering "integrated financial services that socially and economically empower." The social dimension of the group's mission statement caught my eye. They had spent nearly half a billion dollars on social impact investment as of December 2023. (This number was to increase to $693 million as of December 31, 2024!) The online statement further emphasized, "Transforming lives is at the core of our vision."

God was once again opening a door through which I could make a difference for my native country.

With Priscilla's agreement, I joined the board of Equity BCDC as an independent director, chair of the board audit committee, and a member of its risk and credit committees.

God continues to chart my path. And I will remain open to His leading until He calls me home.

The Hall of Angels

God has given each of you a gift from his great variety of spiritual gifts. Use them well to serve one another.
1 PETER 4:10 NLT

IN THE NEW TESTAMENT, THE ELEVENTH CHAPTER OF HEBREWS IS often referred to as "the Hall of Heroes." It lists those who, by faith, listened to and obeyed God's call on their lives.

I would like to end my story with "the Hall of Angels." This is a list of some of those whom God placed in my life to love and guide me, people whose very presence alongside me made an indelible impact on the man I became. I write of them with love and still-unplumbed depths of gratitude.

My father, Alphonse Ngandu Kashala:
Even on his deathbed, my father had God-given wisdom to keep our fates away from his brothers' hands. When he defied his culture and traditions by instructing my mother that she was not to marry any of his brothers, he safeguarded our futures. Even in his death, he gave us a chance at life.

My mother, Julienne Ngalula Kayibabu Wa Kanda:
Where would I be without this incredible woman of courage and resourcefulness? From the time she brought me into the world to the time I introduced her to another woman of valor, the beautiful Minnesotan who became my life's companion, my mother is the reason I am who I am today. Much of the discipline and character traits I saw in her have served me well in my personal and professional life.

My brother Robert Kanyiki:
This eldest male sibling in the Ngandu family took on the role of the father I had lost at three years of age. He counseled me, provided for me, and nurtured me selflessly. His deep love for me was manifest in all our interactions.

My sister, Godelieve Kayowa:
The eldest sibling in our family, she became my second mother. After marrying very young, she took me to live with her and her family in the diamond mining town of Tshikapa to give our mother a break. It was in Tshikapa, years later, that she surprised me with the bundle of Congolese francs she had been saving under her mattress, part of which was for my immediate need (school tuition), and part of which was to be saved for when I would need a dowry to give to my future in-laws, following our tribal customs.

My brothers Antoine Tshiyombo Muka and Honore Ngandu Kashala:
Out of their limited means, they both went out of their way to contribute toward my education, often simply by sharing a pair of shorts or a shirt they were no longer going to wear. My mother and my elder siblings all passed away in the late 1980s and early 1990s, save one, Antoine Tshiyombo Muka, chief of the Bena Kadiamba clan, who died in October 2024 at the age of eighty-nine years.

Eric Bolton:
My tough and caring high school principal, who harshly disciplined me with *la gymnastique Tshibakienne* (Tshibakian gymnastics), became both my mentor and God's instrument to open the door for me to study in America.

Ann Anderson:
What a joy it was to reconnect with my beloved high school professor at the Youth for Christ conference in Atlanta, Georgia, in the summer of 1968. I had been in America for about one year, and speaking with her at that time was truly comforting. Years later, in Kananga during the summer of 1971, she said to Priscilla, "Athanase? My baby!" With those words, Ann welcomed Priscilla and nursed her back to health before sending her on to meet with my family in Mbuji-Mayi, Tshibombo, and Miabi.

Wilder Kim Abbott:
Kim was an incredible leader, a man of integrity and well-anchored principles. He was exceedingly compassionate and yet very strict, serving as an exemplary steward of his critically important responsibility as Citibank's most senior executive in Congo. As managing director during my season of trial and suffering at the hands of President Mobutu, Kim became my go-to counselor, advocate, and friend. I was both honored and humbled to be asked by Alice, his loving wife, to eulogize this man of great compassion and wisdom at his passing.

Our children: Niki, Kelly, Mara, and our grandchildren:
You are true gifts from our Father in heaven. Priscilla and I have myriad reasons for thankfulness, but being your parents trumps the rest. We are grateful that you are following Jesus Christ.

Niki, I fondly remember your participation in church as a young boy, never afraid to speak whatever God put on your heart. After your Harvard law degree, you served as a lawyer before God called you to plant a church with your beloved, Kelly. Both of you are advocates for God's kingdom. I am enormously proud of the man you are, as husband, father, and son. Keep leaning on Jesus through whatever God-given opportunities and challenges this life has on offer for you and Kelly.

Mara Julienne, I know this will be hard for you to accept, but you will always be my darling girl. You remind me of your aunt, Godelieve Kayowa, beautiful inside and out. You care deeply for others, especially for those in need. You model Christ's love and patience for your children. May you flourish and attain all of the Lord's plans for your life, as He has so thoughtfully and graciously equipped you.

Our grandchildren, may you all grow to be men and women after God's own heart, leading lives of impact and significance, always mindful of the real needs around you and not neglecting to respond enthusiastically and generously. As God blesses you, may you all become blessings to many, drawing on and replenishing from the inexhaustible fountain that is Christ Jesus.

My wife, Priscilla Madlyn Johnson Tshibaka:

The love of my life. I fell for you the very first time I saw you serving at the Green Latrine on the Dartmouth campus. Your face radiated both the innocence and the beauty of an angel. Your very demeanor, whether standing by the counter or serving, told me there was something very special about you. When I ate for fifty cents but lavished you with a one-dollar tip, I hoped to spark a conversation, and perhaps a relationship. Alas, it was not to be…at least not that day! Our Lord had other plans for us that neither you nor I could perceive.

When our subsequent encounter on a dance floor began our relationship, a God-ordained union commenced, one that has seen us together in an ever-deepening and loving bond. I am indebted to God and to you for the incredible support and forbearance shown me these past five decades plus. I do not know who or what I would have become without you by my side all these years. You have never ceased to be a loving and generous mother, even to the three hundred or so of my father Ngandu Alphonse's progeny. You are the most beautiful person I could ever have dreamed of as a lifelong soulmate. We have experienced innumerable seasons of exhilarating joy, just as we have gone through untold difficult challenges together. We learned to go to God in prayer, and in the process, we tremendously benefited from His amazing grace. My cup overflows, my love. I am blessed, and I am grateful.

Christ Jesus:
My Lord, my Savior, my Redeemer. You made me. You watched over my childhood. You provided all I have ever needed and so much more. Without You, I could do nothing and would not amount to anything. Thank You for knocking on the door of my heart that day in October 1975. I had so many arguments to offer in resisting Your entreaties, but You would not give up. You persisted until I confessed I was a sinner, falling short—far short!—of the glory of God. Then I invited You into my heart to reign over my life and guide me. I have never been the same. I owe all to You. Words may prove inadequate to express the depth of my gratitude, not only for the assurance of eternal life with You but also for the refining work You continue to do in me as You prepare me for that day.

Amen.

Acknowledgments

WHILE MY "HALL OF ANGELS" ACKNOWLEDGES THE PEOPLE who have accompanied me in life, I'd also like to express my gratitude to those who have helped me refine and complete, publish, and distribute this work.

David Jacobsen, who patiently and diligently collaborated with me in writing this book, meticulously taking notes and recording my story. Thank you.

Becky Nesbitt, who loved my story from get-go and has coordinated within Forefront Books to publish my book. Kia Harris, who oversaw the editing and production phases of the manuscript. Amanda C. Bauch, the professional who diligently poured her time into making this work a first-class product.

My son, Niki, who very patiently worked with his father to clarify and refine the stories. My wife, Priscilla, and my daughter, Mara, to whom I had to recur for confirmation of facts on some of the stories.

Many thanks to all of you who have left your mark on my life—and this book!

About the Author

Athanase Kadita Tshibaka—known affectionately as A.T.—is a son of the Congo, a descendant of Bena Kadiamba chieftains, and a living testimony to the power of divine grace, resilience, and unwavering faith.

Born into hardship, displaced by conflict, and raised amid scarcity, A.T. could have become a footnote in history. Instead, God wrote a different story—one of ascent, service, and purpose. Over a distinguished four-decade career in international finance, he rose through the ranks of Citigroup, eventually overseeing Corporate Risk Management across 77 emerging markets. He later served in executive roles at Lloyds TSB in London and the U.S.

In 2008, answering a deeper call, A.T. brought his leadership to Opportunity International, a global Christian microfinance organization. There, as senior leader and interim CEO, he championed dignity, hope, and economic empowerment in some of the world's most vulnerable communities.

A trusted advisor and board member for corporate and nonprofit institutions alike—including as an IFC Nominee Director for Ecobank and currently Chair of the Audit Committee for Equity Banque Commerciale du Congo—A.T. continues to lead with integrity and a Kingdom-minded heart.

Educated at Dartmouth and the Tuck School of Business, he is a devoted husband to Priscilla Madlyn, proud father to Niki and Mara, and joyful grandfather of seven.

His journey is living proof that adversity can birth purpose, that ashes can bloom with grace, and that the most extraordinary endings often begin with broken beginnings—anchored always in an unwavering belief in God's faithfulness and providence.

Family Tree

Tshitenga wa Nkole or Mbuyi Tshitenga
Mwanza Mukala or Mwanza Luketa
Mbayi Kafwemba
Mwanza Kadiamba
Mwanza Lubala
Mwanza Nkashama
Mwanza Nkala
Kande Mwana Mwenyi
Ntumba Kalonji
Kande Nsanguluja
Kanyiki Mpwanya
Ngandu Kashala Alphonse
Kayowa Godelive
Kanyiki Mutombo Mpwanya Robert Vianney
Tshiyombo Muka Antoine-Marie
6 Children
21 Children
21 Children

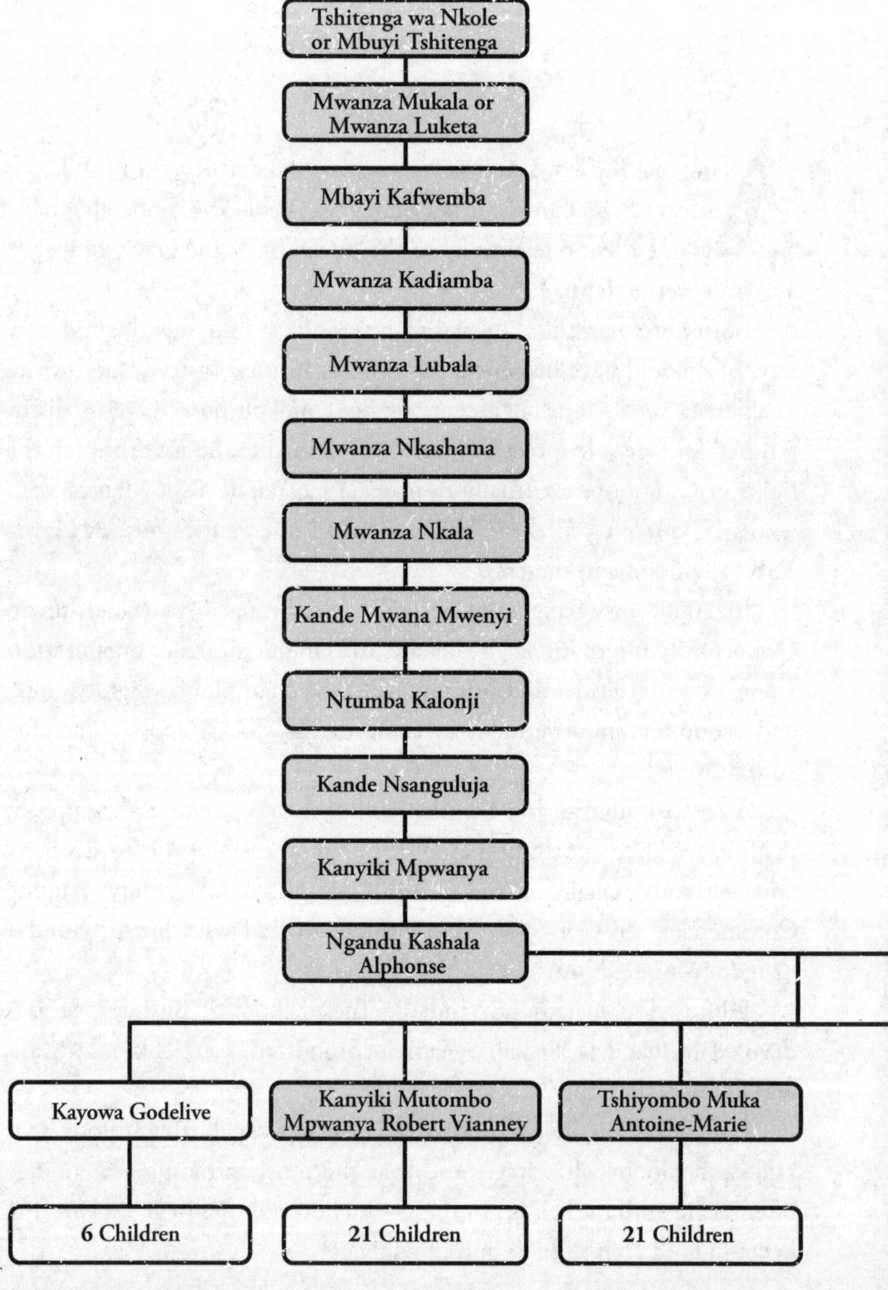

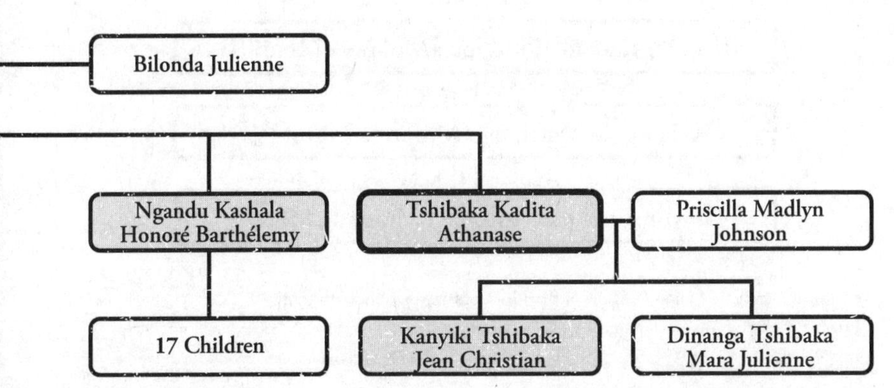
Bilonda Julienne
Ngandu Kashala
Honoré Barthélemy
Tshibaka Kadita
Athanase
Priscilla Madlyn
Johnson
17 Children
Kanyiki Tshibaka
Jean Christian
Dinanga Tshibaka
Mara Julienne

Chieftainship Tree

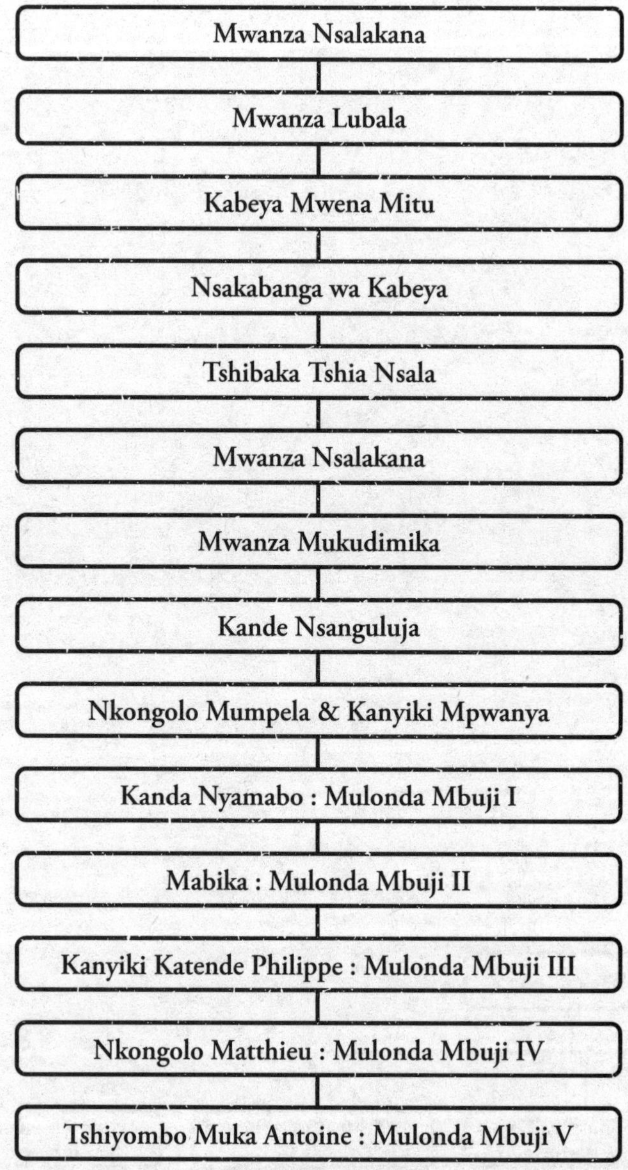

* Matthieu Nkongolo Mumpela, Chief of Bena Kadiamba, word of mouth (early 1970's).
Etienne Ngandu Kashala, eldest nephew, amendment and validation through research and interviews.
Initial design by Karen W. Beall, Genetic Genealogist, FIGG Tree Analytics, LLC.